THE ELECTION OF 1992

Reports and Interpretations

GERALD M. POMPER

F. CHRISTOPHER ARTERTON

ROSS K. BAKER

WALTER DEAN BURNHAM

KATHLEEN A. FRANKOVIC

MARJORIE RANDON HERSHEY

WILSON CAREY MCWILLIAMS

CHATHAM HOUSE PUBLISHERS, INC.
CHATHAM, NEW JERSEY

THE ELECTION OF 1992
Reports and Interpretations

Chatham House Publishers, Inc. / Post Office Box One / Chatham, New Jersey 07928

Copyright © 1993 by Chatham House Publishers, Inc.

Publisher: Edward Artinian
Jacket and cover design: Lawrence Ratzkin
Composition: Bang, Motley, Olufsen
Printing and binding: Arcata Graphics/Fairfield

LIBRARY OF CONGRESS CATALOGING-IN-PUBLICATION DATA

The Election of 1992 : reports and interpretations / Gerald M. Pomper
  ... [et al.].
      p.   cm.
    Includes bibliographical references and index.
    ISBN 1-56643-000-3 (cl) — ISBN 1-56643-001-1 (pa)
      1. Presidents—United States—Election—1992. 2. United States.
  Congress—Elections, 1992. 3. Elections—United States.
  I. Pomper, Gerald M.
  JK526 1992d
  324.973'0928—dc20   93-16269
                                                                 CIP

Manufactured in the United States of America
10 9 8 7 6 5 4 3 2 1

Contents

Politics in Western Europe
United Kingdom, France, Germany, Italy, and Sweden
M. Donald Hancock, *Vanderbilt University,* et al.

The authors discuss the context of each country's politics. Where is the power? Who has the power and how did they get it? How is power used? What is the future of that country's politics? The United Kingdom is explored by Guy Peters. France is the domain of William Safran. Germany is discussed by David Conradt. Italy is the province of Raphael Zariski. And Sweden is reviewed by Donald Hancock. Finally, the European Community is analyzed by Hancock and Peters.
0-934540-30-6   *$33.95 paper*

Public Administration
The State of the Discipline
Edited by **Naomi B. Lynn** and **Aaron Wildavsky**

"Public Administration: The State of the Discipline covers a full range of topics admirably. It is an excellent volume for practitioners and students seeking a broad and thought-provoking overview of the field."   **David H. Rosenbloom,** *The American University*
0-934540-62-4   *$29.95 paper*

The Thinking Game
A Guide to Effective Study
Eugene J. Meehan, *University of Missouri, St. Louis*

"Meehan lays out a teachable model of critical thinking. Students who learn it, enthusiastically use it to improve personal decision making and academic analyses of public policy arguments."
                Larry D. Spence, *Pennsylvania State University*
0-934540-64-0   *$14.95 paper*

Time, Chance, and Organizations
Natural Selection in a Perilous Environment. 2d ed.
Herbert Kaufman

"Uniquely perceptive book as only Herbert Kaufman could write it. A 'must' for all students of organization, indeed for practically any well-read person."   **Amitai Etzioni,** *George Washington University*
0-934540-93-4   *$16.95 paper*

The World of the Policy Analyst
Robert A. Heineman, *Alfred University,* **William T. Bluhm,** *University of Rochester,* et al.

"A valuable contribution to a literature that ought to grow on how we can build bridges between scholarship and practice in public affairs."   **Richard P. Nathan,** *SUNY at Albany*
0-934540-75-6   *$14.95 paper*

The Moral Imagination and Public Life
Raising the Ethical Question
Thomas E. McCollough, *Duke University*

"In a thoughtful and low-key manner, McCollough establishes the relevance—indeed, the necessity—of ethical concern in public life. Through vivid examples from contemporary policy debates, he challenges us to justify our issue preferences in terms of the public interest. Arriving by chance during the Gulf War, the book forced me to test and refine my own views." **Kenneth D. Wald**
0-934540-85-3   *$14.95 paper*   *University of Florida*

Politics in Israel
The Second Generation. Revised Edition
Asher Arian, *Graduate Center, CUNY*

"Arian's *Politics in Israel* is probably the best book on Israeli domestic politics that I have read out of several hundred over a period of 38 years." **Carl Leiden,** *American Political Science Review*
0-934540-80-2   *$18.95 paper*

The Politics of the Administrative Process
James W. Fesler, *Yale University,* and **Donald F. Kettl,** *University of Wisconsin, Madison*

"It is challenging yet user-friendly, comprehensive yet concise—a real bull's eye. The adoption decision has never been simpler."
G. Calvin Mackenzie, *Colby College*
0-934540-81-0   *$29.95 paper*

The Postmodern President
George Bush Meets the World. 2d ed.
Richard Rose, *University of Strathclyde*

"*The Postmodern President* can serve as a fine supplement or as one of a series of core books. It offers much to students and teachers alike, much to ponder, much to argue with, much to reexamine in the light of a rapidly changing world. It is a very good book."
Stephen J. Wayne, *Georgetown University*
0-934540-94-2   *$19.95 paper*

The President as Interpreter-in-Chief
Mary E. Stuckey, *University of Mississippi*

Presidential rhetoric, from FDR to George Bush, is the vehicle by which Stuckey illustrates and explains the evolution of the President's role. A position that was once primarily administrative has become one of aggressive agenda setting and policy advocacy, as revealed in the evolution of presidential rhetoric since the 1930s.
0-934540-92-6   *$14.95 paper*

Britain at the Polls, 1992
Anthony King, *University of Essex,* et al.

A number of prominent political scientists in Great Britain offer their reports and interpretations of the recent general election. Edited by Anthony King (University of Essex), this timely volume features contributions from Ivor Crewe (Essex), Phlip Norton (Hull), Patrick Seyd (Sheffield), David Denver (Lancaster), Kenneth Newton (Essex), and David Sanders (Essex).

0-934540-95-0 $17.95 paper   0-934540-96-9 $25.00 cloth

Dogmas and Dreams: Political Ideologies
Nancy Love, *Pennsylvania State University*

Nancy Love has compiled a comprehensive anthology of political ideologies for students in introductory college courses. Liberalism and Democracy are discussed through the writings of John Locke and J.S. Mill; Conservatism, by Burke, Kristol, and Bloom; Socialism by Marx, Lenin, and Sidney Webb; Anarchism by Emma Goldman, Kropotkin, and Proudhon; Fascism by Mazzini, Mussolini, and Hitler; and Feminism by Phyllis Schlafly and Betty Friedan.

0-934540-84-5 $24.95 paper

The Election of 1992
Reports and Interpretations

Gerald M. Pomper, *Rutgers University,* **F. Christopher Arterton,** *The Graduate School of Political Management,* **Ross K. Baker,** *Rutgers University,* **Walter Dean Burnham,** *University of Texas,* **Kathleen A. Frankovic,** *CBS News,* **Marjorie Randon Hershey,** *Indiana University,* and **Wilson Carey McWilliams,** *Rutgers University*

Seven political scientists probe the electoral impact of issues including the economy, the importance of family values, and questions of character. The authors of *The Election of 1992* examine the results and report their findings, covering the events from the prenomination period to the inauguration of President Clinton.

1-56643-001-1 $16.95 paper   1-56643-000-3 $25.00 cloth

Mastering Public Administration
Brian R. Fry, *University of South Carolina*

"Fry's *Mastering Public Administration* is a fine book. Fry serves the profession admirably by his singularly fair-minded accounts of the systematic thinking of major figures in the development of public administration and by his judicious assessments of their contributions." **James W. Fesler,** *Yale University*

0-934540-56-X $17.95 paper

CHATHAM HOUSE PUBLISHERS

Box One, Chatham, NJ 07928   Phone: (201) 635-2059

Abortion and American Politics

Barbara H. Craig, *Wesleyan University,* and **David M. O'Brien,** *University of Virginia*

O'Brien, author of *Storm Center,* and Craig, author of *Chadha,* examine the impact of the most explosive issue on the social agenda. With sensitivity and coherence they discuss how it has affected the institutions, process, and policies of American politics.

0-934540-89-6 $17.95 paper   0-934540-88-8 $30.00 cloth

Agenda for Excellence

Public Service in America

Edited by **Patricia W. Ingraham,** *Syracuse University,* and **Donald F. Kettl,** *University of Wisconsin, Madison*

Eminently useful for intro courses in public administration, Pat Ingraham and Don Kettl have produced an important volume on public service that is much more than a *Festschrift* for Charles H. Levine. Contributors include Lloyd Nigro, William Richardson, David Rosenbloom, Peter Benda, James Pfiffner, Colin Campbell, Donald Naulls, Hal Rainey, James Perry, Barbara Romzek, Charles Levine, Rosslyn Kleeman, Patricia Ingraham, and Donald Kettl.

0-934540-86-1 $24.95 paper

American Public Policy

Third Edition

B. Guy Peters, *University of Pittsburgh*

One of the leading texts in public policy has been completely revised and updated. Peters provides insights into the policy-making process, from agenda setting to evaluation, and examines substantive policy areas such as health care, energy, and the environment.

0-934540-87-X $27.95 paper

The Bush Presidency

First Appraisals

Colin Campbell, S.J., *Georgetown University,* and **Bert A. Rockman,** *University of Pittsburgh*

For all courses on the Presidency, a timely report on the Bush administration by an impressive list of scholars that includes Joel Aberbach, Giles Alston, Larry Berman, Colin Campbell, George Edwards III, Bruce Jentleson, Charles O. Jones, Anthony King, Paul Quirk, Bert Rockman, and Barbara Sinclair.

0-934540-91-8 $16.95 paper   0-934540-90-X $25.00 cloth

Figures and Tables

Figures

Tables

Preface and Acknowledgments

> I know your mind.
> 'Tis not my speeches that you do mislike,
> But 'tis my presence that doth trouble ye.
>
> — *The Second Part of King Henry the Sixth*
> (I, i)

Readers of this book, the fifth in a series on American presidential elections since 1976, may be tempted to dismiss "expert" reports and interpretations as decisively as American voters dismissed their incumbent president. Candor compels us to admit that the election of 1992 astounded us many times.

Soon after we had agreed to collaborate, the Persian Gulf war seemed to assure the triumphant reelection of George Bush, not the victory of Bill Clinton, an unknown and later embattled governor of Arkansas. Throughout the year, events belied predictions. From the first primaries through the oscillations of Ross Perot down to the election day throngs at the polls, we watched and tried to understand the reversals of commonplace truths.

As much as George Bush, conventional wisdom about American politics took a beating in 1992. Experiencing that election, we have perhaps gained some humility and perhaps learned some new lessons. Incumbency can damage, not always help, a sitting president. Nomination campaigns can overcome adversity and candidate unpopularity. Negative campaigning is no sure-fire road to political success. Voters can pay attention to tough questions and lengthy answers. Congressional power is riskily held, subject to electoral reward and punishment. Voters are able to overcome traditional habits, the constraints of the two-party system, and even their own self-interest when challenged to become citizens.

The national campaigns lead us to a certain optimism that the American people do respond to leadership, in war and in recession. That lesson is the most important meaning of the election of 1992. Yet, the election of Bill Clinton, Al Gore, and scores of new legislators by no means resolves the problems of the Republic. Voter loyalties are uncertain, financial troubles lie ahead, the world order is disorganized, and the deeper meanings of citizenship in the United States are still moot. We must remember Shakespeare's caution:

> If to do were as easy as to know what
> were good to do, chapels had been churches,
> and poor men's cottages princes' palaces.
>
> — *The Merchant of Venice* (I, ii)

The contributors to this book are:

F. CHRISTOPHER ARTERTON, Dean of the Graduate School of Political Management and coauthor of *The Electronic Commonwealth*.

ROSS K. BAKER, Professor at Rutgers University and author of *House and Senate*.

WALTER DEAN BURNHAM, Frank C. Erwin, Jr., Centennial Professor at the University of Texas at Austin and author of *Critical Elections*.

KATHLEEN A. FRANKOVIC, director of surveys at CBS News and president of the American Association for Public Opinion Research.

MARJORIE RANDON HERSHEY, Professor at Indiana University and author of *Running for Office*.

WILSON CAREY MCWILLIAMS, Professor at Rutgers University and author of *The Idea of Fraternity in America*.

GERALD M. POMPER, Professor at Rutgers University and author of *Passions and Interests: Political Party Concepts of American Democracy*.

As has been true throughout this series, we have gained much from others. We acknowledge the help and comments of John Aronsohn, Mark Baldwin, George Beasley, Paul Beck, Kathleen Casey, Anthony Corrado, Patrick Deneen, Kim Downing, Lois Duke, J. Clifford Fox, Dennis Hale, D.A. Hamlin, Pia Christina Hansen, John Hart, Howard V. Hershey, Marla Kaye, Phil Kuntz, Marc Landy, Richard Lau, Peter Lindenbaum, Jane Mansbridge, Joan Martin, William Martin, Maureen Moakley, Carolyn Nestor, Jan-Olof Nyman, Henry Plotkin, Leroy Rieselbach, Florence Riley, Joseph Romance, Jocelyn Shadforth, Paul Skowronek, Bessie Thibodeaux, and John White.

The team of Chatham House—Edward Artinian, Irene Glynn, Katharine Miller, and Christopher Welch—continues to astonish us and the publishing world. Edith Saks tirelessly coordinated the work of seven scattered individualists. Our families, and particularly our former editor Marlene Pomper, provided critical support. I am also personally grateful to my hosts at the national conventions, Ed and Lynn Sternstein, and Jan and Milton Finegold, and to David Pomper for skillful Shakespearean research and Miles Pomper for concerned editing.

The election of 1992 will undoubtedly have major effects on our own lives and on the future of our nation. As a personal heritage, we dedicate this book to the authors' first grandchildren, Aidan Samuel Pomper and Veronica Leigh Burnham, and to their future peers. Surely they come from a place called Hope.

Gerald M. Pomper

1

The Legacy of George Bush: Travails of an Understudy

WALTER DEAN BURNHAM

> O! that I were as great
> As is my grief, or lesser than my name!
> Or that I could forget what I have been!
> Or not remember what I must be now!
>
> — *The Tragedy of King Richard the Second*
> (III, iii)

On 3 November 1992 George Bush was defeated for reelection to the presidency of the United States. His was the fourth such case in the twentieth century, joining William Howard Taft (R) in 1912, Herbert Hoover (R) in 1932, and Jimmy Carter (D) in 1980. Granted that a major third candidate won nearly one-fifth of the popular vote in 1992, the collapse of Bush's 1988 base of support in the electorate was far more spectacular than the size of Bill Clinton's margin over him. But the very presence of Ross Perot as a significant player in this election was a compelling sign that the incumbent was in very deep trouble. From 1860 to the present, major third-party entrants have appeared in seven presidential elections. Candidates of the incumbent party (including four sitting presidents) have lost six of these elections, only Calvin Coolidge (R) breasting the tide in 1924.

Whatever else 1992 was, at its center was the landslide rejection of an incumbent president. It was also a landslide vote of no confidence in the conservative regime that Ronald Reagan and his allies had sought to create on the ruins of interest-group liberalism and that George Bush had been selected (and elected) in 1988 to maintain.[1] This fact makes the 1992 election of far more than usual consequence. Rejections of this order of magnitude have not happened very often over the course of American political history. The task of this chapter is not that of analyzing the election results in any detail, though some mention of them seems inevitable. It is, instead, to evaluate the legacy of George Bush's tenure in office and to identify as clearly as possible what went wrong and why.

The first order of business is to place this particular president in an appropriate "political time." George Bush belongs to a specific, if select, group of presidents who, initially elected with high hopes and considerable popular support, achieved spectacular failure on the job. Including Bush, there have thus far been six such cases across the history of the American presidency. These men, whom I call "third-term understudies," were selected in the first instance, not for their capacity to innovate or for their possession of what President Bush once disparagingly called "the vision thing," but as promising conservators of the "revolution" carried out by others. Each of them, each in his own way and time, encountered mountainous seas of difficulties during his term. Like his predecessors in this group, George Bush found his reelection campaign buffeted by adversity, deep public pain, and massive demands arising from that pain for the one thing that regime conservators are not very good at providing: a coherent policy vision of his own and a positive, sustained leadership in dealing with the country's problems.

Understudy/Conservator Presidents as a Class:
A Historical Overview

From 1900 to the present, twelve presidents seeking reelection have won it, while only four have lost, a success rate of 75 percent. Of initially elected incumbents seeking reelection in this period before 1992, only three had failed to achieve it: Taft in 1912, Hoover in 1932, and Carter in 1980. But these (except for Carter, who does not fit our definitional criteria) are joined by earlier cases: John Adams (Fed), elected in 1796 and defeated in 1800; James Madison (DR), elected in 1808 and reelected in 1812; and Martin Van Buren (D), elected in 1836 and defeated in 1840. There are four criteria, each of which must be met, for admission to our select subiverse of understudy/conservator presidents. First, the president had extensive service in the preceding two-term regime, was thus an "insider," and had an exceptionally full résumé. Second, that regime had been noteworthy for policy innovation/transformation on an extensive scale, and much more usually than not, the understudy president had succeeded one with notable heroic status, charismatic gifts, or both. Third, what was wanted by the party elite and the majority of the public at the time of the understudy's first election was more of the same, continuity. And finally, the incumbent was renominated by his party for a second term. Men meeting all these criteria are found six times from 1796–1800 to 1988–92. They are often very widely spaced in chronological time: Seventy-two years separate Van Buren from Taft, and George Bush was the first such instance since Herbert Hoover sixty years earlier.

In a recent study of some interest, the historian Allan J. Lichtman and his associate Ken DeCell, proceeding from recent Soviet work on pattern recognition, have posited the existence of thirteen "keys" to the presidency. The dichotomous (yes–no or O–X) position of these keys in any given year, they assert, can come close in the aggregate to determining the outcome of American presidential elections.[2] Since 1892, incumbent-party candidates, whether or not themselves incumbents, have always won with five or fewer negative (X) keys of these thirteen, while such candidates have always lost when six or more of the keys turned negative.[3] The keys are grouped in straightforward fashion. The political keys start the sequence (1–4): performance of party at last midterm congressional election, or "party mandate"; nomination contest; incumbency of candidate; presence of significant third-party candidate in campaign. The next six (5–11) are performance keys: short-term and long-term economic trends (5, 6); existence of major policy change initiated by administration (7); social unrest (8); scandal in the administration (9); and two foreign-policy indicators, foreign/military policy success (10) or failure (11). The final two are "charisma" estimates: The incumbent is charismatic or a national hero (12), and the challenger is neither (13).

Obviously, as the authors concede, some of these keys are much more matters of *Gestalt*, or impressionistic judgment, than others. Nor does their schema allow for important institutional change across a century and a quarter (e.g., changes in the basic rules of nominating conventions after 1968). And even when there are numbers, for example with the economic indicators, nagging problems can present themselves. Numerous economics-and-politics models for the 1992 election, apparently centered on incumbency, low inflation, and short-term economic expansion (1991–92), with near-unanimity predicted a Bush victory, in one famous case by a landslide of 55–57 percent of the two-party vote. Yet from the beginning there seemed something strange about such a projection in a year marked by strongly negative public evaluations of the incumbent's performance in office, by enormous public preoccupation with poor economic performance even in the short term, and by a growth in per capita disposable income across Bush's term that was the lowest in six decades.[4] Yet were we slavishly to follow the definitions given by Lichtman and DeCell, we would have to turn these keys positive in 1992 and thus (as Lichtman himself apparently did) project a Bush victory.

Impressionistically utilizing the often impressionistic method of *Thirteen Keys,* I have transcribed that work's conclusions for 1912 and 1932 and provided my own estimates for elections involving third-term understudies before 1860 and in 1992 (see table 1.1).[5]

This estimate of Bush's negative keys in 1992 would seem to be a reasonable minimum. On the one hand, there would surely be some debate about our classification of the short-term economy key, but on the other hand, some case could be made for an even higher negative total than the 7 we provide here.[6] It is worthy of note that our six understudy cases have a mean negative score very close to 7. This stands in sharp contrast to a score of 2.6 for fourteen other incumbents seeking reelection between 1864 and 1984.[7] Let us now put some flesh on these bones by discussing each case in turn before concentrating our attention on the last of them, George Bush.

John Adams, George Washington's vice-president, succeeded him by a very narrow electoral-vote margin over the leader of the Democratic-Republican opposition, Thomas Jefferson. Washington had of course been the supreme "hero" president, "first in war, first in peace, first in the hearts of his countrymen." As most of his contemporaries well understood, he was *the* indispensable man for launching the new constitutional order. By definition, the Federalist regime of 1789–97 was a policy-innovative regime par excellence. But internal tensions within it escalated rapidly from 1793, when American domestic politics became increasingly shaped by the "world war" between Great Britain and revolutionary/imperial France, its two chief protagonists. The war was to last nearly a generation, and all the way down to its termination in 1815 American domestic politics regularly danced to its tune.

Tensions within the Federalist coalition pitted moderates against the "high Federalists" around Alexander Hamilton, the latter pushing for a policy of "thorough" in state building and military armament that the more moderate wing of the party, increasingly centering on the new president, John Adams, found unacceptable. To no small degree, Adams found himself a kind of prisoner to his cabinet, which was heavily populated with Hamilton's allies. Adams's personality—angular, explosive, and rigid—precluded success in dealing with this persistent infighting. Tensions with the French *Directoire* government led in due course to an undeclared but vigorous naval war with that country (1798–1800), which petered out without decisive result, while routine harassments and humiliations from Great Britain continued. At home, efforts to raise new revenues to support a much more vigorous national state than a public made up mostly of yeoman farmers was prepared

TABLE 1.1
"KEY" NEGATIVES FOR UNDERSTUDY PRESIDENTS,
1800–1992

President and previous service	Number of negatives	Content of negatives
J. Adams (Fed) Vice-president 1789–97; defeated 1800	6	No policy change; social unrest (e.g., Fries' Rebellion, 1798); foreign-military failure and lack of success; incumbent lacking charisma, challenger (Thomas Jefferson) having it
Madison (DR) Sec. of State, 1801–09; reelected 1812	6	Party defection (DeWitt Clinton Democrats); short-term economy; foreign-military lack of success and failure; incumbent lacking charisma; no (domestic) policy change
Van Buren (D) Sec. of State, 1829–31; Vice-president, 1833–37; defeated 1840	7	Party mandate; short-term economy; long-term economy; no policy change; no foreign-military success; incumbent lacking charisma; challenger (William Henry Harrison, "hero") having it
Taft (R) Gov. of Philippines, 1902–4; Sec. of War, 1904–8; defeated 1912	7	Party mandate; nomination contest; major third party; no policy change; no foreign-military success; incumbent lacking charisma; challengers (T. Roosevelt, W. Wilson) having it
Hoover (R) Sec. of Commerce, 1921–28; defeated 1932	8	Party mandate; short-term economy; long-term economy; no policy change; social unrest; lack of foreign-military success; incumbent lacking charisma; challenger (FDR) having it
Bush (R) Director, Central Intelligence Agcy., 1976–77; Vice-president, 1981–89; defeated 1992	7	Party mandate; major third candidate; nomination contest; short-term economy; long-term economy; no policy change; incumbent lacking charisma

to tolerate produced unrest, the most notable instance of which in Adams's terms was Fries' Rebellion in Pennsylvania (1798). Dissonance was fueled as well by that piece of Federalist "thorough" legislation, the Alien and Sedition Acts (1798), and, from the Jeffersonian opposition, the Virginia and Kentucky resolutions (1798–99), with their whiff of nullification if not secession.

By 1800 Federalism was becoming increasingly marginalized as voter participation in this mostly yeoman electorate notably rose. The president himself was increasingly isolated within his own party, and the party itself was wracked by personal and ideological conflicts among its top elite. The stage was set for an overthrow having sufficiently large and durable consequences as to be frequently cited as a case of critical realignment. The figure of six negative keys proposed here would certainly rise if one had a way of specifying intraparty-conflict dimensions back to a period whose still-primitive level of institutionalization provided none of the scope for them that emerges with democratized politics in the 1820s and 1830s.

James Madison's reelection in 1812 represents the only example of an understudy's success. The key to this remarkable achievement lay in the fact that the "first party system" after 1801 had no forces that tended to restore nationwide two-party competition.[8] The Federalists were rapidly reduced to local and regional redoubts in the Northeast (especially New England). Under normal circumstances, the Jeffersonians could count on well over two-thirds of the membership in the House of Representatives. That Madison could survive a nearly fourteen-point drop in his share of the total vote from the level he achieved in 1808 reflected the fact that he won 65.5 percent of the ascertainable popular vote in his first election.

Yet, for all that, 1812 was the only seriously competitive presidential election between 1800 and 1824. It is clear that Madison was much less popular than his party that year, receiving only 51.6 percent of the popular vote and 58.7 percent of the electoral vote. Indeed, had Pennsylvania swung into the column of his coalition opponent DeWitt Clinton, he would have ousted Madison from office. The key factor in producing this remarkable slump was clearly the entrance, at long last, of the United States into a great world war by congressional declaration of war against Great Britain in June 1812. We may also note on the personal level that Madison himself believed that he had no aptitude for the presidency, a judgment that contemporaries and later historians were to support. Under his regime the institutional power of the presidency declined, just as Jefferson's cousin and archenemy, Chief Justice John Marshall, had predicted: The party-creating sorcerer, Thomas Jefferson, could command a personal loyalty in Congress that was not transferable to Madison. The creature, rather than the creator, of the Republican caucus that chose him in 1808, Madison found himself something more, but perhaps not much more, than a chief clerk.[9] Nevertheless, the war, with its very heavy if geographically concentrated impact and above all its sociopolitical divisiveness, drove politics in the 1812 election.[10] Madison survived, but as we have suggested, in any later political environment he would very probably have gone down to defeat.

Martin Van Buren's immediate predecessor, the "Old Hero" Andrew Jackson, was the charismatic creator of the Democratic party after his landslide election in 1828. Policy innovation and turmoil were dominant features of his regime. This border aristocrat was, ironically, the chosen vessel of mass democratic impulses and electoral mobilization, as was the Hudson Valley aristocrat Franklin Roosevelt a century later. But at the organizational level, a strong case could be made that the true creator of the Democratic party was his secretary of state and vice-president. Martin Van Buren is a virtually classic case of a conservator of a status quo who almost necessarily had no innovative agenda of his own.

It is probably true of most successors to policy-innovative regimes—in aggregate, a considerably wider group than our six examples here—that theirs is generally a regime-sustaining rather than a transforming role. What probably distinguishes our smaller set is that there is an abnormally adverse intersection in "political time" between the policies and regime commitments to be conserved and the political effects of rapidly changing contexts and their associated demands. Van Buren had two decisive strikes against him. First, he was the first president under democratized political conditions to be in office during a serious economic depression. As with Hoover, the slump virtually coincided with and lasted through his entire term. It could be supposed that this economic slump could be traced by parts of an angry public to the longer-term effects of one of Andrew Jackson's great innovations, his successful war on and destruction of the Second Bank of the United States (1832–34). Connected with this at much shorter range were the strong contractionary effects on the money supply associated with Jackson's issuance of the Specie Circular in 1836, demanding payment to the federal government in gold and silver only.

Second, and what was probably even worse for Van Buren, was the intersection of his public image with the fact that the democratizing revolution, launched in Jackson's time, had not yet run its course to completion. In all sorts of ways, the "second party system" divides into two discrete halves, before and after 1838–39.[11] Down through 1836, national turnout had remained only in the middle 50 percent range. Both the elections of 1838 and 1840 witnessed unprecedented mobilizations of new voters into the electoral system, in the latter year reaching just over 80 percent of the potential electorate of the day. The partisan opposition to Jackson took a very long time to consolidate. Even after the emergence of the Whig party in 1834, its inchoate character was reflected in its fielding not one but three candidates to oppose Van Buren in 1836.[12] The holding of the first Whig national convention in 1839 was evidence that this party was coming of age as serious opposition to the previously ascendant Democrats.[13]

One very significant negative aspect of the members of our understudy group as a whole and individually is that they are exceptionally vulnerable to opposition attack as insider elitists who are out of touch with the problems and concerns of ordinary Americans. Van Buren's plight in 1840 is an almost clinical example of this generalization. Like many "new men" from humble origins then and since, he acquired an elegant lifestyle as he climbed the social ladder. This was brilliantly seized on by the Whig campaign of 1840. The president, drinking wine from a silver goblet while lounging on a cushioned settee, was placed in the sharpest image contrast with their candidate. William Henry Harrison, the "hero of Tippecanoe," was, they said, content to sit on a buckeye bench while drinking hard cider, just like ordinary folks. Nor was Van Buren's appeal broadened by his insistence at the outset of his administration (like Grover Cleveland in the 1890s and Herbert Hoover in the 1930s) that it was the duty of the people to support the government, not that of the government to support the people. The 1840 campaign is has often been derided for its "showbiz" spectaculars and its total lack of substantive issue content. This is a misconception. The substantive issue lying underneath the ballyhoo was the completion of the democratizing revolution. No matter that General Harrison himself was a descendant of one of the oldest aristocratic families of Virginia. Like aristocrats before and after him, he became the chosen vessel for achieving this democratic goal. Yet one should not leave the scene without noting that Van Buren, in losing, still gained a very large share of the new voters for himself and the Democratic party. His decline of just over 4 percent of the total vote between 1836 and 1840 is by far the smallest among our third-term understudies. He gained 8.3 percent more of the potential electorate losing in 1840 than he had had winning in 1836.

We must move fast forward to reach our next example, William Howard Taft. The 1896 realignment had created a hegemonic Republican majority that was to last (with a Democratic interlude produced by Taft's defeat in 1912) until the Great Depression. This realignment conclusively decided one major set of issues, those involved broadly in "the city beating the country" at a certain stage of capitalist development. But the disruptive dynamic of that development was far too great to be thus simply contained. The year 1896 opened the door to a new era of political conflict and adjustment that, while involving the western and southern colonies, was largely fought out within the victorious metropole-Republican coalition itself. Out of these dynamics, that vastly protean phenomenon known as progressivism emerged into clear view not long after the turn of the century.

The chance of an assassin's bullet put Theodore Roosevelt into the White House in time to serve almost a full term before his landslide electoral victory of 1904.[14] This extraordinary man, full of energy and activity, keenly aware of the image-building uses of the new mass media—it was in his time that the White House press corps became a permanent feature of the Washington landscape—was in many respects the first "modern president." With considerable rhetorical trust-busting flourishes and the enactment of early consumer-protecting regulatory measures such as the Pure Food and Drug Act of 1906, Roosevelt successfully rode the progressive tiger in its early stages of development. He also projected a new image of American power on the international stage. Retiring voluntarily in 1908, he literally hand-picked William Howard Taft to carry on his work and continue his policies. Taft himself, then and later, doubted his own capacities in the presidential role. He was much more interested in becoming (as he did in 1921) chief justice of the United States.

The whole period has been thoroughly canvassed by the writing of academic historians, one of the most recent and analytically oriented of whom is Martin Sklar.[15] The details of the period and the setting of the epic struggle between Roosevelt and Taft in 1912 are admirably and penetratingly explored in Sklar's work. It is enough to note here that the continuing disruptive pressure of corporate concentration stimulated ever more exigent debate over the proper role of the federal government in dealing with such concentration and its social effects.[16] Roosevelt, returning from Africa in 1910, promptly staked out a position far to the interventionist left of anything he had espoused while in office. Taft responded with a bewildering set of policy zigzags and by gradually rallying around his own innate conservatism. The developing context of politics had shifted with unusual speed in the years after 1909; the policy "synthesis" that seemed to work so well at Taft's accession was no longer viable by 1912. And Taft himself, the purest case of understudy selection among our six, was also the only one of them repudiated by his predecessor.

The Republican party in that period was hegemonic, but it enjoyed no such lead as the Jeffersonians had had after they came to power in 1801. The nomination contest between Taft and Roosevelt was very nearly the most bitter in party-convention history. Roosevelt's insurgency in the general election pulled voters almost exclusively from Republican ranks, winning about 55 percent of the party vote to Taft's 45 percent. This made Taft's defeat, and his third-place showing, a foregone conclusion. One can note here a president who lacked important presidential qualities, who had no coherent agenda of his own as stress and demands rapidly mounted, and who reversed course on important matters without offering any convincing explanation for doing so. The parallel with George Bush in office seems particularly noteworthy, though unlike Taft, Bush suffered no complaints from his predecessor in office.

Our final pre-Bush case, Herbert Hoover, requires limited comment here. Hoover achieved national prominence under the most favorable possible image auspices during and just after World War I by his effective attempts to organize large-scale relief efforts in Belgium and Russia. Actively considered by both parties as a nominee in 1920, Hoover stayed out of that contest but became secretary of commerce during the Harding-Coolidge "normalcy" regime (1921–28). A description of him as an "understudy" in the Teddy Roosevelt–Taft sense would obviously fall wide of the mark. Indeed, President Coolidge, who disliked most people, also disliked Hoover, whom he called sardonically the "Boy Wonder." But by 1928 Hoover had become the ideal conservator figure for the *collective* leadership of the Republican party. He was the "great engineer" who could further the rationalization of politics and its reduction to technique in an age when corporate capitalism had apparently found the magic key to permanent growth and prosperity. By 1928, any serious policy alternatives to the ascendant politicoeconomic order had all but evaporated. With this, and with the Democrats' nomination of a Roman Catholic (Al Smith), probably any respectable Republican could have been elected.[17] Hoover was chosen as the strongest possible candidate, and, as with all our other examples, he had no serious intraparty opposition to his elevation to the presidency.

Herbert Hoover's failure in office has often been described and even given psychobiographic treatment.[18] We confine ourselves to noting that an overwhelmingly adverse change in the economy—sixteen quarters of uninterrupted contraction!—intersected with a personal image of grimness and rigid inflexibility and, as in the past, of an incumbent uninterested in the plight of the average American. To some extent, that image was inaccurate. Hoover was, as some historians have pointed out, much more open to innovation than it seemed to many of his contemporaries, and some policy adaptations actually occurred (e.g., the Norris-LaGuardia Act and the creation of the Reconstruction Finance Corporation, both in 1932). But this was always within the overarching context of maintenance of the ideological and political-economic status quo. As the objective basis of this status quo had been destroyed by November 1932, he was rejected in a landslide even larger than the one that had originally elevated him to office. The magnitude of this swing may have been the greater because his challenger, Franklin D. Roosevelt, like most regime creators, projected an image of optimism, experimentalism, and success that was the polar opposite of Hoover's.

Before turning to an appraisal of George Bush's presidency in this setting, a certain summary of the ground traversed so far may be in order. As Stephen Skowronek has observed, across the history of the presidency one sometimes finds regime maintainers who are capable of significant innovations in their own right.[19] Far more frequently, we find presidents who more or less successfully maintain the established order with which they are affiliated and leave little trace behind. Not surprisingly, such figures were more likely to arise when the federal government had limited functions, when crises occurred relatively infrequently, and when international relations played only a very small part in our domestic politics. From the emergence of the so-called modern presidency in 1933, the contexts of rule have involved vastly increased vectors of change and thus, in a sense, have altered and perhaps have accelerated "political time." There is some evidence that destabilizations of presidential support in public opinion have tended to increase in the most recent period. This trend seems associated with the accelerating erosion of the old partisan links between rulers and ruled since the vast crisis of the late 1960s. But while all this may be so, our review has underscored the existence of a group of presidents originally selected to conserve a given regime who then founder in the attempt, not merely in modern times, but across the span of "political time" since the earliest days.

We may also note at this point in the argument that this group of understudy/conservator presidents is sharply bounded not only in definitional but in statistical terms from all other groupings of incumbent presidents that may exist. The fourteen other elections in which incumbents of the White House ran for a second full term show a mean of 51.4 percent of the total vote in their first race and 53.1 percent in their second, with an interelection swing of +1.7 percent. Our six understudies, in contrast, enjoyed a mean of 55.0 percent of the total vote in their first contest (52.8 percent if Madison is excluded). Their second election is associated with a catastrophic drop to 38.8 percent (36.3 percent if Madison is excluded). This adverse interelection swing of 16.2 to 16.4 percent has no remote parallel elsewhere in any category of presidential election pairs, with or without incumbents seeking reelection. If we apply a standard t test comparing this group with all other initially elected incumbents as a group, we find, as we would expect, that the t value of 1.363 is statistically insignificant. But in the second election the value of t swells to 4.019, and rises further to 5.104 when the two groups' interelection swings are thus compared—easily significant at the .001 level. Anticipating ourselves a bit, we may note here that in 1988 George Bush received 53.4 percent of the total vote and in 1992, 37.4 percent—with rounding error, an interelection swing of −16.0 percent. As his final showing is so close to the means derived from the five preceding cases, it turns out to be remarkably "typical" for this group. Once identification of him as a member was made, it became altogether possible to make an a priori prediction (long before November 1992) that he would be defeated on the basis of this file of evidence alone.

George Bush in Political Time I:
The Inheritance

Let us now turn to George Bush and the storm that gathered over both his presidency and his bid for reelection. In personality, Bush is clearly a conservator type, yet his commitment to neo-Reaganite shibboleths such as "no new taxes" was anything but ironclad. He was the man with the perfect résumé, having served in the Ford administration before becoming Ronald Reagan's vice-president. No matter what doubts he may have expressed during the 1980 nomination contest about Reagan's "voodoo economics," he was the perfectly loyal supporter of his chief's economic and other policies after he joined the team. In 1988, the last of the really good Reagan years as far as the economy was concerned, Bush became the chosen vessel for continuing the policies (and, it was hoped, the electoral success) of the previous regime. But by mid-1992, Senator Robert Dole (R-Kans.) and many other members of the party elite were complaining that Bush had failed to explain to the public just why he sought reelection; they asked him to spell out the kinds of positive, change-oriented policies he would pursue in a second term. That Bush was not personally charismatic had been obvious in 1988 but was also largely irrelevant: Neither was his hapless Democratic opponent, Michael Dukakis. But lack of the "vision thing," which generally infected the most lethargic administration in many decades, became a progressively debilitating political reality. In the opinion atmosphere of 1992, there was manifest public demand for vigorous and proactive leadership. What was of little consequence in 1988 was central to any possibility of success in 1992.

What happened? To address this question, we must first provide a brief overview of the regime and interests that Bush inherited in 1989. After his election in 1980, Ronald Reagan sought to stop the rot in the American economy and in the country's international position. Here was a classic example of a "conviction politician," a revitalizer in office, a charismatic leader informed by a clear ideological vision. Basic to this vision was the maximum possible dismantling of the interest-group liberal state at home and the pursuit of a massive defense build-up in confrontation with the USSR and other hostile forces in the world. The Reagan coalition, reflecting also the impact of the failure of the Carter years, contained the traditional core of economic conservatives plus a substantial number of less affluent white voters ("Reagan Democrats") who were repelled by a welfarist interest-group liberalism that excluded them. It also included not only traditionally conservative anticommunists but former Democratic neoconservatives who flocked to the new anticommunist crusade. In addition, another force became organized after the Supreme Court's 1973 abortion decision in *Roe v. Wade* and in response to broader destabilization of traditional social mores: the religious right.

Each of these forces contributed its part of the Reaganite synthesis of the 1980s. For each of them, some aspect of the very reproduction of the American domestic and international order had come to be seen by the late 1970s as at serious risk. For corporate business, economic reproduction was at stake; threats to it included the "debt economy," inflation, and real rates of interest hovering close to zero (lenders close to the position of paying borrowers for the privilege of lending money to them). Less affluent segments of the middle class, squeezed by stagnant or declining real income since 1973 and by escalating state and local taxes, struck back by endorsing tax-rollback referendums such as Howard Jarvis's Proposition 13 in California (1978); they were ready adherents to the Reaganite tax-cutting crusade at the federal level.

As for the "good empire," its reproduction potential seemed to many defense conservatives to be put at risk by the inglorious end to the Vietnam war, adversary hearings in Congress directed at the military and the Central Intelligence Agency, and major cuts in defense expenditures. (By the late 1970s, these had reached levels as shares of the GNP not seen since before the Korean war.) What with these developments, along with Soviet intervention in Afghanistan and the Iranian hostage crisis from 1979 on, defense-oriented neoconservatives created an organization called the Committee on the Present Danger and flocked to Ronald Reagan's standard in 1980. Finally, the reproduction of the very foundations of society all the way down to the nuclear family's primordial level was sufficiently problematic as to reflect a deepening crisis many Americans believed (and continue to believe) to be of the first magnitude. Crime, drugs, promiscuous lifestyles, homosexuality, abortion, schools that failed to provide an acceptable education—all seemed to many to be infallible signs of deadly decay in the moral fiber of the country. The organization and mobilization of the religious right by Jerry Falwell, Pat Robertson, and other electronic-church entrepreneurs was one of the most noteworthy of all the important political changes in the late 1970s. It led to an unprecedented Republican majority among white Christians with the strongest pietist/fundamentalist/born-again leanings.

Reagan promised revitalization on all these fronts, and he did his best to deliver on his promises. For corporate business and the wealthy there was the lion's share (and then some) of the massive income tax cuts of 1981. Jimmy Carter had done his part too, by naming Paul Volcker to the chairmanship of the Federal Reserve Board in 1979, for Volcker executed a revolutionary policy change: targeting money supply rather than interest rates—thus producing the highest extended real rates of interest since the post–Civil War Great

Deflation of 1865–80, and in time quite effectively killing the inflation dragon, as it was intended to do. For the economically stressed middle classes, there were crumbs from the 1981 tax-cut banquet table and, of course, large gains to be made in real estate and in income (especially interest income) during the "good" Reagan years of economic expansion (1983–88). The deregulation surge—which, again, got under way not with Reagan but with Carter—further swelled from 1981 on. This led in particular to the "liberation" of savings-and-loan companies from bothersome regulatory constraints. And this in turn led (human nature being what it is, intelligent people know a license to steal when they see one) to the savings-and-loan crisis of the early 1990s and, along the way, to a vast speculative overinvestment in real estate, particularly commercial real estate. All sorts of people with any claims on assets, starting with those able to qualify for a home mortgage in booming real estate regions of the country, could and did profit, often hugely, from these changes in public policy.

The defense industry and foreign policy conservatives won a spectacular "Empire Strikes Back" victory with Reagan's huge defense build-up. This build-up naturally added its own considerable stimulus to the economy as it went on line after 1982. The new "forward" foreign policy was pursued on a global scale, supporting the El Salvador regime against leftist insurgency, supporting insurgent opponents of the leftist Afghan and Nicaraguan governments, and pursuing similar policies in Africa and the Middle East. To Republicans by 1992 this policy seemed to have produced one of the greatest successes in world history. Not only was El Salvador retained and not only did the inimical governments of Afghanistan and Nicaragua disappear, but the entire collapse of world communism unfolded during George Bush's term in office. At the end of 1991 the Soviet Union itself disappeared into the mists of history, and a supposed "new world order" had come into being.

It has often been said that the social-issue conservatives and the religious right were far less successful in realizing their objectives than the other major beneficiaries of the Reagan revolution. From the vantage point of 1992, such a view might be regarded as at least premature. Naturally, since success for these forces importantly involved capture of the judiciary and gaining ascendancy within the Republican party on all issues about which they were concerned, success required considerably more time to realize. Yet twelve years' worth of Supreme Court appointments by Ronald Reagan and George Bush had in 1992 brought the Court to within a single vote of flatly overturning *Roe v. Wade*,[20] and to the emergence of a very large majority within the Court in favor of substantial state restraints on the "right to privacy" that *Roe* had proclaimed to be constitutionally protected. And the judicial right turn so clearly visible by the early 1990s had a much wider reach across Supreme Court jurisprudence than this. It oversimplifies, of course, to say that this jurisprudential shift sacrifices the claims of individuals to the benefit of the state or congressional claims to the benefit of the executive when they are in conflict; but something of the sort is not too far from the heart of the matter. By 1992 the religious right could well suppose that with another four years of George Bush, their cause would finally go over the top.

By 1992, as the Republican platform abundantly showed, abortion had become a prime talismanic issue, subsuming a far wider range of social-issue politics. Both the Houston platform and the first-night speeches by such leading apostles as Pat Buchanan and Pat Robertson projected a theological tone more in keeping, one would have thought, with Ecumenical Councils of the early Christian church than with a political party in a popularist country whose founding charter explicitly separates church and state.[21] Both Presidents Bush and Reagan—each in an earlier incarnation favorable to the general doctrine of *Roe v. Wade*—became rock-solid champions of the religious right's position on the abortion question. Countermobilization on the part of those who believed their views to the contrary were constitutionally protected could reasonably be expected to emerge, of course; but that too would be a sign not of failure but very considerable success for socioreligious conservatives. It is clear, especially in the wake of George Bush's defeat, that these conservatives will engage in an epic struggle with other conservatives for outright control on the Republican party.

George Bush in Political Time II: Contradictions and Ironies of Success

Every victory in politics has its ironies; and these, if substantial enough, take on the character of contradictions that may actually contribute to defeat in the longer term. Many gallons of ink have been spilled by academics, journalists, and others about each component of the Reaganite effort to revitalize the economic, political, and social system, and America's position in the world, through an attempted right-wing "revolution." By 1992, this impulse had clearly reached a dead end, and the Reaganite synthesis was on its way to the same discard pile that interest-group liberalism had reached a dozen years earlier. Our discussion here primarily deals with economics, for economics drove the election from beginning to end; but it addresses as well the domestic political ironies embedded in the total ideological victory of capitalism over communism that was a basic feature of Bush's years in office.

By 1992 there was exceptionally broad consensus that the American economy was in serious crisis. The recession that began in 1990 had been relatively shallow by the usual numerical measures; 1980–82 had been notably worse. But recovery was far more feeble than in the immediate aftermath of any preceding postwar downturn. Moreover, it was evident not merely to economists and policy elites but to the public at large that the economy was undergoing a radical restructuring. Hundreds of thousands of good jobs, especially in manufacturing, had disappeared forever. Substantial parts of the middle class now experienced or were directly threatened by the pink slip, and this development was something new.

Reaganomics ultimately had not solved the long-term problems of American capitalism but had displaced them onto a new plane. Since the tax cuts of 1981 had permanently unbalanced the federal budget, and since continuing Democratic control of congress made impossible the drastic domestic program cuts originally called for, the consequence was an explosive increase in federal deficits as a share of the gross national product and, thus, in the federal debt. These revenue cuts—and other policy changes, such as the deregulation of the savings-and-loan industry—did not produce a massive new force for investment in the domestic productive economy, as had been promised. Instead, very much as in the 1920s, they led to a speculative boom in preferred commodities and a hugely visible increase in conspicuous consumption by the rich.[22] The total mix of fiscal, monetary, interest-rate, and deregulatory policies made an impressive contribution not only to mushrooming debt acquisition by the federal government but by all major sectors of the political economy from households to business corporations. The Federal Reserve Board's figures (see table 1.2) tell the story for the Reagan-Bush years.

Ronald Reagan (and Congress, it may be added) seemed to have found the politicians' version of the philosopher's stone. The federal policy mix broke historically unprecedented ground. New Dealers and interest-group liberals had often been criticized by Republicans for tax-and-spend policy mixes. Now, jettisoning the fiduciary responsibility that had been the GOP's stock in trade for decades, the new conservatism produced a mix based on borrow and spend. What was worse, the borrowing was essentially for maintaining consumption at levels considerably in excess of what the productive economy could any longer support. The something-for-nothing deal was sealed, it seemed, with George Bush's 1988 pledge: "Read my lips: no new taxes." It seemed the party could go on forever. But by 1992, according to the Organization for Economic Cooperation and Development's account, the U.S. government's debt had quadrupled to somewhat over $4 trillion (about $2.7 trillion of which was publicly held) and was the largest among twenty-three more or less advanced capitalist democracies. The annual budget deficit was also the largest in raw numbers and among the largest as a share of

TABLE 1.2

CREDIT-MARKET DEBT IN THE USA, 1983–90

(YEAR-END OUTSTANDINGS)

Category of debt sector (Public and private)	Percentage of GNP		
	1983	1987	1990
Government			
Federal	33.2	42.2	46.5
State and local	10.1	12.0	11.8
Subtotal	43.3	54.2	58.3
Private domestic nonfinancial			
Corporate business	28.8	37.1	39.4
Nonfarm noncorporate business	18.2	23.1	21.9
Farm	5.3	3.1	2.6
Households	51.1	61.9	69.5
Subtotal	103.5	125.2	133.4
Foreign held	6.4	5.3	5.2
All domestic nonfinancial plus foreign held	153.2	184.8	196.9
Financial sector	24.2	39.5	45.7
Total credit-market debt, percentage of GNP	177.4	224.3	242.5
Note:			
Percentage U.S. government of all C-M debt	18.7	18.8	19.2
Household debt of disposable personal income	71.7	87.2	95.8
Ratio of corporate debt to corporate profits (profits = 1)	4.58	6.42	7.22

SOURCE: Federal Reserve Board, *Flow of Funds Accounts, Year-End Outstandings*, various years.

gross domestic product. State, local, and federal taxes as a share of GDP, in contrast, were the second lowest among all these countries; only Turkey's taxes were lower. As morning in America (1984) was replaced by morning after in America (1992), it was strictly to be expected that there were two oppositions to George Bush's reelection, the one (Clinton) stressing the urgent need for investment and job creation, the other (Perot) stressing the equally if not more urgent need for an immediate and comprehensive assault on the debt-deficit problem.

Table 1.2, however, makes clear that it was in the private sector that the lion's share of debt acquisition occurred in the 1980s. In only two previous years—1932 and 1933, when the productive economy collapsed—had total long- and short-term credit-market debt reached higher levels than the nearly two and a half times GNP reached by 1990. There is probably no magic number defining the precise moment when debt levels have grown too high to be sustained, but it is worth noting that historically, except for the Great Depression, the usual level has hovered somewhere around 150 percent of GNP. One of the important contributing factors to George Bush's defeat was a virtually flat economic growth rate across his entire term, with per capita disposable income actually in marginal decline from 1989 through mid-1992. If we consider that about two-thirds of the GDP passes through the private-consumption sector and that total household debt had climbed by 1990 to just under 100 percent of disposable personal income, those facts plus poor corporate profits and massive job-sacrificing restructuring together go a long way to accounting for this persistent stagnation.

The fact of long-term decline and the lack of a sustained Reaganomic bounceback from it can be put in summary form by examining the gross share of pretax corporate profits in the national income and product accounts (NIPA) over the past thirty years, along with the share of net interest payments (see table 1.3). Earlier material is provided in the table for comparison. Whether or not Karl Marx was right when he claimed the existence of a *law* of a falling rate of profit under capitalism, there is no doubt at all that as an empirical *fact*, gross corporate profit rate has fallen heavily for American capitalism over the past generation. Naturally, this trend has been followed repeatedly by cuts in the rate of corporate taxation, and rhetoric has become ever more insistent that corporations do not really pay taxes, only the consumers of their products do. Equally naturally, this continuing long-term profit squeeze provided President Bush with an important incentive for his repeated insistence on cutting the capital-gains tax.

A note should also be added about the implications of the net interest segment in table 1.3. As the 1929 figure indicates, rates of interest before the New Deal were substantial. A major objective of the post-1933 policy regime had been the drastic reduction in these rates (cf. John Maynard Keynes's call for the "euthanasia of the *rentier* class"). This goal was fully achieved during and after World War II. The post-1945 extended-mass-consumption state was predicated on these extremely low interest rates: Net interest payments in NIPA did not exceed 3 percent until 1962. The consumption-oriented network of financial regulations (e.g., Regulation Q, which for more than a generation limited the interest payments permitted on passbook accounts) pursuing that end was tied to a Federal Reserve Board policy that targeted interest rates.

Conjunctural change occurred in the later 1970s and was consolidated in the 1980–91 period, first stimulated by the inflationary price revolution of the 1970s and then by Paul Volcker's reversal of Federal Reserve Board mon-

TABLE 1.3

CORPORATE PROFITS AND NET INTEREST PAYMENTS AS
PERCENTAGES OF THE NATIONAL INCOME, 1929–30

Year	Corporate profits (with IVA & CC Adj)	Net interest payments	CP – NI
1929	10.7	5.5	+5.2
1932	–4.3	10.9	–15.2
1939	7.5	5.0	+2.5
1950	14.6	1.3	+13.3
1960	11.6	2.7	+8.9
1970	9.7	5.2	+4.5
1980	8.0	9.1	–1.1
1990	6.7	10.6	–3.9

SOURCE: *Economic Report of the President,* various years.

etary policy. There were implications. An old Wall Street saying goes to the effect that 10 percent will draw money from the moon. Net interest payments in NIPA, hovering around this magic number, exceeded corporate profits in each of the twelve years between 1980 and 1991, a situation without precedent in the modern history of the American economy. Involved was a relative shift in the aggregate incentive structure from the entrepreneurial productive-investment side (with its attendant risks to capital) to a more passive income-receiving side of the political economy. If Keynesians had ever come close to his goal of eliminating the *rentier* class, the policy mix of the 1980s resurrected it. Parallels could be and were drawn to similar imbalances between risk and reward in the eighteenth-century age of great decline in the economies of the Netherlands and Venice. And if the Federal Reserve Board reversed policy again in 1991 under the stimulus of recession, cutting short-term rates to their lowest levels by 1992 to the lowest levels since John F. Kennedy occupied the White House, the stimulative effects on the economy were still invisible by election day 1992.

Taken all in all, an overview of economic policy in the Reagan-Bush years leads this observer to depressing conclusions. Ronald Reagan and his table of economists, intellectuals, and policy makers were a kind of collective Pied Piper of Hamlin. The tune was sweet and most agreeable to American ears. Government is the problem. It produces nothing. Taxes are too high and can and should be cut without anyone in particular having to give up anything very much that government outlays provide. We can look the other way as far as deficit and debt are concerned, and anyway we can grow out of them. Decline will thus be reversed: Let free enterprise be free enterprise. The tune was sweet, but perdition eventually loomed. Books proliferated during George Bush's term in office with titles such as *Day of Reckoning, The Age of Diminished Expectations, The Bankrupting of America,* and *America: What Went Wrong?*[23] And the authors were far from being economic cranks.

Perhaps the most telling indictment of this era is that it leaders systematically and fatefully miseducated the American public into believing that it could really have something for nothing and that it could indefinitely consume without penalty more than it produced. As political economy is also moral economy—any old-fashioned conservative would insist on the point —one can even dare to invoke a parallel from the scriptural history of Israel, whose kings (quite a few of them, it would seem) taught the people to sin a great sin. Days of reckoning, apocalypse style, are happily very rare events. Times of reckoning are less so. George Bush's reelection campaign of 1992 coincided with such a time.

But what about foreign policy where, in sharpest contrast, success seemed absolute and conclusive? The wildest dreams of Americans, and particularly of American conservatives, were exceeded during the Bush years. Soviet Communism, its empire, its very heartland, had abruptly vanished from the world scene, and the United States was now the only superpower on the planet. Never since 1917 was free enterprise more widely received as the touchstone of economic wisdom around the world. Never was liberal democracy more universally accepted as the appropriate political counterpart. And never had the left—*all* the left, it might be said—been in greater eclipse or disrepute. What more could anyone ask?

As we have said, irony is the essence of politics. We are in the midst of one of three great revolutions in world politics to occur in our collective lifetime as a nation. During it, the Soviet Union collapsed in explosive decompression. But is explosive decompression confined just to the ex-Soviet world? Consider that this, like other revolutions, has left great disorientation in its wake. Consider that fighting world-class totalitarian dictatorships had shaped two generations of Americans—not to mention governmental demands on individual citizens and their resources—from 1940 to 1990. The cold war was strikingly expensive and burdensome, and it had important constraining effects on American domestic politics. For half a century it was the centerpiece of international politics, ordering the world and America's place in it. But on what might be called the positive side, the cold war provided us with a powerful external threat that was the virtually Manichean negation of America and all that it stood for. The existence of these "children of darkness" did us the very great favor of focusing America's collective identity and its sense of national purpose. For a country as deeply fragmented as the

United States now is, this was no small gift. In a variety of ways whose pattern is not yet clear, politics in the years immediately ahead will center on the need to construct a definition of our collective selves as exigent as that which the cold war provided us. Symptoms of decompression and disorientation accompanying it seemed abundant indeed in the public opinion landscape of 1992; withdrawal symptoms, one might have said.

The strains imposed by the cold war, culminating at one point in its history with the failed Vietnam venture, made a fundamental contribution to the realignment of the late 1960s and the emergence of a quarter century of normal Republican control of the White House. This Republican "lock" in the foreign military policy domain was signally reinforced by reaction against the perceived weakness of the Carter administration on this dimension. This "lock" remained as an important ingredient of George Bush's 1988 electoral triumph over Michael Dukakis: Foreign policy was and is the jewel in Bush's crown. But, as Sidney Blumenthal stressed in his valuable survey of the 1988 election, it was in fact the last cold war election.[24]

How rapidly the mighty can fall—this is one of the oldest themes in literature. Issues as well as men can endure sudden deflations. In 1992 foreign policy issues and public concerns about them played the smallest role in any American presidential election since 1936. The problem of maintaining formidable international-threat figures as electoral anchors is displayed abundantly enough in the case of one of President Bush's great triumphs, the Gulf war against Saddam Hussein of Iraq. Mobilization against Saddam's seizure of Kuwait in 1990, and George Bush's proclamation of him as a Hitler figure, justifiably rallied not only the troops but the nation. But the mobilization could hardly last. Hitler had Germany behind him, after all, while even before the war Iraq had a gross domestic product the size of Kentucky's. If you are the sole surviving superpower in the world, you have difficulty by definition in defining geopolitical enemies who are in your own class. Nor could ideology work very efficiently as a fixative: Whatever else Saddam Hussein is, he is no communist. Thus, as public opinion evaluations about George Bush's performance in office swung rapidly against him in the second half of 1991, it could readily be seen that the Gulf war was but the palest and most evanescent reflection of what the cold war provided the United States (and the Republican party) for decades on end.

The real threat from foreigners these days comes not from a defunct world communism but from our great economic rivals who are as capitalist as ourselves, if arguably more successful. One interesting feature of opinion during the Bush era was a rapid upsurge of Japan bashing as the economic situation at home soured. This may very well reflect our contemporary tendency to form a coherent picture of the world and ourselves by contemplating alien threat figures. A former enemy that is, moreover, nonwhite and has been a notably successful economic competitor—here is an evidently useful target for one's frustrations. But this particular threat imposes very tight constraints on manifesting such sentiments too widely or too publicly. Japanese money has sustained our debts and deficits, and the Japanese economic interpenetration with the American domestic productive scene has created friends and clients aplenty here at home. They, like the Europeans, use the state in close support of favored economic sectors and exports.

As the 1992 campaign season has made very clear, the paradoxical result of "total victory" in the Fifty Years War has not been a rallying around the incumbents in charge when the victory occurred. Conservatives are perplexed because their usually successful electoral stock in trade, the Evil Empire and Democrats too weak willed to stand up to it, have vanished. No comparable enemy figure can be conjured up with even the feeblest credibility. The public's attention in 1992, not surprisingly, had turned overwhelmingly to domestic and particularly economic issues. In this environment, Republican claims that the Reagan-Bush regime had won the cold war traded at a huge discount.

George Bush in Office:
Some Defining Moments

One of the most fundamental characteristics of the regime order that has emerged out of the critical realignment of the late 1960s has been divided government as a normal rather than an exceptional states of affairs. Only recently, during George Bush's term in office, has this phenomenon begun to attract the substantial attention from political scientists that it has long deserved.[25] Among journalists and much of the general public, divided government has often been stigmatized as leading to conflict, deadlock, and political paralysis. These have surely happened—particularly under George Bush, it may be added—but the problem is more fundamental than this. Divided government compromises and in a real sense corrupts both major parties by making each an "incumbent" party in the branch it controls. The broader pattern of policy making under these conditions includes not only collision but collusion and mutual evasions of responsibility on a large scale. It is basic, for one thing, that the king's government must somehow be carried on. For another, when Republicans occupy the White House, as they have for twenty of the past twenty-four years, the Democratic congressional leaders cannot for political reasons allow themselves and their party to be cast in a wholly negative, obstructionist role.

Thus, as with the 1982 social security agreement or the so-called tax reform act of 1986, divided government produces a novel, semi-institutionalized pattern of high policy making. Key congressional committees and party leaders essentially negotiate treaties with the president and his top aides, and then steamroller the agreed-upon deal thorough the congressional rank and file on a vote-it-up-or-down basis. On other occasions, most notoriously in the 1982 deregulation of the savings-and-loan industry, there was full collusion with eventually disastrous national consequences, but without resorting to this new quasi-institutionalized machinery. In either event, a primary objective for both parties is to ensure that each is "held harmless," as the Washington phrase puts it—to ensure that neither party to the settlement will use either process or result as ammunition in its political wars with the other side. The most conspicuous example of this negotiated treaty approach during the Bush years was the 1990 budget agreement. This had important practical consequences for the president, which we soon canvass.

Complex deals worked out among a tiny group of players are in essence efforts to paper over the fundamental irresponsibility of divided government, but they create legitimacy problems of their own. The process excludes not only the public but also, to a great extent, ordinary members of Congress. The deals are thus very likely to become unpopular both in process and result. Linked as they are with a general environment in which lack of campaign finance reform has helped reelect the overwhelming majority of congressional incumbents, and in which a mixture of partisan and institutional finger-pointing and blame-placing (and blame-avoiding) dominates the political noise emanating from Washington, a considerable part of the public had literally become fed up by the midpoint of Bush's term in office. One could hardly be surprised that new energy went into the drive to secure a constitutional amendment requiring a balanced budget, that a very large-scale movement toward imposing term limitations on legislators got under way, and that Ross Perot—a candidate running squarely on the view that the system had really broken down and needed comprehensive fixing— should enter the 1992 race and win the support of more than 19 million Americans.

Ronald Reagan and, before him, Richard Nixon had coexisted relatively comfortably with Congress. Reagan in particular, despite his ideological differences with the Democrats, got along better on a personal level with the House leadership than Jimmy Carter had ever been able to do. Of course, it helped greatly that Republicans also controlled the Senate for six of Reagan's eight years in office. George Bush had far less success. In part this may have been related to the fact that his party was deeper in a minority position on his accession, particularly in the House (just 173 Republicans, or 39.8 percent of House membership), than at any previous presidential accession in American history. But in considerable part, Bush was far more distant, rigid, and confrontational in his relationship with Congress than Reagan had ever been. He wielded the veto power with extraordinary success (more than thirty vetoes sustained and only one overridden). On the other hand, in 1990 his presidential success score in Congress hit the second lowest (48 percent) recorded since *Congressional Quarterly* first reported this measure in 1953. Even Bush's first-year "honeymoon" success rating (65 percent) was lower than for any incoming president from Eisenhower on, with the sole exception of Gerald Ford, who took office in 1974 under unusually adverse circumstances. Both Bush's sterling veto record and his strikingly poor success record are, of course, two sides of the same coin: a growing ideological polarization built into the dynamic of this divided-government interregnum state's recent evolution.

Let us now examine several particularly defining moments in the Bush presidency. The first of these was the Iraqi conquest of Kuwait in August 1990 and the American-led countermobilization that was to result in the Gulf war of January–March 1991. Here was a situation in which the president was deeply and passionately committed: "This aggression will not stand," and it didn't. George Bush's skills in weaving the multinational anti-Iraq coalition together have been widely and justly admired. The military build-up and the actual four-day land war were widely perceived to have been splendidly organized, though the military operation's execution fell some distance short of perfection. Tactically, Operation Desert Storm was a brilliant success, and by spring 1991 Bush's approval rating had risen to close to 90 percent. This was to have political consequences, for it cast an aura of invincibility around the president that not only dulled his awareness of impending danger on the electoral front but discouraged the most prominent Democratic hopefuls from entering the ring against him. For reasons we have attempted to identify earlier, the Desert Storm triumph was to stand politically little longer than Iraq's aggression had stood militarily. It was to turn out by 1992, again ironically, that Bush's skill, vigor, commitment, and determination in dealing with foreign policy crises stood in the sharpest contrast to his lack of attention to, or interest in, the domestic side of his job.

The second major defining event of the Bush years was the epochal struggle over the 1991 budget. Ultimately the struggle pivoted on usual domestic issues that divide Democrats from Republicans, but there was an additional ingredient: No deal that purported to attack the budget deficit could pass muster without a tax increase, and the president had therefore to abandon his 1988 pledge on that subject if any agreement were to be had. The consequence was that the negotiations that preceded the obligatory interbranch treaty were the most protracted and excruciating in the short history of this particular policy device. They lasted from the middle of May to the end of September 1990. The treaty then duly proclaimed by both leaderships, it was summarily voted down in the House of Representatives on 5 October by a resounding 179–254 vote. Faced with the imminent shutdown of the government, negotiators went back to the drawing board. A major element in the failure of the first pact was anger among congressional Democratic rank and filers, who keenly resented exclusion from the decision process. The leadership was much more careful to engage in consultation with them on the second round. At the same time, the president's prestige had also been severely damaged by the 5 October rejection, and it became increasingly clear that if any treaty was to be framed, George Bush would find a large majority of House Republicans opposed to him and would thus have to rely on the Democrats for its enactment.

The second version of the treaty was finally enacted on 27 October —scarcely a week before the 1990 congressional election!—by narrow margins in both houses (228–200 in the House, 54–45 in the Senate). Its modifications on the services-cutting side made it acceptable to the large majority of Democrats. But it also included the second-largest dollar volume of federal tax increases in our history, some $150 billion worth, and this enraged Republicans in and out of Congress. George Bush had flip-flopped on an issue of paramount symbolic importance to them, and his treaty carried the day with three-quarters of House Republicans flatly opposed to him. This was to have very long-lasting consequences. Faced with the internal uproar, Bush was reduced to apologizing to the conservatives for his "mistake" in agreeing to a deal that had been urged on him by his own Treasury secretary, Nicholas Brady, and his Office of Management and Budget director, Richard Darman. And however successful this admission and his pledge never to do it again may have eventually been in pacifying the right within the Republican party, it left him vulnerable with the American public throughout the campaign on the very issue of trust with which he hoped to defeat Bill Clinton.

The third defining moment, more than any other, engaged social-issue politics in the fall of 1991. This was of course the nomination of Clarence Thomas to the Supreme Court and the storm of controversy it produced, particularly among women. In the first place, Thomas had shown himself to be a reliably right-wing black, which fact could and did help divide the liberal coalition against him. Second, while there will probably never be any "smoking gun" evidence on the subject, it is reasonable to assume that George Bush selected him to provide another vote on the Court to overturn *Roe v. Wade*. Bush did his credibility no good in proclaiming that he had picked the best-qualified candidate. This was as incredible to the attentive public of lawyers and legal scholars as was Thomas's bland claim before a much larger public that he had never talked to anyone or really formed any opinion about that famous case.

But as the history of Supreme Court appointments across two centuries amply demonstrates, mediocrity of background or record has hardly been a barrier to the elevation of a person to the nation's highest tribunal. The detonating feature of this case lay elsewhere. Thomas's confirmation hearings before the Senate Judiciary Committee culminated explosively when Anita Hill, a black professor at the University of Oklahoma Law School and a former subordinate of Thomas's, charged that he had engaged in sexual harassment of her repeatedly and over an extended period. Neither race nor ideology were involved here: just his word against hers. The result was a media spectacular in which Ms. Hill, facing a Senate panel composed exclusively of well-off, middle-aged white males, was eventually left alone with her point of view. The confirmation strategy, ably and aggressively led by three Republican senators (Orrin Hatch of Utah, Alan Simpson of Wyoming, and Arlen Specter of Pennsylvania) aimed to prevail by destroying Hill's credibility and as much of her character as necessary. Helped considerably by the Democrats' paralysis in the face of a black nominee before them, and by Clarence Thomas's own very deft playing of the race card in his testimony, the strategy prevailed.

In the aftermath, a certain outraged consciousness-raising was easily visible among many women. The theme was repeated over and over again: "They just don't get it." In this view, white middle-class males, particularly conservative ones, are so sunk in a culture of patriarchy, of gender subordination, that they have no remote clue as to the outrage and deprivation that so many women feel over the myriad impacts that gender discrimination inflicts on them. As one consequence—specifically cited as such by one incoming U.S. Senator, Carol Mosely Braun (D-Illinois)—1992 came rather early to be called "the year of the woman candidate." Some of these women, like Senator Braun, were in fact elected; others were not. And it is only appropriate to note that the only one of the big three Republican senators in the Thomas-Hill controversy who ran for reelection in 1992, Arlen Specter, was in fact reelected. But as far as George Bush's election prospects were concerned, the whole affair was a net minus, even if it was not an overwhelming disaster that could be clearly identified as such. He did not need any further sources that conveyed the public impression that he too was out of touch or "just didn't get it."

The final pre-1992 event of the Bush years that we have selected for discussion is the election campaign to fill a Senate vacancy that occurred in Pennsylvania in the fall of 1991. There are certain occasions when by-elections of this sort convey unusually strong signals about the public mood. The

Pennsylvania Senate election, occasioned by the untimely accidental death of Republican Senator John Heinz, is a prime example of this rather unusual set of by-election cases. For it was here that the dominant themes of the presidential election exactly one year later were first clearly and dramatically raised, and with the special force that only an election provides.

George Bush's attorney general, Richard Thornburgh, entered the race as the overwhelming favorite. Having also been twice elected to the governorship, his name recognition among Pennsylvania's electorate was nearly total. Republicans began the campaign with high hopes. After all, no Democrat had won a Senate election in the state since Joseph S. Clark in 1962, and Republicans had won no fewer than thirteen of the fifteen contests for the Senate between 1946 and 1988. Thornburgh faced a Democrat who had had lower-level experience in the executive branch as far back as the Kennedy administration, Bryn Mawr president Harris Wofford. In brief, the tables were very promptly turned. Thornburgh, stressing his record and connections as a Washington insider, ran a wooden campaign as though he were an incumbent. For his part, Wofford found magic-button issues among a middle-class electorate that was undergoing considerable economic stress. His campaign slogan, "It's time to take care of our own," landed right on target, as did his chief campaign issue, a call for a national health-care program. It is also worthy of note that this campaign was brilliantly orchestrated by a young political operative, James Carville, who went on to greater things in 1992.

Wofford not only won but secured a landslide margin, 55 percent of the vote, which was the largest that any Democrat had received since the first popular Pennsylvania Senate election in 1914. The coalition he put together was particularly striking, prefiguring as it did the one that Bill Clinton was to forge in defeating George Bush in this state and in the nation one year later. In particular, Wofford benefited from an enormous swing in the Philadelphia suburbs. Hugely Republican, these counties normally produced a lead of somewhere around 300,000 votes for Republican candidates, usually enough to carry the state. Thornburgh's margin in these suburbs was cut to just 558 votes; the Democratic swing from 1988, less than 5 percent elsewhere in the state, approached 15 percent in these suburban counties. What Wofford's campaign had managed to do was to connect forcefully and effectively, and on strictly economic-issue grounds, with middle-class suburbanites, many of whom had never before cast a Democratic vote. *Congressional Quarterly Weekly Report's* headline concisely summed up the situation: "Domestic Discontent—Wofford Win Sets Tone for '92 Elections: Angry Voters Want Help on Home Front."[26] This Senate election was a crystal-clear warning to George Bush and his reelection campaign aides. It was very characteristic of him, and of at least some of them, that this warning went unheeded.[27]

Toward 3 November: Bush's Rocky Road
to Defeat in 1992

In terms of initial voter volatility and with loud expressions of disgust and anger easily picked up by pollsters, 1992 was an election year without modern parallel. Despite these and other abundant storm signals, the president himself was remarkably serene, not to say confident, about his prospects in what he himself called "this crazy election year." Was he out of touch? Or did he believe that at the end, the public's fear of change would outweigh all the vocal clamor for it? Whatever the explanation for George Bush's calm and self-assurance, neither were widely shared within the leadership cadres of his own coalition. While most of these people rallied around him at the end, as could be expected, conservatives in particular had for a time risen in revolt against him and his presidency. Following the huge Clinton "bounce" in July after Ross Perot temporarily bowed out of the race, unease among top Republicans produced vocal demands that Bush retire from the field and let the Republican part nominate someone who could win. Such dismay and disarray within the governing party has occurred frequently enough with our other understudy presidents as well.

Such old conservative faithfuls as Richard Viguerie, Paul Weyrich, and George Will, along with the *Orange County (CA) Register,* joined the call for Bush to step down. Their arguments may be worth reviewing here:

1. From 1989 onward, George Bush and his administration have not given movement conservatives the time of day. They are essentially the old crowd of "country-club Republicans," totally out of tune with the larger public, though this public has given abundant proof of its dedication to Ronald Reagan's right-wing populism. (Weyrich)

2. George Bush betrayed the conservative cause when, to resolve the budget impasse of 1990, he abandoned his solemn pledge against tolerating any new taxes. He broke his word on a subject that conservatives believe to be of fundamental importance and demonstrated thereby his lack of principle. (All)

3. The president seeks reelection but has given no clue about what he would do in a second term. The administration—including George Bush but excluding Dan Quayle—has been unable to define a clear forward course of any kind during the past four years. He and his advisers are essentially managers in temperament and outlook. Moral zeal and commitment to anything are conspicuous by their absence. (All, but especially Will)

At a point just three months before the election, the pages of the *Wall Street Journal* contained assessments of often very similar import by three of its own people.[28] Paul A. Gigot argued that the president should retire, his mission accomplished and nothing else definable on the horizon. "Bill Clinton is now soaring in the polls because voters sense that Mr. Bush is a spent president." The editor of the *Wall Street Journal,* Robert Bartley, advocated instead that Bush use the convention podium and the campaign to define what he intended to do substantively during a second term, and why. "The president, in short, is on the floor. To recover, he has to use his concentration, and his power as president, to define himself and show that he stands for something." A third tack was suggested by Karen Elliott House, vice-president (international) of Dow Jones, the newspaper's publisher. She urged George Bush to take a leaf out of Harry Truman's book in 1948 and to go on the offensive as he had done, by calling an opposition Congress back into session, and (as Truman had done) to take controversial actions that Congress could not block. "In short, if George Bush decided to demonstrate his willingness to go down fighting, he, like Harry Truman, might surprise the pundits and pollsters and wind up winning."

Conservative commentary of this sort highlights more effectively than anything but survey evidence the depth of the problems this president had to deal with in his bid for reelection. It must be stressed that there was nothing foreordained or deterministic about Bush's defeat. In fact, at the end of the campaign he seemed to take fire and opt for the third strategy, the one suggested by Ms. House and others; and there was a time, about a week before the end, when he seemed to be drawing even with Bill Clinton. We deal throughout with balances of probabilities, not with certainties. But the balances did indicate, granted what kind of president Bush was, that the probability of electoral failure was very high: on the gross performance of past understudies, about .8, in fact. This was intuitively obvious to leading figures in Bush's camp, and their commentary is thus particularly revealing.

Summed up, this commentary reads very like a composite definition of the kind of person who has filled the presidency in the wake of an innovative and successful predecessor. Each understudy/conservator successor, chosen to provide continuity, found himself in rapidly accumulating difficulties. Many of these difficulties had grown directly out of decisions (and nondecisions) of the immediate past. Most of these understudies were overwhelmed by them and lost their bids for reelection. In each instance, the fissures in their coalition had become clearly visible months or even years before the election, as was the swelling popular discontent with the incumbent's performance in office. In Bush's case, his critics within the conservative camp provided the litany of complaint that was specific to 1992. They assailed the incumbent for having been grossly out of touch with a larger public, for being an insider elitist, for undercutting if not betraying the legacy he had inherited, and for lacking the political imagination to provide leadership or even a minimally adequate definition of himself and his purposes. What was once a source of strength in his appeal was now irrelevant if not an outright source of weakness. Qualities that scarcely mattered in the first election, qualities this conservator, like his predecessor, did not have, became of the essence for success in the second election.

In considerable part, this remarkable outburst of soul searching was occasioned by keen awareness among the participants about the extent of presidential weakness in the court of public opinion. Leaving the ebb and flow of the horse race to other contributions to this volume, this chapter concentrates on the deeper structure of this public opinion as it emerged on the eve of the Republican convention in Houston. Our text at this point is taken from an article by John Morin, director of polling for the *Washington Post* in its weekly edition of 17–23 August 1992.[29] Morin's evaluation begins with the telling summary comment that "President Bush staggered into ... Houston this week as the most unpopular incumbent president to seek re-election in the past five decades." He then enumerates the negative historical survey-research records that had been broken in 1992.

1. *The greatest sustained drop in presidential popularity ever recorded,* with Bush's ratings falling 57 percent from the end of the Gulf war to the eve of the Republican convention. The runner-up was Harry Truman, who was to become George Bush's exemplar on the comeback trail. Truman's rating fell by as much as 55 percent in a period after World War II, but that fall occurred much earlier in his presidency and had been reversed by the time the 1948 campaign got under way.

2. *The lowest job approval rating of any president at a similar point in his presidency.* Since World War II, in fact, only three of the nine incumbents (including Bush) have had lower approval ratings at *any* point in their terms.

3. *The highest disapproval rating of any incumbent president seeking re-election.* As Morin notes, "Bush arguably is as unpopular with the American people as Richard Nixon was in the worst days of his presidency."

4. *The biggest advantage that any challenger has ever enjoyed over an incumbent president at a similar stage in his campaign.* This of course was in mid-August, with Perot out of the picture and before the Republican convention, a moment at which Bill Clinton led George Bush by a twenty-six–point margin in the *Washington Post* poll. As Morin

notes, from the earliest days of survey research in 1936 to the present, only 1964 Republican *challenger* Barry Goldwater was further behind in the summer horse-race polls than was George Bush in 1992.

As our earlier schema makes clear, the last third-term conservator case before Bush was Herbert Hoover sixty years earlier. Survey research has come into being since that time, giving us an indispensable portrait of individuals and their political attitudes. There is strong reason to suppose that, had such techniques been available in 1932 and on earlier occasions involving this group of presidents, very similar attitudinal profiles would have appeared. We may say, for want of parallel information for earlier elections, that the survey-research findings for 1992 may be thought of as representative for the entire class, which should make them of particular analytic interest not just for students of public opinion and elections, but for students of the history of the American presidency as well.

At the end of the day, George Bush's electoral showing—particularly his share of the total vote—faithfully reflected what the summer polls had been telling us. This showing was also almost uncannily typical for a member of this select group of third-term understudy presidents. Between 1988 and 1992 Bush's share of the total vote fell by 16.0 percent, very close to the mean for the group as a whole with or without including him in it. His 1992 share of the total vote (including minor-party candidates) was 37.4 percent. Except for Taft's 23.2 percent in the special party-bolt circumstances of 1912, this was the lowest ever recorded by an incumbent president seeking reelection. Finally, we may note that Bush lost just under 30 percent of his 1988 voting base. Only Herbert Hoover in 1932, John Adams in 1800, and, of course, Taft in 1912 presided over worse coalitional collapses, and in the cases of Hoover and Adams they were not very much worse.

Conclusion: George Bush and the American Presidency

Our discussion has identified several commonly recurring factors that seem to come together with particular virulence among a certain well-bounded group of presidents whom we have labeled third-term understudies or conservators. Rapid change in the contexts and issues of politics collides with the personal traits of presidents who are for one reason or another defective, missing something, in their total makeup as chief executives. John Adams was incapable of the political suppleness needed to ride herd over fractious coalitional infighting within his party and his own cabinet, a talent that such regime-order creators as Jefferson, Lincoln, and Franklin Roosevelt had in such abundance. James Madison, superb political theorist and Founding Father though he was, was also the very definition of a weak president subordinate to Congress and unable to control his own administration; and he himself recognized that he had practically no aptitude for the job. Martin Van Buren, an organizational genius, could lay real claim to the title Father of the American Party System; but he could not translate his talents into those needed for effective executive leadership. William Howard Taft himself recognized his lack of aptitude for or real interest in the presidency. His highest goal was not the White House but the Supreme Court. Herbert Hoover, like another ill-fated president, Jimmy Carter, was technician and engineer by training and temperament. His ideal of leadership was to convert politics into technique and administration at a time when something very different was called for. And among a number of these men, rigidity and an inability to adapt to changing circumstances were significant personality characteristics.

What, finally, are we to say of George Bush? A retrospective view of his tenure in office reveals certain clearly parallel features. He conceived of his role essentially in terms of management and administration. He had very feeble interest in any aspect of American domestic politics. His chief political passions—apart from the very fact of being president, an important consideration for him—lay in the realms of foreign policy and diplomacy, areas in which he had undoubted and considerable gifts. But in the changed economic and political setting of 1992, these could not compensate for the image of disinterest, punctuated by standpattism, that had grown up around him. In his whole involvement with the domestic political arena, Bush displayed a striking mixture of rigidity and policy zigzags, all in an overarching context of profound indifference.

In certain important aspects, the American presidency bears some comparison with the principate of Imperial Rome. In the sharpest distinction to most advanced democratic capitalist political systems, what the British theorist Walter Bagehot a century ago called the Dignified and Efficient functions of government are not sharply separated as they are there, but are here fused in a single person. Americans vote for a political leader who, in addition to his other functions, is the *pontifex maximus,* not so very different, perhaps, from Augustus Caesar. The president is the chief priest of the American civil religion.[30] Theodore Roosevelt, a particularly adept practitioner of the arts associated with this important presidential function, had the insight to refer to the presidency as a "bully pulpit." Ours is, in truth, an elective principate. The office and its incumbents preside over a country that is by a wide margin the most religious of any of the advanced capitalist democracies.

Performance of the thaumaturgic functions of the American presidency probably reached its apogee with Abraham Lincoln, a man often described as the Christ figure in America's Passion Play. As Garry Wills has pointed out in a brilliant study of Lincoln's rhetoric, his exceptional gifts were used for something even more fundamental than order maintenance. They were used to produce a permanent and vitally significant realignment in American public discourse.[31] Each in his own way, every president retrospectively judged by historians to be "great" or "near great" has been able to comprehend this role and to perform it in an effective, and very often transforming, way. Closely connected to it is that elusive quality, presidential "vision," through which focus on "the good society" is attempted and often achieved. But it is strikingly characteristic of third-term understudy-successor presidents that each in his own way lacked the perception, the innate talent, or both, to exploit this fundamental dimension of presidential power. Needless to say, they shared this deficiency to greater or lesser degree with most American presidents. But for them, in their own "political time," the deficiency became critical. So it was with George Bush, the latest avatar of this species.

With perhaps some license, we can push our Roman comparison a little further. It seems to this writer that a certain parallel exists between George Bush as a leader and the masterly description of the Roman Emperor Galba (reigned A.D. 68–69) left to us by the great historian Cornelius Tacitus.[32]

> In the course of seventy-three years he had led a successful life spanning the reigns of five emperors—reigns that proved luckier for him than his own. He came of a family that could boast ancient nobility and great wealth. His own personality was something of a compromise. While free from serious faults, it scarcely achieved real virtues. Having won a reputation, he neither despised nor exploited it. He harbored no designs on other people's property, was thrifty with his own, and where the state was involved showed himself a positive miser.... Distinguished birth and the alarms of the time disguised his lack of enterprise and caused it to be described as wisdom.... Indeed, as long as he was a subject he seemed too great a man to be one. In the opinion of all he was capable of rule—had he never ruled.

Each of our failed American understudies had perhaps this much in common with the hapless Galba: Each was chosen to continue a recently glorious past, and each had an exceptionally splendid résumé. To each of them, and not least to George Bush, the summary judgment of Tacitus's last sentence applies: *Omnium consensu capax Imperii, nisi imperasset.*

Notes

1. As for the policy-transformative character of the Reagan regime, see (among many other accounts) the essays in *The New Direction in American Politics,* edited by Paul Peterson and John Chubb (Washington, D.C.: Brookings Institution, 1985).

2. Allan J. Lichtman and Ken DeCell, *The Thirteen Keys to the Presidency* (Lanham, Md.: Madison Books, 1990).

3. From 1892 to 1992 there have been fifteen incumbent party wins (of which twelve involved sitting presidents) and ten incumbent party losses (five of which involved sitting presidents seeking election or reelection).

4. Sometimes the victims of elections include not only defeated politicians and parties but analysts as well. The notorious failure of the *Literary Digest*'s straw-poll technique in 1936 was paralleled later by the pollsters' conspicuous misfires in the 1948 presidential election here and the 1992 general election in the United Kingdom. The chief analyst/academic losers in the American election of 1992 were, without question, those engaged in the thriving cottage industry of constructing predictive economics-and-politics models. (For a general account of modern political forecasting, see a recent study by one of the losers, Michael S. Lewis-Beck and Tom W. Rice, *Forecasting Elections* [Washington, D.C.: CQ Press, 1992]; and for a summary review of these efforts during the campaign, see *Business Week,* 3 August 1992, 15.) All or virtually all these models projected a victory for George Bush by margins ranging from 51 percent to as high as 55–57 percent of the two-party vote. One suspects excessive preoccupation with short-term (say, 1991–92) economic change and inflation levels. Needless to say, such projections were in stark contrast to the message that surveys were so insistently telling us, including evidence of considerable public anxiety about longer-term economic performance.

By midsummer I had become thoroughly dissatisfied with all this, and it occurred to me that the fact of incumbency was significant and that a long-term variable (growth in per capita disposable income) from the first to the fifteenth quarter of an initial presidential term should be included. The economic-growth–electoral-outcome database was thus confined to six cases of presidents seeking reelection in the postwar period (1956–84), 1948 being rejected since the long-term component was uniquely distorted by the economic effects of World War II and reconversion. Having run several equations on this basis, I found rather to my surprise that the long-term component (X_1) contributes about two-fifths to the whole result. The best-fit equation measured δPCDI from quarters 1 to 15 of the presidential term (X_1, LT) and δPCDI from the immediately preceding year to the election year (X_2, ST). This produced an r^2 of .856 and the equation

$$Y = 42.504 + 1.061X_1 + 1.662X_2.$$

Assuming what may well have been an overestimate from available data and projections that LT growth was 1.0 percent and ST growth was 1.6 percent, the model projected that Bush would receive 46.2 percent of the two-party vote. The actual figure was 46.6 percent of the two-party vote, far within the mean empirical deviation of ±2.1 surrounding this equation. Needless to say, this is a very simple-minded model and no predictive clairvoyance is claimed for it. Still, it is clear that it came much closer in the end to the real-world result, and what the surveys were telling us, than the "consensus forecast" given us by the economics-and-politics modelers.

5. It will surely be noted by some readers that Hoover (1928) succeeded a two-term regime that had two presidents rather than one, as in every other case in our group. Moreover, it might seem whimsical by modern standards to posit that Hoover's immediate predecessor, Calvin Coolidge, was in any sense "charismatic." Yet the regime itself was certainly policy innovative: Restoration of "normalcy" was the right turn of the 1920s, and it reversed course very substantially from that dominant in the Wilson/Progressive years. As for Coolidge, say what one will, he dominated politics in Washington in his own time, both in image and policy terms, far more than is often remembered today. He set a "tone" for politics in his day not far inferior to Ronald Reagan's tone-setting in his, and it is not in the least surprising that Coolidge's portrait held a place of high honor in Reagan's White House.

6. Despite his well-canvassed problems, it is not impossible that Bill Clinton might turn out to have "charisma" retrospectively, assuming a successful presidency. (How really "charismatic," after all, was Franklin Roosevelt *in 1932*?) And what about key 8, "social unrest"? Would the Los Angeles riots of 1992, the flare-up of unrest in New York City just before the Democratic convention in mid-July, the massive pulling and shoving in front of abortion clinics by Operation Rescue and its opponents over the course of Bush's presidency, or all of them together, be enough to "turn" this key? Cases could be made either way. It is also noteworthy that there is no key in the Lichtman-DeCell scheme for the kind of massive popular unhappiness with "the system" that was a striking feature of the American electorate in 1992.

7. This includes, by the way, another small set: those initially elected as vice presidents and succeeding through death or resignation and then running for election in their own right. There have been five such cases, all in the twentieth century (Theodore Roosevelt, 1904; Coolidge, 1924; Truman, 1948; Lyndon Johnson, 1964; and Gerald Ford, 1976). All of these men except Ford achieved their goal, and they have a mean "negative key" score of just over 4.

8. There are quite fundamental differences as well as some very intriguing continuities in the structure of American electoral politics before and after the democratizing transition of 1828–40. As indicated, one of these fundamental differences was the structural absence of forces tending to restore two-party competition over a series of elections. For a seminal discussion of the contrary situation in the period 1966–1932, see Donald E. Stokes, "On the Existence of Forces Restoring Party Competition," in Angus Campbell, Philip E. Converse, Warren E. Miller, and Donald E. Stokes, *Elections and the Political Order* (New York: Wiley, 1966), 180–93.

9. The *locus classicus* for the history of the entire period from 1901 to 1817 is Henry Adams, *History of the United States of America during the Administrations of Thomas Jefferson and James Madison* (1903), recently reprinted in 2 vols.

in the Library of America Series (New York: Literary Classics of the United States, 1986). Despite a distinct "Adams family party" slant, this is a masterwork, an indispensable resource for anyone interested in studying the "lost Atlantis" of American party politics before the rise of Andrew Jackson.

10. One notes, for example, that turnout in the March 1814 New Hampshire gubernatorial election reached 81.4 percent of the estimated potential electorate, a level of mobilization not again equaled until the Civil War realignment forty years later.

11. William G. Shade, "Political Pluralism and Party Development: The Creation of a Modern Party System, 1815–1852," in Paul Kleppner et al., *The Evolution of American Electoral Systems* (Westport, Conn.: Greenwood, 1981), 77–112.

12. Daniel Webster in Massachusetts, William Henry Harrison in the other free states plus Kentucky and Maryland, and Hugh L. White in the remaining slave states.

13. An important and very recent account of this process of institutional development and mass mobilization is Joel H. Silbey, *The American Political Nation, 1838–1893* (Stanford: Stanford University Press, 1991), esp. 1–71.

14. Lichtman and DeCell, *Thirteen Keys to the Presidency*, 191–97, identify 1904 as "the perfect election" from their perspective: the only instance from 1968 through 1988 in which all thirteen keys turned in favor of the incumbent.

15. See Martin J. Sklar, *The Corporate Reconstruction of American Capitalism, 1890–1916* (New York: Cambridge University Press, 1988), esp. 332–82, his penetrating comparison and analysis of the presidencies of Theodore Roosevelt and William Howard Taft.

16. Obviously, another and very important set of issues turned on the drive for a radical restructuring of political institutions whose legitimacy in the new corporate America was in question, and especially of the major parties themselves. But these issues are not central to our discussion here.

17. A useful discussion of the Democratic party as a warring jumble of parochial outgroups in the 1920s is David Burner, *The Politics of Provincialism* (New York: Knopf, 1965).

18. James David Barber, *The Presidential Character: Predicting Performance in the White House,* 3d ed. (Englewood Cliffs, N.J.: Prentice-Hall, 1985), 18–25, 39–41, 58–65, 81–84. George Bush might be reasonably classified in Barber's terms as a semipassive-negative personality (though he certainly displayed occasional outbursts of intense activity). Barber classifies Taft as a classic passive-positive; perhaps one could fit Van Buren in or close to that category. In Barber's view, Hoover was an active-negative personality type; and so, pretty clearly, was John Adams. As with many premodern presidents, James Madison seems hard to categorize in these terms. In office at least, he usually displayed most of the traits of the passive-negative, though he could be surprisingly purposeful and energetic on occasion, as he was in the annexation of West Florida in 1810. As the classic case of Coolidge demonstrates, passive-negatives can work out quite well in the presidency as long as their inactivity matches public demand.

19. Stephen Skowronek, "Notes on the Presidency in the Political Order," in

Studies in American Political Development, vol. 1, edited by Karen Orren and Stephen Skowronek (New Haven: Yale University Press, 1986), 286–302. The cases
he cites of these "super-conservators" who produce important innovations of their
own are James K. Polk (D, 1845–49), Theodore Roosevelt (R, 1901–9), and Lyndon B. Johnson (D, 1963–69).

20. *Planned Parenthood of Southeastern Pennsylvania v. Casey,* decided 29
June 1992 (slip opinion no. 91–744). To the great distress of the religious Right
and the manifest displeasure of President Bush, Justices O'Connor, Kennedy, and
Souter resisted the call to overturn *Roe v. Wade* 410 U.S. 113 (1973) outright. On
this particular point the decision was 5–4, with Chief Justice Rehnquist and Justices Scalia, Thomas, and White in favor of discarding it. The specific state law
imposing some restrictions on abortion was, however, upheld by a 7–2 majority,
only Justices Blackmun (the author of the majority opinion in *Roe*) and Stevens
(appointed by President Ford in 1976) dissenting. The opinions on all sides are
marked by a level of often personal rancor that is quite extraordinary by normal
judicial standards. Reading is believing!

21. Jackie Calmes, "Tougher GOP Stance Reflects Surge of the Religious
Right," *Wall Street Journal,* 10 August 1992, A8

22. One of the most interesting of the many accounts of this development
—not least because of the author's impeccable Republican credentials—is Kevin
Phillips, *The Politics of Rich and Poor* (New York: Random House, 1990). See
also the penetrating examination of the career of junk-bond king Michael Milkin
and other Wall Street "masters of the universe" by *Wall Street Journal* reporter
James B. Stewart: *Den of Thieves* (New York: Simon and Schuster, 1991). For
those who may not wish to invest time in reading a 493-page book, the same atmosphere is convincingly depicted in the movie *Wall Street* (1987).

23. Benjamin Friedman, *Day of Reckoning* (New York: Random House,
1988); Paul Krugman, *The Age of Diminished Expectations* (Cambridge, Mass.:
MIT Press, 1990); David P. Calleo, *The Bankrupting of America: How the Federal
Budget Is Impoverishing the Nation* (New York: Morrow, 1992); James Dale Da-
vidson and Lord William Rees-Mogg, *The Great Reckoning: How the World Will
Change in the Depression of the 1990s* (New York: Summit, 1991); and Donald
L. Bartlett and James B. Steele, *America: What Went Wrong?* (Kansas City: An-
drews and McMeel, 1992). This last book originally appeared as a series of ar-
ticles in the *Philadelphia Inquirer,* stimulating a huge public demand, which was a
media event of the time. Politicians such as retiring Republican Senator Warren
Rudman (N.H.) and Democratic presidential hopeful Paul Tsongas (Mass.) ener-
getically joined in raising the alarm. The ground was thoroughly prepared not
only for Bill Clinton but, of course, for Ross Perot.

24. Sidney Blumenthal, *Pledging Allegiance: The Last Campaign of the Cold
War* (New York: HarperCollins, 1991), a typically perspicacious account.

25. One of the earliest of these recent academic inquiries is Gary Jacobson,
The Electoral Origins of Divided Government (Boulder, Colo.: Westview Press,
1990).

26. *Congressional Quarterly Weekly Report,* 9 November 1991, front cover.

27. Curiously enough, this same state had sent a very similar warning to

John Adams and the Federalist party in an event extremely noteworthy in its time: the narrow but—as it turned out—decisive defeat of Federalist James Ross by the leader of the Jeffersonian forces in Pennsylvania, Thomas McKean, in the 1799 gubernatorial election. As with a number of other phenomena, the "by-election" with unusually general political significance can be detected across the span of American electoral history. By no means all of them have occurred in Pennsylvania!

28. *Wall Street Journal*, 3 August 1992, A14.

29. John Morin, "George Bush in the Land of Way Down Under," *Washington Post Weekly Edition*, 17–23 August 1992, 37.

30. The decisive conceptual breakthrough on these issues was made a generation ago by the anthropologist Robert N. Bellah. See his seminal article, "Civil Religion in America," reprinted in *Daedalus*, 117, no. 3 (Summer, 1988): 97–118. This essay was originally published in the Winter 1967 issue of the same journal. See also the analysis of presidential "bully pulpit" activity by Jeffrey K. Tulis, *The Rhetorical Presidency* (Princeton: Princeton University Press, 1987).

31. Garry Wills, *Lincoln at Gettysburg: The Words That Remade America* (New York: Simon and Schuster, 1992).

32. Tacitus, *The Histories*, trans. Kenneth Wellesley (New York: Penguin Books, 1986), no. 49 in any edition, p. 51 of this text. On the "noble family" front, it is worth a marginal note that, genealogically speaking, George Herbert Walker Bush is the most "noble" president the United States has ever had. He can trace undisputed ancestry on a number of lines back to the Plantagenet English Royals (1154–1399) and thus back to the truly imperial figures of Charlemagne (d. 814) and Otto I, creator of the Holy Roman Empire (d. 973). See Gary Boyd Roberts (comp.) *Ancestors of American Presidents* (Santa Clarita, Calif.: Boyer, 1989), esp. 94–101, 163–65. In this particular setting, only George Washington and Franklin D. Roosevelt are runners-up.

2

Sorting Out and Suiting Up: The Presidential Nominations

ROSS K. BAKER

And choice, being mutual act of all our souls,
Makes merit her election, and doth boil,
As 'twere from forth us all, a man distill'd
Out of our virtues . . .

— *Troilus and Cressida* (I, iii)

It had become an article of faith among political professionals in the 1980s that the front-runner among the presidential hopefuls at the beginning of the primary election season could be counted on to win the nomination at the end of it. And looking back on the three contests of the past decade, it would be difficult to contradict that conventional wisdom or be reluctant to apply it to the outcome in 1992.

One sign that pointed to a firm connection between early standing of candidates and their ultimate success was the presence in the race of an incumbent president. Both Jimmy Carter in 1980 and Ronald Reagan in 1984 were heavy favorites to win renomination, and both won easily—Carter less easily than Reagan. But even in the final primary cycle of the decade, 1988, when there was no heavily favored incumbent in either party, little doubt existed from the New Hampshire primary onward that George Bush, the incumbent vice-president, and Michael Dukakis, with his incomparable organization, would become the nominees.

So if all that needed to be done in 1992 was to consult the list of hopefuls in January, look for the names mentioned most commonly by experts as the front-runners, and then in June tally the delegate votes, you would have found George Bush and Bill Clinton at the top of both lists. This might lead you to conclude that the primary season was not noteworthy (and that this should be the shortest chapter in *The Election of 1992*).

But that would be a little like saying that the expected winner of the American Civil War at the time it began was the North, and that, because that side won in 1865, the story of the intervening four years does not need to be told. While America's great conflict and the 1992 primaries are certainly not of comparable magnitude, the paths taken by George Bush and Bill Clinton to the nominations were noteworthy because in both campaigns doubts emerged —small in Bush's case but considerable in Clinton's—that the early front-runner would prevail in the end. Also, the manner in which Bush and Clinton conducted themselves in the primaries told much about them as men and politicians and the parties they represented; and the primaries provided a testing ground for the issues and strategies they would use in the general election.

This chapter discusses this doubt-plagued primary process and the considerably less suspenseful conventions that followed it by examining the prehistory of the two campaigns; the rules of the game; the sorting-out process—the primaries; the significant role of Ross Perot; and the great robing ceremonies at Madison Square Garden in New York and the Houston Astrodome, where the two candidates suited up for the general election, and, finally, a summation of what it all meant.

The Prehistory of the Republican Primaries

No particular date can be assigned to the commencement of the Bush reelection campaign, but it would probably not be too far off the mark to place it on the day after he won his forty-state victory over Michael Dukakis in the presidential election of 1988.[1] Bush's first year in office was spent dispelling the image he had earned in 1988 of a man so consumed with winning that no means of achieving victory was beneath him. As a veteran White House observer described the first phase of the Bush administration: "Conciliation and congeniality were the watchwords of Bush's presidency. Good times, and his determination not to give offense, brought him high ratings in the polls.... After he had been in the White House a year, the Gallup Poll found that 84 percent of those surveyed approved of him as a person; by contrast even Reagan, still enjoying the nation's thankfulness for his recovery from the attempt on his life, reached a personal approval score of only 73 percent at a comparable time."[2]

By late 1990, however, the signals were more ambiguous, although by no means negative. For a perceptive observer, they might have pointed to troubles down the road for Bush because the period from August 1990 to March 1991 was the most eventful of Bush's presidency, the time of his most enduring achievement and his most troubling action as president.

In August 1990, Iraq invaded and annexed its neighboring state of Kuwait, a small, underpopulated country that is a major supplier of petroleum to the West. To counter a similar threat to Saudi Arabia, America's long-time ally in the Persian Gulf region, and to expel Iraqi forces from Kuwait, President Bush dispatched troops to the area. In January 1991, they formed the major part of the UN forces that began the military campaign to eject the Iraqis from Kuwait.

At roughly the same time, budget negotiations were going on between the Bush administration and congressional Democrats on deficit reduction. In June 1990 the president had reluctantly conceded that a tax rise would have to be part of any deficit-reduction agreement. By agreeing to a tax increase, the president had broken his categorical pledge of the 1988 campaign: "Read my lips: no new taxes." Most outraged by this broken pledge were conservative Republicans in Congress and in the media. Eternally mistrustful of George Bush, this group of Reagan loyalists saw in the breaking of the tax pledge a retreat from a fundamental tenet of Reaganomics: Only by starving the government of tax revenues could its size be reduced. Using a favorite conservative example of an historical sellout, the conservative commentator Patrick Buchanan referred to the breaking of the tax pledge as "the Yalta of the Republican party."[3]

But in the afterglow of the military triumph against Saddam Hussein's forces, Buchanan and other critics of Bush were buried in an avalanche of favorable ratings for the president. At the conclusion of the war in March 1991, Bush received some of the highest approval ratings on record. A survey by the *Los Angeles Times* on 9–11 March 1991 found that 86 percent of respondents said that Bush had strong qualities of leadership.

In politics, as in physics, what goes up must come down. And in some ways, these remarkably strong showings by Bush in a variety of polls masked a more sober reality. By the time of the war, the country was already deep in recession. It took little time for the euphoria of the Gulf war victory to wear off. Beginning in mid-March 1991, the Bush popularity curve began to head downward, and his disapproval ratings began to rise; by January 1992, a month before the primaries began, the lines crossed (see figure 2.1).

Dragging Bush's ratings down most forcefully was the state of the economy. Back in the palmy days of March 1991, 65 percent of those questioned

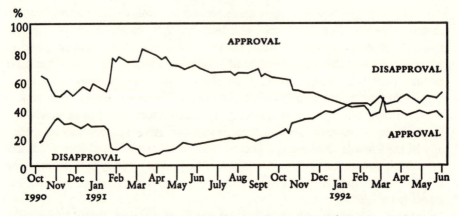

SOURCE: Surveys by the Gallup Organization, *American Enterprise* 3 (July/August 1992): 82–83.

FIGURE 2.1

APPROVAL RATINGS OF GEORGE BUSH AS PRESIDENT

in an ABC News/*Washington Post* poll approved of Bush's handling of the economy; that number was down to 24 percent in January 1992. Even Bush's conduct of foreign affairs, approved by a whopping 85 percent of those questioned in a CBS/*New York Times* poll in March 1991, declined in January-February 1992 to 59 percent. When Patrick Buchanan on 10 December 1991 announced his candidacy for the presidency, there was not only a substantial measure of discontent in the country with Bush's policies, but a new readiness on the part of the public to consider an alternative to the president. Within the Republican party, however, only Buchanan, along with former Ku Klux Klan leader David Duke, who had announced a week before, was available as a vehicle for discontent.

The Prehistory of the Democratic Primaries

Pinning down the first evidence of presidential candidate activity among Democrats is less precise because six of that party's hopefuls were in the field on New Year's Day 1992. In terms of announced candidacies, the early bird was former U.S. Senator Paul Tsongas of Massachusetts, who had left the Senate in 1984 when he was stricken with cancer. On 10 March 1991, Tsongas made his presidential announcement in a Lowell, Massachusetts, living room to a small group of supporters.

The dimness of Tsongas's prospects at the time and the lack of attention paid to his announcement were understandable in view of the fact that on that date President Bush had the approval of more than three-quarters of the American people for his performance in office. But even as Bush's popularity rating began heading downward in the spring of 1991, it was hard to take seriously the campaign of this dour ex-senator.

The year 1992 was not the first time that Bill Clinton formulated presidential plans. He had actually set an announcement date for a 1988 campaign, but the event was called off, reportedly because of what was called "the Gary Hart problem." Like the former Colorado senator, who was revealed in 1987 to be having an extramarital affair after defiantly denying it, Clinton was rumored to have skeletons in his closet. Clinton's own explanation at the time was that he was not ready. But by 3 October 1991, when he announced for the 1992 race in an address from the steps of the Old State House in Little Rock, the old inhibitions were cast aside.[4]

The best-financed Democratic hopeful at the dawn of 1992 was Senator Tom Harkin of Iowa, who occupied the most liberal part of the political spectrum in the Democratic field. By his 15 September 1991 announcement in Winterset, Iowa, Harkin had already launched a remarkably successful direct-mail fund-raising campaign. This effort placed Harkin near the head of the pack of hopefuls to qualify for matching public funds. (To become eligible for these funds, a candidate needs to raise at least $5000 in each of twenty states. The only contributions that qualify, however, are those of less than $250. Direct mail is an ideal way to raise sums of that size.[5])

The most unusual presidential announcement was not a conventional announcement at all, but a letter dated 2 September 1991 from former California governor Jerry Brown to 5000 supporters, enlisting their aid in "an insurgent campaign against the entrenched leadership that is either unwilling or unable to restore real democracy and vitality to the system." Brown, who had sought the Democratic nomination as early as 1976, rejected all contributions larger than $100. He made campaign finance reform a centerpiece of his campaign and characterized excessive political spending as "the root of all political evil."[6]

The 1992 field was rounded out by a genuine American hero, Senator Bob Kerrey of Nebraska, whose campaign was kicked off on 1 October 1991 in Lincoln to the strains of the Bruce Springsteen song "Born to Run." Kerrey was the holder of the nation's highest military decoration, the Congressional Medal of Honor. In the eyes of many observers, this decoration immunized Kerrey against one of the most effective traditional Republican attacks on Democratic presidential candidates, that they placed insufficient emphasis on the utility of military power in the conduct of foreign policy; they were "soft" on defense.

The Reluctants of 1992

As interesting, in some ways, as those who chose to enter the 1992 race for the nomination were those who chose to sit it out. The Reverend Jesse Jackson was at the top of the list of potential candidates, but decided instead to become the host of a talk show and run for "shadow" member of Congress for the District of Columbia, an unofficial post more akin to lobbyist than lawmaker. Jackson's largely black constituency might have been inherited by Virginia's Governor Douglas Wilder, the nation's first popularly elected black governor. Wilder declared for the nomination, but he dropped out on 8 January 1992. Accordingly, African American voters who had supported Jackson so loyally in 1984 and 1988 were up for grabs.

Unlike Jackson, New York's Governor Mario Cuomo had never before sought the nomination, but his speech to the 1984 Democratic National Convention so electrified the audience that it made him a natural focus of speculation. Big-state governors are always considered among the most eligible hopefuls, and Cuomo was taken very seriously. But New York was in serious financial difficulties, and Cuomo cited his need to attend to these problems when he announced his refusal to run on 20 December 1991.

The reluctant Democrats also included Senator Jay Rockefeller of West Virginia, Senator Bill Bradley of New Jersey, Representative Dave McCurdy of Oklahoma, and House Majority Leader Richard Gephardt. The lateness of some decisions to run and the outright abandonment of others, in large measure reflected the remarkable success of Operation Desert Storm, the identification of President Bush with the victory, and the belief that Bush would be unbeatable in 1992.

The Rules of the Game

The ground rules for Democrats and Republicans for the 1992 primary elections reflected the considerable differences between the two parties. The Democratic rules for primaries and caucuses have changed greatly in the years since the tumultuous convention of 1968. The early reforms promoted participation by minorities and women. More recent rule changes made it easier for a party consensus to build around a broadly acceptable candidate and, at the same time, gave certain factional candidates an opportunity to carry on their campaigns somewhat longer. The Reverend Jesse Jackson forced the party to accept the principle that those who received modest percentages of the popular vote in primaries were entitled to a fairer share of delegates.

Republican rules changed in a more evolutionary way. But Republican rules were subject to change from outside the party—paradoxically, by changes in the Democratic rules. When a party alters its delegate-selection rules so as to have an impact on elections, the states must write the party rules into their election laws. Since most legislatures have been under Democratic control in recent years, their willingness to incorporate the Democratic rule changes into statutes has been an incentive to Republicans to conform to Democratic changes in such things as the dates of primary elections.

Another trend initiated by the Democrats and followed by the Republicans is the practice of "front-loading" the primary process. What this means is that the most important events of the primary season take place early in the process. Such Democratic innovations as "Super Tuesday" have prompted the GOP to front-load its process as well. Both sets of primary rules make it extremely difficult for candidates to enter the primaries late in the game.

In recent years, and particularly in 1992, presidential hopefuls had a powerful incentive to raise their money well before the election year dawned and to have well-developed organizations in the early primary states. As party rules shifted the emphasis to the first events, the media also concentrated their attention on the first primaries and caucuses. Indeed, it was noted that in 1988, one-third of all media coverage in the primary season was devoted to stories about New Hampshire and Iowa.

The most notable feature of all these rule changes is that party leaders have been stripped of any significant impact on the choice of the ultimate nominees. That power rests squarely in the hands of the primary voters. Accordingly, a brokered convention, where party leaders step into a deadlocked primary process and pick a nominee, is a thing of the past. Speculation about such a possibility emerged briefly when Bill Clinton was struggling through the various scandals that plagued him, but quickly abated when he was able to ride out the storms. Moreover, Democratic "superdelegates" (mostly elected officials), who were intended by party officials to act as a kind of counterweight in the event that primary voters seemed to be favoring a controversial or vulnerable nominee, also played no major role in the nomination process.

The New Hampshire Primary: The Prototype Event

Toward the middle of the primary election season, Kevin Phillips, a respected conservative commentator, wrote: "As the 1992 presidential campaign unfolds, it is increasingly evident that the United States has entered a period of political alienation and turmoil the likes of which have been experienced only a few times in our history."[7]

The Persian Gulf war euphoria was breathtakingly short, as the U.S. economy descended into recession. A bad economy always spells trouble for an incumbent president. Indeed, the last two incumbent chief executives not to win reelection were Herbert Hoover in the Great Depression year of 1932 and Jimmy Carter in a period of economic stagnation in 1980. The economic recession of 1973–74 also was a major element in the defeat of an unelected president, Gerald Ford, in 1976.

The impact of the Persian Gulf war on public opinion was so fleeting that when a poll was taken of New Hampshire primary voters, a mere 7 percent indicated that the Persian Gulf war had played any role in their voting decision in the primary in that state.[8] The preeminent issue was the economy: a deficit projected to reach $400 billion by 1993 and a $4 trillion overall debt. Unemployment was at more than 7 percent, with joblessness in some towns at 10 percent.

New Hampshire would set a pattern for the primary season in establishing the economy as the dominant issue of the campaign. Eighty-two percent of New Hampshire voters ranked the economy as the top issue. The state's primary, then, was both the first and the defining event of the 1992 primary season. The Granite State's contest had symbolic importance because no candidate since 1952 who had lost this primary had been able to win the presidency.

Bush versus Buchanan

George Bush consistently misread the nature of the challenge from Patrick Buchanan or, perhaps, read the challenge very well but chose not to heed its implications. Buchanan's attack on George Bush from the political right evoked in the president a desperate political fear—that one of the core groups of Republican voters he had inherited from Ronald Reagan and that had served as a foundation of his 1988 victory might be lost. This segment of the electorate is variously referred to as "social conservatives" or "moralists"—voters whose support of Republican candidates derives from their opposition to abortion, gun control, and gay rights and their support for school prayer and strict controls on immigration.[9]

With little evidence to suggest that he was suffering much slippage among such highly conservative New Hampshire voters—the Times-Mirror survey showed him beating Buchanan by 63–24 percent with this group—Bush nevertheless veered toward the political right and spent the primary season shoring up his conservative support.

Republicans who were associated neither with Bush nor Buchanan argued that the conservative columnist enjoyed little popular support except as a vehicle of protest; it was the economy, not social issues, that most deeply troubled the electorate. Appraising the results of the New Hampshire primary, in which Buchanan won 37 percent of the vote to the president's 53 percent, Representative Newt Gingrich of Georgia, a former ally of Buchanan but a backer of Bush, described the challenger's strong showing as "a primal scream" from the people on the state of the economy.[10]

Buchanan's most devastating attacks on Bush in New Hampshire were repeated television spots showing close-up shots of George Bush's mouth speaking the 1988 words, "Read my lips: no new taxes." When the results were sifted after New Hampshire, it became clear that the outcome was a reflection on the president and his performance on the economy rather than an endorsement of Buchanan. An exit poll by Voter Research and Surveys showed that Bush had captured decisively only those voters who felt that their financial situations were better off in 1992 than they had been four years earlier. Those who felt that they were keeping pace were split more evenly. But among those whose financial problems were greater than they had been in 1988, Buchanan overwhelmed Bush 57–39 percent (see table 2.1)[11]

Never again in the 1992 primaries would Buchanan's vote rise as high as in New Hampshire. But in laying down the challenge there and having it misunderstood, or simply ignored, by President Bush, Buchanan influenced the course of the entire campaign in ways that he could not imagine and would not have desired.

New Hampshire: The Survival of Bill Clinton

In years to come, when memories of the 1992 New Hampshire primaries have become dim in the minds of all but the *cognoscenti,* people may find themselves reflecting on the "victory" of Bill Clinton in that state. He did not win; he survived. And if your principal objective is to persist so that you carry the battle to more friendly terrain, saying that Clinton won might not be too wide of the mark. The vote totals show Paul Tsongas with 55,000 votes and 33 percent, and Clinton with 41,000 and 25 percent. Bob Kerrey and Tom Harkin barely broke double digits with 11 percent and 10 percent, respectively. Jerry Brown got 8 percent. The vote in New Hampshire and in later primaries is detailed in tables 2.1–2.3 (pp. 48–50).

In being perceived as a victor by finishing second, Clinton seemed to be in the tradition of such second-place seeming winners as Eugene McCarthy in 1968 and George McGovern in 1972, who did better than they were expected to do against formidable front-runners. Clinton, however, had been considered by many the early front-runner. Why was the New Hampshire primary not a disaster for him as it had been for other front-runners? The

TABLE 2.1

THE REPUBLICAN VOTE IN NEW HAMPSHIRE

% of total vote		Voted for	
		Bush	Buchanan
	Family financial situation		
19	Better today than four years ago	71%	27%
40	About the same	67	31
40	Worse today than four years ago	39	57
	Those who said the national economy is ...		
7	Good	86	13
49	Not so good	69	29
43	Poor	38	58
	Political identification		
64	Republicans	62	36
35	Independents	48	48
11	Liberals	55	39
35	Moderates	59	38
55	Conservatives	55	43
	Those who voted for a candidate mainly ...		
72	Because he would make the best President	73	25
25	To send a message	11	83
	Views of President Bush		
51	Approve of the way he is handling his job	93	6
45	Disapprove	14	81
29	Said his breaking "No new taxes" pledge was a very important factor in vote decision	13	85

SOURCE: Poll conducted by Voter Research and Surveys of 1848 Republican voters leaving voting places throughout New Hampshire. *New York Times,* 20 February 1992.

answer lies in the challenges Clinton faced in the weeks before the New Hampshire primary and how he coped with these challenges.

On 16 January, a month before the New Hampshire primary, Clinton's campaign aides learned that the *Star,* a supermarket tabloid, would print a story that Clinton, a married man, had had a twelve-year affair with a woman named Gennifer Flowers. Clinton and his wife, Hillary, gambled that a joint appearance on the top-rated CBS program "60 Minutes," to be seen just after the Super Bowl game, would give them a chance to tell their story and, perhaps more important, to present a more complete picture of the candidate than voters had yet seen. A parallel effort began to discredit the source of the story, and Clinton's favorable ratings actually rose to 67 percent in a poll taken after the "60 Minutes" program.[12]

TABLE 2.2

THE PRIMARY VOTE — DEMOCRATS

Date	State	Clinton	Tsongas	Brown	Other	Total vote
18 Feb.	New Hampshire	24.7%	33.2%	8.1%	34.0%	167,815
25 Feb.	South Dakota	19.1	9.6	3.9	67.4	59,794
3 Mar.	Colorado	26.8	25.6	28.8	18.8	239,441
	Georgia	57.1	24.0	8.1	10.8	452,570
	Maryland	33.7	40.5	8.2	17.6	551,184
	Utah	18.3	33.4	28.4	19.9	31,638
7 Mar.	South Carolina	63.0	18.5	6.0	12.5	114,191
	Arizona	29.2	34.4	27.5	8.9	36,326
10 Mar.	Florida	51.7	34.0	12.3	2.0	1,117,878
	Louisiana	69.3	11.1	6.6	13.0	380,568
	Massachusetts	11.0	66.5	14.6	7.9	789,856
	Mississippi	73.4	7.9	9.6	9.1	191,755
	Oklahoma	70.5	—	16.6	12.9	415,067
	Rhode Island	21.3	53.4	18.9	6.4	50,349
	Tennessee	67.4	19.3	8.1	5.2	313,745
	Texas	65.4	19.2	8.0	7.4	1,492,371
17 Mar.	Illinois	51.5	25.9	14.7	7.9	1,471,284
	Michigan	50.6	16.6	25.8	7.0	582,309
24 Mar.	Connecticut	35.6	19.6	37.2	7.6	171,198
5 Apr.	Puerto Rico	95.6	.1	1.6	2.7	63,398
7 Apr.	Kansas	51.1	15.2	13.2	20.5	159,424
	Minnesota	32.7	22.8	31.7	12.8	185,465
	New York	40.5	22.8	26.0	4.7	976,465
	Wisconsin	37.9	22.2	35.0	4.9	748,908
28 Apr.	Pennsylvania	56.6	12.7	25.6	5.1	1,225,222
5 May	Indiana	63.5	12.3	21.1	3.1	467,464
	North Carolina	64.0	8.3	10.4	17.3	681,327
	District of Columbia	73.8	10.5	7.2	8.5	60,411
12 May	Nebraska	47.9	7.5	22.1	22.5	142,261
	West Virginia	74.1	6.9	11.9	7.1	304,019
19 May	Oregon	49.6	11.4	34.8	4.2	299,957
	Washington	51.5	15.9	28.9	3.7	111,565
26 May	Arkansas	68.1	—	11.1	20.8	497,446
	Idaho	49.3	—	16.9	33.8	54,792
	Kentucky	56.9	4.9	8.3	30.8	369,438
2 June	California	47.5	7.4	40.2	4.9	2,750,281
	Alabama	68.1	—	6.8	25.1	436,122
	Montana	46.9	10.8	18.5	23.8	116,899
	New Jersey	59.2	11.1	19.5	10.2	399,913
	New Mexico	52.8	6.3	16.9	24.0	180,770
	Ohio	61.2	10.6	19.0	9.2	1,032,851
	Percentage of total vote	52.1	20.0	18.2	9.7	
	Total votes	10.41 mil.	3.63 mil.	4.00 mil.	1.93 mil.	19,990,780

NOTE: Totals based on later, adjusted values, including caucus outcomes.

TABLE 2.3
THE PRIMARY VOTE — REPUBLICANS

Date	State	Bush	Others	Total vote
18 Feb.	New Hampshire	53.0%	47.0%	174,165
25 Feb.	South Dakota	69.3	30.7	44,664
3 Mar.	Colorado	67.5	32.5	195,673
	Georgia	64.3	35.7	451,059
	Maryland	69.9	30.1	240,895
7 Mar.	South Carolina	66.9	33.1	148,130
10 Mar.	Florida	68.0	32.0	894,273
	Louisiana	61.9	38.1	134,589
	Massachusetts	66.1	33.9	267,648
	Mississippi	72.0	28.0	153,062
	Oklahoma	69.6	30.4	217,188
	Rhode Island	63.2	36.8	15,690
	Tennessee	72.6	27.4	244,252
	Texas	69.8	30.2	792,218
17 Mar.	Illinois	76.5	23.5	831,447
	Michigan	67.1	32.9	445,378
24 Mar.	Connecticut	66.5	33.5	96,921
5 Apr.	Puerto Rico	99.1	.9	254,109
7 Apr.	Kansas	62.0	38.0	212,579
	Minnesota	67.5	32.5	123,705
	Wisconsin	77.5	22.5	464,807
28 Apr.	Pennsylvania	76.8	23.2	983,769
5 May	Indiana	80.1	19.9	465,100
	North Carolina	70.9	29.1	283,329
	District of Columbia	81.4	18.6	5,107
12 May	Nebraska	83.5	16.5	186,062
	West Virginia	80.6	19.4	123,128
19 May	Oregon	75.9	24.1	249,341
	Washington	82.3	17.7	97,341
26 May	Arkansas	87.4	12.6	52,287
	Idaho	63.7	36.3	115,049
	Kentucky	74.6	25.4	101,061
2 June	California	73.5	26.5	2,090,880
	Alabama	74.4	25.6	152,964
	Montana	71.6	28.4	90,471
	New Jersey	83.3	16.7	282,500
	New Mexico	63.7	36.3	85,569
	Ohio	83.2	16.8	924,572
Percentage of total vote		73.4	26.6	
Total votes		9.35 mil.	3.38 mil.	12,739,981

NOTE: Totals based on later, adjusted values, including caucus outcomes.

More serious and less easy to resolve by a single brilliant stroke was a story in the *Wall Street Journal* just a week before the New Hampshire primary alleging that Clinton had been a draft evader during the Vietnam war. Clinton responded that he had done nothing wrong in seeking to avoid military service. He argued that he had voluntarily placed himself back in the pool of draft-eligible men and had simply been lucky in drawing a draft lottery number that made it unlikely that he would have to serve.

Clinton airily dismissed the newspaper's charges and headed home to Little Rock, thinking that the issue had been disposed of. But tracking polls showed a huge drop in Clinton's support and a corresponding rise in the ratings of Paul Tsongas. Clinton's advisers told him to deal with the draft issue in the same manner as he had the infidelity problem: Be public and forthright. He appeared on the ABC-TV show "Nightline" and listened while host Ted Koppel read a letter that Clinton had written to an ROTC recruiter in 1969, thanking him "for saving me from the draft" by finding a vacancy in the military reserve unit. The "Nightline" appearance did not vault Clinton back into the lead, but it limited the damage to his campaign and allowed him to continue.[13]

Paul Tsongas, the actual winner, who had been largely ignored by the Clinton campaign until the final days in New Hampshire, gained new credibility and the momentum to allow him to challenge Clinton outside Tsongas's home region of New England.[14] The Tsongas message was that the economic problems of the country required stringent, even harsh, measures. Saying that he was "no Santa Claus," Tsongas gained a reputation as the "truth-telling candidate" by scoffing at Bill Clinton's proposal for a middle-class tax cut. Tsongas also depicted Clinton as the prisoner of the various interest groups that make up the Democratic coalition. Tsongas directed his message at the best educated and most affluent Democrats. But Clinton's skillful defense of himself and his strong showing in Tsongas's backyard enabled Clinton to continue the battle where he would have the home-court advantage.

Between New Hampshire and Super Tuesday: The Warm-up Primaries

After New Hampshire, all candidates looked to states where they either had exceptionally strong organizations or where they thought they might simply be natural favorites. Jerry Brown targeted the Maine caucuses, receiving the help of antinuclear groups. Although great things had been predicted for Bob Kerrey, he proved to be a wooden and uninspiring campaigner, but he got his first win in South Dakota, beating Harkin. Weakened by the poor showing, Harkin saw his money begin to dry up. For Tsongas, the next immediate target was Maryland, with its white-collar suburbs; his appeal to upscale Democrats might have considerable effect. For Clinton, the target was Georgia, a keystone of the Old South where Clinton's Arkansas roots were an asset and where his accent was not foreign.

On the Republican side, Georgia became a real battleground between Bush and Buchanan. Buchanan continued the attack first mounted in New Hampshire against Bush for reneging on the "no new taxes" pledge, but he expanded it to the area of morals and values when he ran commercials accusing the National Endowment for the Arts of funding pornographic and blasphemous art. (The implication was that the Endowment, a federal agency directed by a Bush appointee, was supporting pornography with the president's approval.)

The 3 March primaries and caucuses established Bill Clinton and George Bush as solid front-runners based on solid numbers (see tables 2.4 and 2.5 for running scorecards on convention delegate commitments). Clinton won Georgia, but Tsongas defeated Clinton in Maryland and Utah and tied him for second place in Colorado, a state won by Brown. At this point, Clinton led in delegates with 198, with Tsongas second at 100. With 2145 delegate votes needed to nominate, Clinton was still far short of his goal on 3 March, but there was an unmistakable trend in his favor. Tsongas seemed to be the only cloud on the horizon. Before the next primaries, both Kerrey and Harkin withdrew. On the Republican side, George Bush won convincingly in Georgia, Maryland, and Colorado. His delegate vote total was 148 to Buchanan's 20, with 1105 needed to nominate.

The Sunbelt Sweepstakes: Super Tuesday

"Super Tuesday," when most southern states hold primaries, was an invention of Democratic leaders from that region in 1988. The intention of its architects was to have a large set of primaries early in the process in a region of the country that would favor a moderate-to-conservative Democrat. In fact, liberal Michael Dukakis got the big prizes in 1988, Florida and Texas. But on 10 March 1992 Super Tuesday's results would more nearly map the intentions of its inventors. The big winner was Arkansan Bill Clinton.

In anticipation of the event, Clinton had spent considerable time organizing the Super Tuesday states. Only in Florida did Paul Tsongas feel he had a chance of defeating Bill Clinton. There, Tsongas began to attack Clinton in earnest. Characterizing Clinton as a "pander bear" who "will say anything, do anything to get votes," Tsongas predicted that "the American people are going to find out how cynical and unprincipled Bill Clinton is."[15]

Republicans on Super Tuesday had eight contests in the South and bor-

TABLE 2.4

ACCUMULATING CONVENTION DELEGATE COMMITMENTS
—DEMOCRATS

Date	State	*New delegates*		*Cumulative delegates* [a]		*Clinton %*
		Clinton	*Other*	*Clinton*	*Tsongas/Brown*	*of delegates*
18 Feb.	New Hampshire	9	9	9	9	.2%
25 Feb.	South Dakota	3	12	12	21	.3
3 Mar.	Colorado	14	32			
	Georgia	54	22			
	Maryland	29	38	148	25	6.7
	Idaho	0	18			
	Utah	5	18	198	145	4.6
7 Mar.	South Carolina	36	7	184	25	8.3
	Arizona	15	26			
	Wyoming	4	9			
	Democrats abroad	0	7			
8 Mar.	Nevada	5	12			
10 Mar.	Florida	87	61			
	Louisiana	59	1			
	Massachusetts	0	94			
	Mississippi	39	0			
	Oklahoma	38	7			
	Rhode Island	6	16			
	Tennessee	56	12			
	Texas	94	33			
	Delaware	3	11			
	Hawaii	16	4			
	Missouri	34	43			
	Texas	0	69	707	428	16.5
17 Mar.	Illinois	107	57			
	Michigan	74	57	947	559	22.1
24 Mar.	Connecticut	21	32	991	589	23.1
5 Apr.	Puerto Rico	51	0			
7 Apr.	Kansas	27	9			
	Wisconsin	35	47			
	New York	101	143	1265	803	29.5
28 Apr.	Pennsylvania	112	57	1586	857	37.0
5 May	Indiana	55	22			
	North Carolina	72	12			
	District of Columbia	17	0	1735	880	40.5
12 May	Nebraska	13	12			
	West Virginia	31	0	1784	888	41.6
19 May	Oregon	29	18	1860	945	43.4
26 May	Arkansas	30	6			
	Kentucky	34	18	1977	944	46.1
2 June	California	191	157			
	Alabama	43	12			
	Montana	8	8			
	New Jersey	80	25			
	New Mexico	17	8			
	Ohio	113	38	2511	1159	58.6

a. Cumulative totals include delegates chosen in second-level caucuses and superdelegates.

TABLE 2.5
ACCUMULATING CONVENTION DELEGATE COMMITMENTS
—REPUBLICANS

Date	State	New delegates		Cumulative delegates		Bush
		Bush	Other or un-committed	Bush	Other or un-committed	% of delegates [a]
18 Feb.	New Hampshire	14	9	14	9	.6
25 Feb.	South Dakota	14	5	28	12	1.3
3 Mar.	Colorado	26	11			
	Georgia	52	0			
	Maryland	42	0	148	25	6.7
7 Mar.	South Carolina	36	0	184	25	8.3
10 Mar.	Florida	97	0			
	Louisiana	32	0			
	Massachusetts	26	12			
	Mississippi	33	0			
	Oklahoma	34	0			
	Rhode Island	10	5			
	Tennessee	23	10			
	Texas	121	0	560	52	25.3
17 Mar.	Illinois	75	0			
	Michigan	72	0	711	52	32.3
24 Mar.	Connecticut	35	0	750	52	33.9
5 Apr.	Puerto Rico	14	0	764	52	34.6
7 Apr.	Wisconsin	35	0			
	Minnesota	22	10			
	Kansas	30	0			
	New York	68	0	963	62	43.4
28 Apr.	Pennsylvania	72	0	1092	59	49.4
5 May	Indiana	30	0			
	North Carolina	45	12			
	District of Columbia	14	0	1211	71	54.8
12 May	Nebraska	9	0			
	West Virginia	16	2	1255	73	56.8
19 May	Oregon	18	5			
	Washington	35	0	1350	77	61.1
26 May	Arkansas	27	0			
	Idaho	12	6			
	Kentucky	25	10	1414	93	64.0
2 June	California	201	0			
	Alabama	35	3			
	New Jersey	60	0			
	New Mexico	18	7			
	Ohio	83	0	1846	105	83.5

a. Cumulative totals include changes and decisions of previously uncommitted delegates.

der states. A strong showing for President Bush could put him across the halfway point to his goal of 1105 delegate votes. Buchanan dismissed the numbers by saying, "We may be losing the battle for delegates, but we're not losing this national debate—and everyone knows it."

But it was numbers that made the news on the morning of 11 March when the results were in. Clinton had swept the South. Tsongas, in his targeted state of Florida, had managed to win only 34 percent of the vote to Clinton's 51.7 percent. Tsongas's effort to portray Clinton as a captive of special interests had failed its most decisive test. Only in Massachusetts and Rhode Island did Clinton lose to Tsongas, whose dream of a victory in Clinton's southern redoubt had failed. In five southern states, including Texas, Clinton won more than two-thirds of the vote. He beat Tsongas 12–1 in the key black vote and finished ahead with lower-income whites. Brown's best showing in Super Tuesday primaries was a shade under 19 percent in Rhode Island. More than ever, it looked like a Clinton-Bush match-up in November.

Shakeout: The Rustbelt and the East

By Tuesday, 17 March, fifteen primary elections had taken place and 10 million votes had been cast. The events had drawn varying levels of interest. In New Hampshire, turnout had been high—almost 67 percent of registered voters had turned up at the polls. The average turnout for all the contests, however, was slightly more than 30 percent.

Both Tsongas and Brown hoped to stop Clinton's momentum. Clinton looked unbeatable, and they were reduced to questioning Clinton's ultimate electability. While both men conceded Clinton's lead in delegate votes, they both argued that Clinton was so tainted by scandalous allegations that he would be easy prey for the Republican nominee in November.

But for all the dire predictions of future disaster, Clinton won majorities in both Illinois and Michigan. Tsongas finished second in Illinois, and Brown, who had assiduously courted Detroit auto workers, took second spot in Michigan. Tsongas had once again fared poorly with a group of Democratic voters whose support was critical. He received only 12 percent of the black vote in Illinois and a meager 9 percent in Michigan. Clinton's support among blacks in both places was in excess of 70 percent. Tsongas was weak among blue-collar workers. More devastating still in terms of his targeted constituencies, he did not run well even in some upper-income suburban communities.

Tsongas suspended his campaign on 19 March saying, "The resources are not there." He had won all six eastern primaries and three caucuses in the West, but his strength remained largely regional. His appeals to sacrifice were greeted skeptically, and his ability to marshal traditional Democratic groups was limited. As one observer noted, "He seemed to relate better to editorial boards than to voters."[16]

Tsongas's withdrawal before the Connecticut primary on 24 March seemed to leave the door open to a quick leap across the 50 percent mark in delegates by Clinton, but that state applied the brakes to the Clinton bandwagon when Jerry Brown, the only remaining alternative, captured the state's popular vote. Clinton actually picked up more delegates than Brown, but the outcome in Connecticut forced yet another reappraisal of Clinton.

George Bush suffered no such setback. Indeed, in the aftermath of the Illinois and Michigan primaries Pat Buchanan announced that he would be scaling back his campaign activities in other states to concentrate his resources on California. This was a virtual admission that Bush would be renominated.

Jerry Brown's surprise victory over Bill Clinton in Connecticut might have been looked on as merely a minor glitch in Clinton's otherwise triumphal procession to the nomination except for some disquieting votes in New York and Wisconsin. While Clinton won New York, his first big northeastern state, after a nasty contest, and Wisconsin, an important midwestern state, the combined totals for Jerry Brown and the now-inactive Paul Tsongas in both states were greater than Clinton's. A majority of Democratic voters in both states was saying no to Clinton, even though he had captured a plurality. Clinton was rolling up the delegates, but as the tally mounted, so did the fear among some Democrats that he might encounter disaster in the general election.

The three weeks between the New York and Pennsylvania primaries gave both candidates a breathing spell. For Bill Clinton, there was a shift in emphasis—away from attacking Jerry Brown to concentrating his fire on George Bush and an opportunity to begin sounding presidential. Incidents from Clinton's past that had cropped up at embarrassing intervals throughout the primary season no longer bedeviled his campaign. Speaking of Pennsylvania, Clinton said it was "my kind of state and my kind of campaign."[17]

Clinton's own confidence was not necessarily reflected in the attitudes of voters. Exit polls taken throughout the primary season indicated that substantial doubts existed in the voters' minds about Clinton's honesty. Almost half of the Pennsylvania voters who cast ballots for Clinton expressed reservations about him.[18] Among party professionals, however, Clinton was seen as unstoppable. Casting aside his impartiality, Democratic National Committee chairman Ronald H. Brown said, "I cannot imagine a set of circumstances that would keep Bill Clinton from having a majority of the delegates by the end of the primary season based on his performance today."[19]

For several days at the beginning of May, the primary campaign was dramatically upstaged by several days of violent riots that swept the Los Angeles area after a Ventura County jury acquitted four members of the Los Angeles Police Department of charges that they had used excessive force on a black motorist whom they had stopped for speeding. The balance of the month was given over to relatively unimportant political events: five primaries, all won by Clinton. But the resolute march of Clinton and Bush each to his party's nomination was to encounter in the next set of primaries a wild card with the face of an undeclared candidate, Ross Perot.

Ross Perot: The First Incarnation

On 20 February, just two days after the New Hampshire primary, Ross Perot, a Texas businessman, appeared on the Larry King talk show and told the host that he would consider running for president if supporters could get his name on the ballot in all fifty states. The computer services billionaire had won a national reputation for his work in behalf of U.S. prisoners of war during the Vietnam war and his rescue of a group of his executives from Iran. With his statement, he began a kind of minuet with an electorate that had tired of conventional politicians and was primed for an alternative.

From the night of his television appearance to the point when he withdrew temporarily on 16 July, Perot entered not a single primary, won not a single Republican or Democratic delegate, and did not even offer a formal platform. Yet Perot, like another unsuccessful candidate, Pat Buchanan, influenced the campaign profoundly.

Perot's rise in the polls was phenomenal. In a survey taken at the end of April he had moved to within five points of Clinton in terms of voter preference.[20] Perot tapped into national discontent over the economy, such scandals as the "Keating Five," and revelations of numerous overdrafts on the House bank by members of Congress. His speeches were filled with somber warnings about the state of the country. "We are no longer the No. 1 economic superpower in the world"; the United States had become "the most violent crime-ridden society in the industrialized world"; and "we have 5 percent of the world's population and 50 percent of the world's cocaine use" —these were some of the phrases used to invoke a sense of national danger. But Perot could also be inspirational with his calls for national renewal.[21]

Perot used unconventional tactics to propel his candidacy. He shunned paid political advertising in favor of appearances on morning news and talk shows. His organization consisted largely of volunteers. Most pleasing to many voters was the fact that Perot was promising to foot the bill for his own campaign costs.

What Perot lacked was a set of specific proposals to remedy the problems he had highlighted. This did not become a problem for Perot until after the primaries, when more attention came to focus on him. From late February until the third week in June, however, the Perot trajectory was straight up. Even more remarkable than the trend line itself was that a *Time/*CNN poll conducted on the evening of 13–14 May showed, for the first time, that Perot was in the lead with 34 percent and Bush and Clinton in a virtual tie at around 30 percent each. By the end of May a consistent pattern of Perot dominance had emerged in all major polls. Some showed Perot more than ten points ahead of Clinton.[22]

Perot's candidacy also overshadowed the final primaries. In Oregon on 18 May Clinton again triumphed, and Brown again finished a strong second. But the big story in Oregon concerned not Clinton and Brown nor even President Bush, who once again gained a lopsided victory over Buchanan. It came instead from Ross Perot who, for the first time, garnered real votes in a write-in effort rather than merely percentages in public opinion polls. Perot captured 13 percent of the vote; exit polls showed that Democratic voters preferred him to Clinton by 57 to 43 percent.

In the three weeks between Oregon and Washington and the 2 June finale in California, New Jersey, and Ohio, the Clinton campaign was devoted to two tasks. First, Clinton shored up the Democratic base by addressing core party groups such as students, blue-collar workers, and gays and lesbians. Second, he tried to adjust his campaign to what now seemed to be a three-sided race with Bush and Perot.

In the interval between these late primaries Clinton devised the technique for dealing with Perot that he would follow consistently throughout both phases of the Perot campaign; simply put, he decided not to criticize Perot. What the Clinton campaign feared above all else was that voters would turn away from Clinton as the agent of change and embrace Perot instead. The Clinton people did not want to antagonize the alienated voters that Perot was attracting. A substantial number of Perot supporters were the very Reagan Democrats whom Clinton would need to win in November.

The final three primaries were anticlimactic. The front-loaded primary process had made the late primaries in these populous states little more than icing on the cake. When the votes were counted on the last big primary night, the only surprises were the margins of the Clinton and Bush victories. Clinton did well in Ohio and New Jersey, finally winning his majority for the nomination. Only in his home state of California did Brown draw a considerable vote total. Pat Buchanan had failed in his effort to unseat George Bush.

But Ross Perot, still undeclared, threatened to turn the predictability and symmetry of a two-man race into a more problematic three-way contest. Almost half of California Republicans and an identical fraction of Ohio Democrats said in an exit poll that if Perot had been on the ballot, they would have supported him rather than the presumptive nominees of their own parties.[23]

At the very time that he was about to win the Democratic nomination, Bill Clinton was eclipsed by a man who had not won a single major party convention delegate and, indeed, had never even declared his candidacy. Clinton had become the third candidate, but in one of the greatest ironies of the 1992 political year, that very obscurity benefited Clinton. In those critical six weeks between the end of the primaries and the beginning of the Democratic convention, Clinton had the time and the protection from media attention to recast his image and his message.

Perot's desire to preserve his amateur status and outsider credentials led to the collapse of the first phase of his campaign. On 3 June, Perot announced that he had engaged the services of two political professionals to run his campaign, Republican Ed Rollins, who had run Ronald Reagan's 1984 campaign, and Hamilton Jordan, a man who had been chief of staff to Democratic President Jimmy Carter. Perot, however, was still expressing reluctance to get very specific about his policy positions. There were also stories about Perot's penchant for having his enemies investigated. Perot began to display a dismissive and temperamental manner as he came under increasing pressure to set forth his policies.

The Perot effort came apart completely following a speech on 11 June in Nashville to a convention of the National Association for the Advancement of Colored People. There Perot used a number of expressions that his black audience considered demeaning and patronizing. Four days later, Rollins quit the campaign, saying that Perot had refused to accept his advice. On 16 July, the day of Clinton's acceptance speech to the convention, Perot called a press conference to announce the end of his noncandidacy. He explained his decision by saying that, "Now that the Democratic party has revitalized itself, I have concluded that we cannot win in November and that the election will be decided in the House of Representatives."[24]

This curious anointment of Clinton did not set off any stampede of Perot supporters in Clinton's direction, but there is little doubt that the terminal stages of Perot's first political incarnation gave Clinton a critical breathing spell that marked a turning point in the campaign.

Uncertain Victories: The Primaries of 1992

Considered in isolation, the political statistics of the winners of the 1992 Democratic and Republicans primaries were impressive. President George Bush ran in thirty-nine primaries and won all of them. Governor Bill Clinton of Arkansas entered thirty-six primary contests and won thirty of them. The six that Clinton failed to win were generally states with small populations. In his winning column were all of the nine most populous states in the country. Clinton carried every demographic group by impressive margins (see table 2.6). By any conventional measure, the absolute majorities of delegates achieved by Bush in May and Clinton in June, which assured their nominations, were great triumphs. No rival to Clinton or Bush came anywhere near amassing their delegate totals. Moreover, Bush and Clinton were the candidates who had been the clear front-runners even before the first votes were cast.

But over the five months of campaigning, voters seemed to have an acute case of buyer's remorse. Buyer's remorse often strikes people when they have placed a down payment on a major purchase such as a car and, on sober reflection, come to doubt the wisdom of their decision. American voters had a bad case of buyer's remorse after they placed their primary votes as down payments on Bush and Clinton. It was not just because the models on the Democratic and Republican showroom floors were less than exciting; it was because of the appearance of a 1992-and-a-half model in the form of independent candidate Ross Perot, whose formal declaration of candidacy had not even taken place at the time the Bush and Clinton nominations were sewn up.

Throughout the long campaign there was evidence of a lack of enthusiasm for the field of primary candidates. One of the most telling indicators of voter apathy was the percentage of voters who turned out. According to Curtis Gans, director of the Center for the Study of the American Electorate, only 18.9 percent of the voting-age population participated in the primaries in states that held them. Gans also observed that "I know of no state where there's been an increased turnout and many where it has declined" since 1988.[25] When it became likely after the New York primary election that Bill Clinton would be the Democratic nominee, television coverage of both him and President Bush plummeted; in early June, the three broadcast networks refused the president's request for prime-time coverage of his press conference. Whether the media's declining interest in the major-party candidates intensified the public apathy or was merely a reflection of it, Clinton and Bush were victors without voices. The campaigns of the presumptive nominees of the Democratic and Republican parties had vanished from the public consciousness.

Seventh-Inning Stretch: From the Primaries to the Conventions

Despite having been shoved aside by the media, the major-party winners now began preparations for the national conventions that would formally nomi-

TABLE 2.6

THE DEMOCRATIC VOTE IN THE PRIMARIES

% of total vote		Clinton	Voted for Brown	Tsongas
100	Total, 29 states	50%	21%	20%
	Gender			
47	Men	50	22	20
53	Women	51	20	21
	Race			
80	Whites	47	23	25
14	Blacks	70	15	8
4	Hispanics	51	30	15
	Age			
12	18–29 years	47	24	19
33	30–44 years	45	26	22
25	45–59 years	51	19	20
30	60 and older	59	15	18
	Religious affiliation			
50	Protestant	55	14	21
30	Catholic	44	24	24
6	Jewish	45	15	33
	Education			
8	Without a high school diploma	67	14	10
27	High school graduate	61	17	15
27	Some college	48	23	18
20	College graduate	42	24	26
18	Some postgraduate education	38	23	28
	Family income			
15	Less than $15,000	62	17	13
25	$15,000 to $29,999	55	19	18
30	$30,000 to $49,999	48	23	21
18	$50,000 to $74,999	45	23	25
11	$75,000 and over	38	23	29
	Those who identify themselves as ...			
67	Democrats	57	19	17
29	Independents	36	25	27
4	Republicans	34	18	32
35	Liberals	47	26	20
45	Moderates	54	18	19
20	Conservatives	48	17	23
	Those whose say their family's financial situation is ...			
14	Better today than four years ago	44	24	22
39	Same today as four years ago	50	20	20
45	Worse today than four years ago	53	20	18

SOURCE: This table constructs a Democratic primary electorate for the nation from exit polls conducted in twenty-nine Democratic primary states from February to June by Voter Research and Surveys. *New York Times,* 12 July 1992, 18.

nate them. Clinton's problem in this interim period was somewhat more complicated than that of George Bush. The president's sole primary challenger, Pat Buchanan, had been little more than a minor annoyance after the Super Tuesday southern primaries, but Clinton was forced to deal with rivals who were still unreconciled to his nomination and who had persisted as serious challengers for a longer time.

Jerry Brown hinted that he might attempt a floor fight on issues on which he considered Clinton to be too moderate. Tsongas continued to express reservations about Clinton's readiness to grant what Tsongas considered extravagant favors to Democratic interest groups. But noncandidate Jesse Jackson caused Clinton the greatest amount of discomfort in the interval between primaries and convention because, unlike either Brown or Tsongas, Jackson had a large and loyal following among a critical segment of voters, African Americans.

Clinton had captured the vast majority of black votes in the primaries, but in no state was black turnout higher than it had been in 1984 and 1988, when Jackson himself had been a candidate. In some states black voting was down 75 percent from 1988. The overall Democratic primary turnout was down 16 percent from 1988; Republican turnout fell by a mere .7 percent. It was critical, then, that Clinton move to solidify his position with a key Democratic constituency.

This was no easy task for Clinton because he needed, simultaneously, to reach out to Reagan Democrats, an overwhelmingly white group of voters, who saw many of their own interests at odds with those of blacks. This was especially true in the South, where many Reagan Democrats lived. There, in an ominous development for Democrats, many whites chose to avoid the Democratic primaries altogether. In Mississippi, for example, 59 percent of the white voters who went to the polls cast their votes in the GOP primary. In South Carolina only 30 percent of white voters cast Democratic ballots.[26]

Clinton's task, then, was to hold on to his black support without seeming to appear overly submissive to it and to reach out to white Reagan Democrats without gratuitous offense to African Americans. A June meeting of Jesse Jackson's political organization, the Rainbow Coalition, provided Clinton with an opportunity to execute one of the shrewdest maneuvers of the season.

In the aftermath of the Los Angeles riots, a little-known rap singer named Sister Souljah was interviewed by a *Washington Post* writer and reportedly said that blacks should stop killing one another and devote some time to killing whites. Clinton gambled that criticizing the remarks of the rap singer before a black organization whose work he had praised might reassure whites without greatly offending blacks.

Clinton's critical remarks drew high praise from the media and placed Jackson in an awkward position. While he had long regarded Clinton as far too conservative and insufficiently supportive of the Jackson agenda, he could not really defend the rap singer. He complained that he had been set up by Clinton, but could do little more than sulk.

Clinton's problem, however, was greater than just calibrating an appeal that would win whites without offending blacks. His overall poll numbers showed that his problem was broadly based. At the close of the primaries, a *New York Times*/CBS News poll found that only 16 percent of registered voters nationally viewed Clinton favorably, while 40 percent viewed him unfavorably. At the root of the problem was that at the conclusion of the primaries, few people knew much about Clinton and much of what they did know was negative. So, beginning on 2 June, a four-member team of Clinton's top advisers began the task of telling Bill Clinton's story to the American people.

The picture that the advisers presented was of Bill Clinton as a husband and father. Many focus-group members had even been surprised to learn that Clinton had a daughter. Others, knowing vaguely about his education in such fashionable schools as Georgetown, Yale, and Oxford, assumed that Clinton was wealthy. Clinton's media advisers encouraged him to request time on television entertainment shows ranging from "The Arsenio Hall Show" to MTV programs. They also developed the biographical film that would run at the convention that depicted Clinton as the poor son of an alcoholic and abusive father. Clinton's acceptance speech also rang with recollections of the difficulties of his early years.[27] Clinton further contributed to the upswing in his fortunes by the astute selection of Tennessee's Senator Al Gore as his running-mate.

The National Conventions and Platforms: Old Realities in New Packages

The tones of the Democratic National Convention that opened in New York on 10 July and the Republican National Convention that kicked off in Houston on 17 August could hardly have been more different. At both conventions, the presidential nominations were only formalities: Clinton received 79 percent of the delegate votes (see table 2.7, pp. 64–65), and Bush 98 percent. But they were very different conventions.

For the Democrats, the watchword was moderation; for the GOP, it was hard-edged conservatism. For the Democrats, the task was to expand their base beyond the core constituencies of labor and minority groups and attempt to win back the nominal Democratic voters who had defected to Ronald Rea-

TABLE 2.7

DEMOCRATIC CONVENTION PRESIDENTIAL ROLL CALL

State	Electoral votes	Delegate votes	Clinton	Brown	Tsongas	Abstentions/ Others
Alabama	9	67	67			
Alaska	3	18	18			
Arizona	8	49	23	12	14	
Arkansas	6	48	48			
California	54	406	211	160		35
Colorado	8	58	26	19	13	
Connecticut	8	66	45	21		
Delaware	3	21	17	3	1	
District of Columbia	3	31	31			
Florida	25	167	141	3	15	8
Georgia	13	96	96			
Hawaii	4	28	24	2		2
Idaho	4	26	22		1	3
Illinois	22	195	155	9	29	2
Indiana	12	93	73	20		
Iowa	7	59	55	2		2
Kansas	6	44	43			1
Kentucky	8	64	63			1
Louisiana	9	75	75			
Maine	4	31	14	13	4	
Maryland	10	85	83		2	
Massachusetts	12	119	109	6	1	3
Michigan	18	159	120	35		4
Minnesota	10	92	61	8	2	21
Mississippi	7	46	46			
Missouri	11	92	91	1		
Montana	3	24	21	2		1
Nebraska	5	33	24	9		
Nevada	4	27	23	4		

Continued ...

gan in 1980, stayed with him in 1984, and transferred their allegiance to George Bush in 1988. The Republicans saw their job as shoring up their base of socially conservative voters who had never been terribly enthusiastic about George Bush and who had been a tempting target for Buchanan's campaign.

The manner in which the losers were treated gave some clue as to the contrast in convention styles and proved to be straws in the wind as to the conduct of the fall campaign. Democratic losers Paul Tsongas and Jerry

TABLE 2.7 – CONTINUED
DEMOCRATIC CONVENTION PRESIDENTIAL ROLL CALL

State	Electoral votes	Delegate votes	Clinton	Brown	Tsongas	Abstentions/ Others
New Hampshire	4	24	17		7	
New Jersey	15	126	102	24		
New Mexico	5	34	30	3		1
New York	33	290	155	67	64	4
North Carolina	14	99	95	1		3
North Dakota	3	22	18			4
Ohio	21	178	144	34		
Oklahoma	8	58	56	2		
Oregon	7	57	38	19		
Pennsylvania	23	194	139	43	4	8
Puerto Rico		58	57			
Rhode Island	4	29	27	2		
South Carolina	8	54	54			
South Dakota	3	21	21			
Tennessee	11	85	85			
Texas	32	232	204	4	20	4
Utah	5	29	20	9		
Vermont	3	21	14	7		
Virginia	13	97	94	3		
Washington	11	84	49	18	14	3
West Virginia	5	41	41			
Wisconsin	11	94	46	30	18	
Wyoming	3	19	18	1		
American Samoa		5	5			
Democrats Abroad		9	9			
Guam		4	4			
Virgin Islands		5	5			
Totals	538	4,288	3,372	596	209	111

SOURCE: *Congressional Quarterly Weekly Report* 50 (25 July 1992): 2220.

Brown sulked in their tents and were offered little opportunity to express their reservations on the floor of the convention. Jesse Jackson, still smarting from Clinton's rebuke of rap singer Sister Souljah, gave a muted speech. The Republicans, by contrast, gave Pat Buchanan a prime-time speech slot that he used to deliver a blistering—some disgruntled Republicans said mean-spir-ited—attack on Clinton and the Democrats.

Historical ironies abounded in the manner in which the conventions were conducted. The normally feisty and disputatious Democrats were models of harmony. Their platform had been toned down and many controversial planks had been removed. One indication of the effort to make the platform a mainstream document was the manner in which national defense was handled.

Since the 1972 campaign that nominated George McGovern, Democratic platforms had been notably vocal in their calls to limit the use of force in international politics; but in 1992, a platform plank said bluntly: "The United States must be prepared to use military force decisively when necessary to defend our vital interests."[28] The selection of a Vietnam veteran, Senator Al Gore, as vice-presidential candidate provided additional assurance that the Democrats would not be called "soft on defense." But this apparent modification must be viewed in the light of the fact that these were the first post–cold war conventions. The political context had been altered. Sounding more resolute on defense for the Democrats was simply easier in the absence of hostile nuclear rivals.

The normally well-drilled and disciplined Republicans were in a state of uncharacteristic disarray. The day their convention opened, delegates could read in their morning copy of the *Houston Chronicle* that in the normally safe Republican state of Texas, George Bush's adopted home, a poll showed the president trailing Bill Clinton by fourteen points.

Bush also seemed, temporarily, to have lost control of the platform-writing process to a group of economic conservatives led by Representative Vin Weber of Minnesota, who managed to place in the draft platform a statement condemning as a mistake Bush's support of the 1990 tax increase.[29]

But it would be erroneous to conclude that the slates of both parties had been wiped clean of traces of the past. Continuity, more than dramatic change, marks American politics, and certain classic patterns were still in evidence, albeit in altered states.

A notable instance was the role of the large labor unions in the Democratic party. A traditional source of Democratic money and votes, the unions had become something of a burden to Democratic presidential nominees, who were often depicted as captives of union bosses. The Clinton campaign's message to these traditional allies was, "We want your money, but play a low profile, guys—we don't want to turn people off. We'll meet with you, but at night behind closed doors."[30]

But while this may have been a message to the industrial unions such as the auto workers and machinists, it surely did not apply to such white-collar unions such as the National Education Association (NEA). So while many education reformers called for competency testing of teachers, Clinton backed off from the support he had given the practice when he was governor of Arkansas because of sizable contributions from the NEA and the fact that 10 percent of all Democratic convention delegates were NEA members.[31]

Republicans in convention resembled delegations of the recent past in their strongly conservative coloration, but this year the mark of the religious right was even more indelible than that of the economic conservatives.

An organization called the Christian Coalition, the remnant of the 1988 presidential primary campaign of television evangelist Pat Robertson, dominated the GOP Platform Committee and brought in a strong antiabortion plank asserting that "we believe that the unborn child has a fundamental individual right to life which cannot be infringed." They called for a constitutional amendment banning abortion. They also opposed homosexual marriage or adoption of children by gay couples, prevented platform debate on abortion, and denounced the use of public funds to support art deemed obscene and blasphemous.

The platform, together with the Buchanan speech and addresses by Robertson and Marilyn Quayle, wife of the vice-president, gave to the convention a harsh and combative tone that might not have been conveyed so forcefully if the event had been better managed. There is reason to believe that no one was really in charge. The convention was held after the resignation of White House Chief of Staff Samuel Skinner but before the arrival of his successor, James A. Baker. Reportedly, no one at the highest decision-making level in the campaign had read Buchanan's speech and vetted it for extremist language. The "family values" emphasis of the convention, accordingly, came to be considered a serious mistake by most GOP professionals.[32]

Since recent conventions have done little but crown, ceremonially, the winners of the primaries, their continuance has been justified not so much as decision-making or even platform-writing exercises but as as media events that provide the nominees with "bounce" or momentum. If these prime-time events do nothing else, they send forth the ticket in a flurry of good feeling among party professionals. The Democrats bounced out of Madison Square Garden as if they had been made of Silly Putty. Various polls put the Clinton lead over Bush in the 17–20 percent range. A *Newsweek* poll conducted after the Houston convention found that Bush had reduced the Clinton lead by only 3 percent, causing some commentators to remark, "Bush had gotten not a bounce but a dribble."[33]

Perhaps the most striking similarity between the two conventions was in the finales of each, the acceptance speeches of the presidential nominees. Clinton's objective was to introduce himself to the American people; Bush's, in a sense, was to reintroduce himself. Clinton, through the skillful use of biographical films and autobiographical recollections hammered home the message of his humble origins in Hope, Arkansas, established himself as a loving family man, and achieved his objective of burnishing his image. President Bush had the more complex job. He needed to come up with some convincing set of remedies for the faltering economy. What he did offer in the way of new proposals was an across-the-board tax cut paid for by reductions in spending. He accused the Democrats, who controlled Congress, of blocking his efforts to help the economy and even apologized for his violation of the "read my lips" pledge.

It was unlikely that the president's plan could produce a positive impact on the economy before November. He was counting on his credibility with the American people to persuade them that he could bring the nation out of recession in the near future. Failing that, he would need to undercut Clinton's claim that he could do a better job or raise doubts that Clinton was even morally fit to assume the presidency. But as the last shots at the character of Bill Clinton were fired from the convention podium and the last diatribe was aimed at the Democrats for being out of the cultural mainstream, a feeling of uneasiness and even foreboding about the general election settled over Houston. Referring to attacks on groups ranging from single mothers to feminists to gays and lesbians, Senator Richard G. Lugar, a moderate Republican from Indiana, told reporters, "You don't build majorities by excluding whole groups of people, and you don't have to be nasty to be conservative. I wish they'd cut it out.... I'm not comfortable with that at all.... It's not a winning message."[34]

What It All Meant: Summing Up
the Nominations

THE CLINTON ASSETS: PERSONALITY AND POSITIONING

The problems that befell Bill Clinton in the weeks before the New Hampshire primary would have destroyed a lesser candidate. Three major accusations were hurled against him: He was an adulterer, a draft evader, and a one-time user of marijuana who gave an equivocating defense of his conduct by claiming not to have inhaled. Collectively, these charges saddled him with the unfortunate nickname of "Slick Willie"—a man of dubious honesty but indubitable glibness who claimed innocence on technicalities and could not give a straight answer to a question. Combined with the impression that he was a boring technocrat, these negatives might well have brought Clinton's campaign to an early end in New Hampshire. His survival there, which enabled him to carry the fight to friendlier terrain, reveals much about his remarkable fortitude and the role it would play in his ultimate success in the primary process.

But American politics is never short of tough and thick-skinned candidates. Why was this candidate so successful? At first glance, it might seem that he was simply lucky: He emerged at a time when Democrats had become so tired of being out of power that they were willing to set aside their habitual factional quarrels and get behind someone who could take back the White House from the Republicans. That explanation, however, applies only to the period after the convention. Indeed, if Clinton was dogged by any single doubt during the primaries, it was that he would be acutely vulnerable to a Republican in the general election.

Luck may have played a part in the particular set of Democratic rivals that Clinton faced in the primaries. All proved to have flaws greater than his own: Harkin was too strident, Kerrey too wooden, Brown too erratic, and Tsongas too solemn. None seemed to possess the indefatigable spirit and toughness that Clinton displayed. There was more to the outcome, however, than personality and luck.

The front-loaded nature of the Democratic primary process was made to order for a moderate southerner like Clinton, with his splendid organization, his abundant funds, and his ability to establish very early that he was the man to beat. By the Illinois and Michigan primaries on 17 March—less than a month after New Hampshire—Clinton had really sewn up the nomination by denying his main rivals, Paul Tsongas and Jerry Brown, any southern or midwestern base. Tsongas was to remain a largely regional candidate and Brown a factional one.

Clinton, moreover, had astutely positioned himself to be acceptable to a Democratic primary electorate markedly more liberal than he. At the same time, he managed to preserve the impression that he was not one to simply knuckle under to the various Democratic interest groups. In the weeks before Super Tuesday, Tsongas was almost successful in depicting Clinton as the captive of special interests, but Clinton was so strong in his native region and Tsongas so weak that the message had little effect.

The strategic genius of the Clinton campaign was that the candidate was able to convince the various groups whose activists play an important role in Democratic primaries that their optimal choices for Democratic nominee would be less successful than he. So while Harkin would have been the first choice of the unions, Brown the preferred candidate of the party's left wing, and Tsongas of gays and lesbians, Clinton convinced all groups that an acceptable nominee with a good chance of winning the presidency was preferable to an optimal candidate who would lose in November. The weakness of Clinton's rivals gave credibility to this message.

Clinton applied the rule to his own constituencies as well. While he was clearly the choice of black voters in the South, he avoided giving the impression that he was in the pocket of black leaders. He embraced a younger generation of African American politicians such as Mike Espy of Mississippi and

John Lewis of Georgia, and avoided a close identification with the Rev. Jesse Jackson, who makes some white voters uncomfortable.

The logic behind this approach was clear: In order to win the Democratic primaries, you must find a way to earn the support of the groups that make up the primary electorate, but you must win that support without positioning yourself so far to the left that you become unacceptable to the more moderate voters who come to the polls in November. Clinton achieved both goals brilliantly.

George Bush's Pyrrhic Victory

On the Republican side, it almost seemed as if George Bush were reading Bill Clinton's playbook—backwards. Clinton finessed and co-opted the left wing of his party, persuading them that he was sympathetic to their goals but managing to avoid being seen as their "cat's paw." Bush, however, openly capitulated to his party's right wing and came closer than any incumbent president to finding himself on the threshold of the general election in the position of a factional candidate. By allowing the conservatives to showcase such issues as "family values" at the convention, Bush allowed the moralistic tenor of the party to degenerate into fanaticism and meanness of spirit, repelling the middle-of-the-road voter. How ironic for the man who was once seen as the ultimate centrist, the establishment moderate, and the man with the longest curriculum vitae in the Republican party.

The hollowness of President Bush's victories in the primaries can be traced to a weakness in his character: His opportunistic conversion to conservatism as Ronald Reagan's vice-president never convinced the right wing of the party that he was truly one of its own. When challenged from that wing of the party by Pat Buchanan, Bush's impulse was to ingratiate himself with party conservatives by becoming more like Buchanan than Buchanan himself. Yet whatever modest success Buchanan achieved in the early primaries had little to do with ideology and much to do with the state of the economy. Feeling that he could do little—indeed feeling that little needed to be done—to cure the recession, Bush diverted his energy to a pointless ideological squabble that only diminished his stature.

As in Clinton's case, however, reference to the personal qualities of the candidate is insufficient to explain why things happened as they did. A differently constituted Republican electorate might have complemented Bush's personal characteristics rather than clashing with them. The fact is that George Bush was an anomaly in the Republican party, or, more kindly, the noble relic of another day. No element of the party felt spiritually bonded to Bush as conservatives had felt bonded to Ronald Reagan. Economic conservatives in the party who might have championed him lost much of their enthusiasm when he defaulted on his "no new taxes" pledge. Worse, from the point of view of the bankers and brokers who vote in Republican primaries, he bungled the economy.

In one sense, Bush was lucky: He drew as his only serious primary opponent a man so extreme in his views that many of those disenchanted with the economy would have had trouble supporting him. Even those most inclined toward a deep-dyed conservatism rejected Buchanan in favor of Bush. But Bush's insecurity about his own conservative credentials and his overestimation of the importance of social issues to the voters kept him clinging tightly to the conservatives even as the less ideological members of the party expressed their disapproval.

Clinton, then, was admirably positioned after the Democratic convention to woo the moderate voters who make up the bulk of the November electorate, while Bush was seriously out of touch with these voters and their concerns. In a year of serious recession, almost any other issue will be subordinated to the state of the economy. No amount of preaching that character or public morality should be the paramount concern of the voter will make much headway. Clinton needed to come out of his convention as an acceptable alternative to the incumbent. That he did. Bush, however, needed to a dramatic improvement in the economy, a plausible plan for economic renewal, or a strategy to depict the alternative as unacceptable. As the GOP convention closed down and the general election campaign began in earnest, it appeared that only the last option offered any hope that Bush might yet achieve a second term.

Ultimately the voters and their peculiar mood of gloom and rebellion shaped the outcome. Frustrated by the passivity of the Bush administration in the face of a serious recession, they looked not only for agents of change but also for truth-tellers. They showed uncharacteristic interest in the campaigns of Paul Tsongas and Ross Perot, who prescribed bitter-pill cures for the economy after the experts had pronounced that only good-news candidates could win. But 1992 was not a year for good-news candidates. The incumbent president, having to defend his administration's record, tried to play the role of the good-news candidate. The more President Bush minimized the rigors of the recession and pleaded for voters to look on the bright side, the more they became enraged because the realities of their lives and those of their neighbors told them otherwise. That they wanted change was beyond doubt. The only question that remained for the general election was what kind.

Notes

1. Bush waged a fierce and aggressive campaign in 1988 that was marked by its negativity. But in his inaugural address on 20 January 1989, Bush sounded a note of conciliation when he said, "America is never wholly herself unless she is engaged in high moral principle.... We as a people have such a purpose today. It is to make kinder the face of America and gentler the face of the world."

2. Robert Shogan, *The Riddle of Power* (New York: Penguin, 1992), 258, 286.

3. Margaret Carlson, "Thorn in Bush's Side," *Time*, 17 February 1992, 22.

4. David Maraniss, "Bill Clinton, Born to Run," *Washington Post National Weekly Edition*, 20–26 July 1992.

5. Elizabeth Kolbert, "Fighting Obscurity on Tight Primary Budgets," *New York Times*, 24 November 1991, and Elizabeth Kolbert, "Harkin Seeks to Recall Democrats' History, Though Some Fear It," *New York Times*, 26 December 1991.

6. Robert Reinhold, "Ex-California Governor to Seek the Presidency," *New York Times*, 4 September 1991; and B. Drummond Ayres, Jr., "Brown Hopes One-Note Campaign Strikes a Responsive Chord," *New York Times*, 28 December 1991.

7. Kevin Phillips, "The Politics of Frustration," *New York Times Sunday Magazine*, 12 April 1992, 38.

8. *New York Times*, 20 February 1992.

9. The term "moralists" to describe this group consisting of roughly 12 percent of the electorate, comes from the Times-Mirror topology that divides voters into nine categories or clusters based on their value orientations. See *The People, the Press and Politics: Campaign '92, New Hampshire and the Nation* (Washington, D.C.: Times Mirror Center for the People and the Press, 22 January 1992).

10. R.W. Apple, Jr., "Ill Wind for the President," *New York Times*, 19 February 1992.

11. *New York Times*, 19 February 1992.

12. Eleanor Clift, "Testing Ground," *Newsweek*, 30 March 1992.

13. Ibid.

14. Clinton and Tsongas received nine delegates each.

15. Richard L. Berke, "Saying Clinton Is Cynical, Tsongas on the Attack," *New York Times*, 7 March 1992.

16. *Congressional Quarterly Weekly Report*, 21 March 1992, 749.

17. *New York Times*, 29 April 1992.

18. Ibid.

19. Ibid.

20. *New York Times*, 26 April 1992.

21. *New York Times*, 9 July 1992.

22. *Public Perspective* 3, no. 5 (July/August 1992): 84.

23. *New York Times*, 3 June 1992.

24. *Congressional Quarterly Weekly Report*, 50 (18 July 1992): 2131.

25. David S. Broder, "When Winning Isn't Everything," *Washington Post National Weekly Edition*, 8–14 June 1992.

26. Thomas B. Edsall, "Southern Primaries Reveal Contradictions for Democrats," *Washington Post*, 23 March 1992.

27. Gwen Ifill, "Discipline, Message, and Good Luck: How Clinton's Campaign Came Back," *New York Times*, 5 September 1992; and Elizabeth Kolbert, "Test-Marketing a President," *New York Times Sunday Magazine*, 30 August 1992.

28. Christopher Madison, "Issue in Waiting," *National Journal*, 15 August 1992, 1889.

29. Jack W. Germond and Jules Witcover, "GOP Eyeing Two Anti-Clinton Themes," *National Journal*, 15 August 1992, 1914.

30. *National Journal*, 15 August 1992.

31. Chris Mitchell, "Gang of Three," *Washington Monthly*, September 1992, 24–25.

32. *New York Times*, 21 September 1992.

33. Howard Fineman and Ann McDaniel, "Bush: What Bounce?" *Newsweek*, 31 August 1992, 26.

34. R.W. Apple, Jr., "G.O.P. Is Flirting with the Dangers of Negativism," *New York Times*, 19 August 1992.

3

Campaign '92: Strategies and Tactics of the Candidates

F. Christopher Arterton

'Tis policy and stratagem must do
That you affect; and so must you resolve,
That what you cannot as you would achieve,
You must perforce accomplish as you may.

— *Titus Andronicus* (II, i)

Presidential campaigns are fought on many levels. They are, above all, competitions over ideas; candidates advance their convictions as to their personal strengths and their policies, agendas, diagnostics, and solutions. The campaign organizations struggle to maintain a base of supporters while expanding their appeal among segments of uncommitted voters. The competitors allocate their time, money, and staff resources unevenly, neglecting states that are sure losers and sure winners while concentrating on the possibly winnable. Each side employs polling to design the advertising programs that will consume the preponderance of their cash. The campaigns also attempt to orchestrate abundant news coverage that, at a minimum, does not harm their position. Meanwhile, "on the ground," the local campaign organizations work to identify supporters and ensure that they actually make it to the polls on election day.

This chapter examines the 1992 presidential campaign from the viewpoint of the contending candidates and their organizations, scrutinizing the various levels of the contest under two broad rubrics: strategy and tactics. The two concepts obviously overlap, and rather than belabor a definition of the differences between strategy and tactics, I start with an informal notion and let a more complicated appreciation emerge from the discussion.

Strategy concerns the development of a campaign's persuasive message and the delineation of groups of voters for which the message is particularly designed. Tactics, in contrast, involves the operational level of campaigns through which strategic decisions become implemented, especially managing the delivery of messages to target audiences. Both strategy and tactics must build on a base of circumstances that are more or less objectifiable because at some level campaigns must confront reality . The competing candidates and their strategists can exercise only minimal influence over these factors. Consider, for example, the demise of the Soviet Union, the poor performance of the domestic economy, the commercial challenges from Japan and Europe, and the number of candidates in the 1992 race. These factors established a basic framework for the 1992 contest, a framework that the candidates could not ignore.

These realities are somewhat less than totally objectifiable because, in politics, perceptions can become more important than the actualities. If campaigns are anything, they are competitions to manage the perceptual environment within which the competition occurs.[1] Thus questions such as who could legitimately claim credit for the demise of the Soviet Union, how serious was the economic downturn, and whether Ross Perot had a real chance to win the presidency were very much within the influence of the contending candidates. The struggle over ideas that comprises a presidential campaign takes place against a background that must be understood before the strategies and tactics of the contenders become clear.

Campaign Strategies

Shortly after the election, a Haitian priest revealed that for more than a year George Bush had been laboring under a voodoo curse.[2] While the priest was uncertain who had put the curse on the president, he was sure that from the moment when Bush fell ill during a state banquet in Japan right up to his election defeat, he was a marked man.

The validity of the Haitian's assertion may well be demonstrated not in the president's personal comportment but in the curse of inevitable business cycles combined with twelve years of "supply side" economic policies. Ironically, the wisdom of Haitian pundits serves as an echo of Bush's own campaign rhetoric of 1980, when he labeled as "voodoo economics" the very policies that eventually lead to his predicament in 1992.

IT'S THE ECONOMY, STUPID!

Ultimately all three campaigns developed the fundamental component of a campaign strategy: a message. To a greater or lesser extent, these messages related to the central question hanging over the election, namely the economy. Each campaign tried to satisfy two somewhat contradictory requirements of a politically potent message. The theme must be simple enough to be communicated to a vast electorate, yet the same message must be capable of being phrased in many different ways. Since journalists quickly lose interest in the same old ideas, the campaign theme needs to be constantly bolstered with new data or dramatized in different ways or surfaced in new contexts.

On being appointed communication director of Clinton's presidential campaign, George Stephanopoulos hung a now famous sign over his desk. In a blunt message to himself, *It's the economy, stupid!*, Stephanopoulos reflected his determination to focus the campaign's manifold rhetoric on a single theme. Polling results indicated that if, on election day, voters thought that the 1992 elections constituted a referendum on the U.S. economy, George Bush would lose. As the campaign evolved, Stephanopoulos learned just how difficult it could be to keep to this simple message. Samuel Popkin, who collected and analyzed state-level polls for Clinton's polling firm, Greenberg-Lake, spoke of "the complexity of simplicity," referring to the need to deal with numerous other issues as they arose while struggling to return to talking about the economy. He noted that a single comment about the draft would knock a full eighteen hours of talk about the economy right off the evening news.[3]

For his part, Perot clearly saw his mission as a crusader against Washington, but the central thrust of his message varied somewhat. During the spring and early summer, "Perot I"—in the terminology of Campaign '92—cultivated a process message, attacking the workings of Washington: the power of lobbyists, the corruption of political action committees, the remoteness of incumbents, and the insularity of the two parties. In the fall, Perot II's attention focused squarely on the budget deficit as the central failing of Washington's leadership: Only someone from outside the sphere of routine politics, someone with a strong record of entrepreneurial leadership, could fix the mess.

To the Bush strategists, the message of the campaign was always "my opponents are worse." The president's campaign became a virtual cornucopia of attacks on Bill Clinton, but it took Bush's strategists several faltering attempts before they zeroed in on exactly the anti-Clinton message they needed to deliver, and by then it was too late.

To some extent, recent election history might indicate that campaigns can invent these messages out of whole cloth. During the past decade, increasingly nasty congressional and senatorial contests featured negative ad-

vertising in which campaigners demonstrated the power of selecting an isolated, trivial act or statement and ballooning it into a charge of fundamental
betrayal or substantial misjudgment by an opponent. In presidential contests,
both the Reagan campaign in 1984 with its "Morning in America" theme
and the 1988 Bush assault on Michael Dukakis demonstrated that campaigns
could be waged, and won, on themes that many perceived as vapid, misleading, and somewhat irrelevant.[4]

The 1992 campaign was different. In case we had forgotten, we have
learned that while campaigners have great latitude in selecting a message, in
order to be successful their message must respond to the underlying dynamics
of public opinion. When public thinking is scattered and diffuse, it may be
possible to win by riveting the attention of enough voters on smaller issues,
particularly when one's opponent does little to respond effectively. When,
however, citizens are focused on a single major issue, particularly one perceived as directly affecting their lives, then a campaign ignores that question
at its peril. From the perspective of strategy, therefore, the story of the 1992
campaign is fundamentally shaped by the failure of Bush's campaign to address voter concerns about the economy. Stephanopoulos's message was directed to himself; it could more appropriately have been directed at the Bush
campaign.

The issue that plagued George Bush all year was, of course, a composite
question; voters who lamented the economic downturn worried about at
least three distinct elements. First, consistent with models of aggregate analysis and the theories of retrospective voting,[5] a short-run downturn in growth
rates and an upswing in unemployment cursed the incumbent's reelection
campaign. The president tried to argue that the state of the economy was not
as bad as many perceived, particularly in the context of a worldwide slump.
Indeed, in the immediate postelection period, a quick turnaround in consumer confidence and improving aggregate statistics seemed to validate his
point. Though confirmation may be a small comfort to the loser, at the time
his argument proved a weak rejoinder to Clinton's attack. Throughout the
year, Bush was working uphill against almost daily headlines of further job
layoffs, continual economic bad news.[6] His plea for perspective only left him
open to the charge that he was out of touch with the plight of the average
voter.

The second component of economic worries concerned the competitive-
ness of the United States as challenged by Japan and Germany. Here again,
perception proved as powerful as reality. President Bush had unwittingly ex-
acerbated these worries during his 1991 trip to Japan. The symbolism of his
illness during a state dinner mirrored the enfeebled response of American industry to public-private cooperation employed by competitors with vigorous

industrial growth policies. In this domain, the conservative ideology that had held the Republicans together for twelve years blinded them to the potential of Clinton's challenge. As they saw it, free trade unquestionably benefited the nation, while industrial policy or public-private investment strategies smacked of centralized planning in which government, not the marketplace, would choose winners and losers.

Finally, the Democrats were able to play on vague concerns among voters of a longer-run decline in the American standard of living. This anxiety was best capsulized in the charge that a family now requires two wage earners to secure the same lifestyle that Americans grew accustomed to in the 1950s when most women were not part of the regular workforce. More palpably, Clinton's speeches and ads accused Republican policies of leading to the first generation of Americans who would be worse off than their parents.

As we learned after the election from several detailed reports, George Bush never considered that the economy would be his undoing or even that he could be defeated.[7] When the surprising strength of Patrick Buchanan's candidacy demonstrated that the economy could hurt him at the polls, Bush concentrated primarily on the short-term component on which he could plausibly argue that the beginnings of improvement were visible. Strategically, the Bush campaign rarely gave much credence to the symbolic importance of international competition and never grasped the nagging fear of a longer-run decline in the American standard of living. It took the resurgent Perot campaign with its long "infomercials" to drive these points home to the American public.

Basically, from April to November, the Bush campaign tried everything it could think of to divert voters' attention from the economy. The president began by trying to argue back on the economy. In bringing James Baker over from the State Department to coordinate the White House, the president proposed that in the next four years the Republicans could achieve in the domestic economy the same victorious bounty their policies had achieved in foreign policy. Then, campaigning on 10 September in Michigan, Bush offered the Detroit Economic Club a detailed economic "Agenda for American Renewal." Although Bush changed his stump speech in subsequent campaign events to tout his plan, once press coverage had highlighted the fact that he had issued an economic plan, rather than the details of it, the campaign references to the plan ceased and it quietly disappeared.

For a brief period, Bush tried to claim the mantle of Harry Truman, arguing that once the people understood that he too had faced a "do-nothing" Congress, he would show a similar surge in popular support. He furiously attacked the "liberal-Democratic" Congress that had stymied his programs. He pleaded for a Republican Congress as the antidote to gridlock until that argument began to turn against him. News commentary began to point out that the chances of breaking the Democratic stranglehold on Congress were exceedingly slim; thus a Bush reelection became synonymous with four more years of stalemate.

Throughout the campaign, however, Bush's primary strategy was to direct voter attention toward Clinton's character, underscoring doubts that already existed in voters' minds. Campaign strategists started by trying to focus attention on Clinton's lifestyle. For a time, "traditional family values" became the catchphrase, a concept that the Republicans hoped would serve as a two-edged sword, energizing conservatives and none too subtly pointing attention at Clinton's marital problems. While the vice-president complained that much of Hollywood was promoting both Clinton and alternative lifestyles, Marilyn Quayle attacked Hillary Clinton's view of the role of women in contemporary society. That ploy failed. The issue of family values unsettled as many voters in the center as it reassured loyalist supporters on the right.

Next, the essence of the choice faced by voters—as projected by the Bush campaign—became a matter of trust: Which candidate do you trust more to be president of the United States? To give this notion concreteness, Bush aggressively and continually attacked Clinton's explanation of his effort to avoid draft induction twenty-five years ago. As one Bush aide opined in September, Clinton's efforts to avoid the draft were to be hung around his neck like an albatross. The nation could not trust a draft dodger to be commander-in-chief of the military. At one point, Bush extended his onslaught by charging that, as a student in England, Clinton had organized anti-American demonstrations on foreign soil. Then he went so far as to insinuate that, while a student at Oxford, Clinton might have met with Soviet intelligence agents during a holiday trip to Moscow.

Near the end of the campaign, Bush shifted ground again, turning to a list of indicators that placed Arkansas near the bottom of the fifty states on a host of measures. By Bush's telling, Clinton's record demonstrated that his opponent was the failed governor of a floundering state.

Bush had opened this line of attack in late September during a whirlwind tour through the six states that border on Arkansas. Taxation, the environment, education, child care, civil rights, and crime, all came under his harsh attack. But this assault never really developed the power of a similar swing against Dukakis in 1988, perhaps because the Clinton campaign was busy pouring out statistics to refute the Bush attack.[8]

In the third debate, Bush tried to bring these instances together to demonstrate a "pattern" of deceit and waffling in Clinton's positions. On a campaign train tour after the debates, Bush slugged away at the trust issue. He simultaneously sought to restate his political differences with the Democrats as a rerun of the 1980 and 1988 campaigns. Arguing that the economy could be a lot worse, he cited the poor economic performance of the last "tax-and-spend" Democrat, Jimmy Carter. "Trust and taxes" became the twin prongs of Bush's standard speech, amplifying the message delivered by his advertising.

Nothing worked. Nothing worked for George Bush because the voters stayed riveted on the economy. Nothing worked because of George Stephanopoulos. Nothing worked because of Ross Perot.

Once Perot returned to active candidacy, he helped Clinton, if only by keeping the economic debate alive. In televised appearances, in long infomercials, and in his arguments during the presidential debates, the Texas billionaire asserted even more single-mindedly than Clinton that the American economy was clearly in trouble. Perot's advocacy placed the federal deficit front and center as the source of the nation's problems, a perspective that led him to an indictment of many policies pursued over the past twelve years by Reagan and Bush. Though he trained his guns partially on Clinton in the campaign's last week and though Clinton's economic plan never squarely addressed the deficit, Perot's real ire and scorn were directed toward the Bush administration. If Bush's strategy was to direct voters' attention away from the economy, then all the attention Perot received during October worked to the president's disadvantage.[9]

Candidates and their advisers are often accused of preparing for the last campaign. Though the critique is often unfair, nevertheless it does appear accurate to observe that by 1992 the Republican strategists running the Bush campaign had come to believe in the invincibility of rhetoric. Who can blame them after eight years of the teflon presidency of Ronald Reagan plus a convincing demonstration in 1988 of the power of attacks to destroy an opponent? Throughout 1992, the Republican war machine, victor in three successful runs for the White House, was confident that words could win it all for them. Almost to the end of the campaign, they confidently looked forward to a repeat of 1988, in which they would pull the Democratic nominee to his knees.

As a result, the Republicans never really developed the necessary response to voter concerns about Bush's leadership on the economy. Only a week after the president's Detroit speech in which he delivered his economic blueprint for a second term, his campaign staff had concluded that they could not win with a positive message alone. "We're not going to start moving until we rip the skin off the guy," said one unnamed campaign official referring to the attacks being readied against Governor Clinton. Another campaign strategist opined that their campaign had to lay a "positive foundation" before they could turn to a full-scale attack on Clinton's credibility.[10]

THE AUDIENCE

At one point during the campaign, the president, ruminating about the mood of the electorate, lamented "It's crazy out there!" In 1992, the voters' disposition was sharply defined: angry, cynical, frustrated, and demanding. Trouble signs were evident early in the year; several studies of voter attitudes recorded unprecedented levels of cynicism toward politics and politicians.[11] Early during the Democratic primary fight, voters signaled that they wanted the candidates to address the major issues facing the nation, a sentiment from which the Tsongas campaign drew its strength. The candidates responded with booklets containing far more detail about their policy proposals than could ever be put into their television ads. Or at least that was the conclusion of the campaign strategists until Ross Perot's half-hour infomercials proved that they could draw an audience. Each candidate identified segments of these troubled voters that loomed particularly large in their calculations of how to achieve victory.

George Bush sought to implement the tried-and-true campaign strategy: "First, reinforce the base, then reach for the undecideds in the center." He never achieved either goal. Bush's natural first instinct was to reach out to the conservative elements of his party, and there were good reasons why a centerpiece of the Bush strategy was a reach rightward. As many observers have pointed out, the conservative movement has never really given Bush its unqualified support. While this wing of the Republican party would blindly follow Reagan through the largest tax increase in U.S. history, many movement conservatives viewed Bush's tax deal with congressional Democrats in October 1990 as the ultimate betrayal.[12]

Early in 1992, the breach was obvious. The primary challenge mounted by Patrick Buchanan demonstrated just how weak Bush was in this critical segment of his constituency. To make matters worse, no sooner had Bush been able to put the Buchanan candidacy behind him than Perot began "plundering the Republicans' conservative base."[13]

The Republican convention was designed as the primary vehicle to accomplish the fundamental strategic need of the Bush campaign to shore up support among the party's right. It worked only marginally, and at great cost. Every presidential campaign has the problem of harnessing the enthusiasm of activists while retaining support among rank-and-file voters, who tend to be more centrist. Though the fiery rhetoric delivered in Houston by Patrick Buchanan, Pat Robertson, and Marilyn Quayle may have played well to the activists inside the convention hall, it alarmed many loyal party voters and repulsed many independents.

Clinton pursued the opposite strategy. Acting on the advice of his chief strategist, James Carville, Clinton went after marginal, persuadable voters and deemphasized the traditional Democratic base vote. Given that Democrats have not done so well in recent presidential elections, losing five of the last six, it is hardly surprising that Clinton decided to try something new. Strategically, he reached for voters in the middle—in the suburbs, among Reagan Democrats, and independent voters—and for voters living in states that Republicans have won narrowly in past elections. He concentrated his campaigning on states and areas within states where Democratic candidates have done moderately well but have not won in recent years. In short, he sought to cut into Bush's marginal voters wherever possible. Evidently, the strategy worked.

Perot reached intuitively for segments of voters who were angry and disgusted with politics. As in many aspects of his campaign, Perot was somewhat unorthodox. Since Perot never liked the professional political managers, whom he dismissed as "handlers," he placed little confidence in polling, which is the primary tool for isolating segments of the electorate that are amenable to persuasion.[14] Instead, Perot relied heavily on contacts developed from calls *into* his campaign headquarters by persons wishing to volunteer their time. Even though the nature of the influence of Perot's campaign is open to question, the volunteer committees that sprang up in each state unquestionably did provide a nucleus of supporters from which a target audience developed.

Campaign Tactics

Most of the tangible activity of the candidates and their staffs can be subsumed under the notion of tactics, since communicating and campaigning are virtually synonymous. All the efforts that the campaign organization puts into delivering persuasive messages to the appropriate audiences define the tactical level of politics. As such, the list of activities on the operational level that might be discussed here is impossibly long. I concentrate on the major areas of campaign performance, which, in 1992, proved to be campaign fund raising, influencing and utilizing the media, participating in the debates, and purchasing television advertising.

CAMPAIGN MONEY

Almost everything a campaign does to deliver its message costs money. Funds are essential, and they are generally scarce, making budgeting the prime ingredient in the rational planning of all campaign tactical operations.

Since the Federal Election Campaign Act (FECA) of 1975, numerous political managers and political lawyers have been hard at work to circumvent the law's strict limits on contributions and expenditures. By the 1992 campaign, they had more or less succeeded in opening enough loopholes so that the presidential campaigns could officially accept and legally spend every dollar that their fund-raising operations could produce. As a consequence, campaign funding has become more complicated and more obscured from public disclosure.[15]

The major pocket of money available to the general election campaigns of Republican and Democratic presidential candidates comes from the public treasury:[16] George Bush and Bill Clinton each received $55.2 million dollars from a fund created by taxpayers who designate one dollar of their income tax. The original act deemed this level of funding sufficient to run the whole presidential campaign and sought to limit the contenders to spending only this amount. But, due to amendments and interpretations of the law over the intervening seventeen years, the public funding is by no means all that presidential campaigns now can spend.

Under other provisions of the law, presidential campaigns can, for example, raise and spend additional money for their legal and accounting fees. The contenders can also use their national party committees to spend money on their behalf[17] and to pay for "institutional ads," which promote all party candidates but do not specifically mention them by name.

That is not all that Bush and Clinton had available to them. The largest component of their funds was the infamous "soft money"[18]—unlimited expenditures by state and local parties for "party building" activities associated with citizen participation in campaigns, including voter registration, grassroots campaigning, and get-out-the-vote efforts. The ground rules for this money are set by state laws, not by federal law. If, for example, an individual contributor is willing to give the candidate $100,000, that money will be graciously accepted by the national campaign and put into states where such a contribution is legal. In 1992 the Democrats were able to do substantially better in raising soft money than in prior years, closing the gap with the Republicans. Through this provision, the Clinton team spent an estimated $40 million in soft money, whereas the Bush campaign brought in $25 million.[19]

In this area as in many aspects of the election, Ross Perot's campaign proved to be an exception. By not accepting federal support for his campaign, he avoided both expenditure limits and the complex accounting. However, contributions to his campaign were limited as the law provides—$1000 from an individual and $5000 from a political action committee. The $69 million that Perot spent, largely out of contributions that he made to his own campaign organization,[20] was roughly equal to the level of funds formally under the direct control of his rivals.

The discussion thus far refers to money that is mobilized more or less under the control of the presidential contenders, but there are many additional ways in which money is spent in electing a presidential candidate, and it would be hazardous to guess at the total amount of money involved. Labor unions and corporations can spend unlimited amounts for "internal communications" with their members and employees, including, for example, phone banks to call voters within this pool. Private individuals who want to help a presidential candidate can spend money that does not come under the candidate/expenditure limits. Organized groups can form political action committees to engage in "independent expenditures" designed to influence the voters' choice. Finally, many groups work to encourage voter participation without having to report their activities as designed to influence the election.

In short, the full costs of electing a president will never be known. Based on the financial reports submitted to the Federal Elections Commission (FEC) thirty days after the election, the major categories of funds for the three presidential campaigns are estimated in table 3.1. These data lead to two observations: If the ability to entice people to make a contribution to one's campaign is a measure of political support, Clinton matched Bush on the fund-raising circuit; the two major-party nominees had approximately equal resources. Second, after all the discussion about how much of his own money the multibillionaire Perot was willing to spend on his campaign, some may find it surprising that he was so outgunned by the major-party nominees.[21]

TABLE 3.1
MAJOR CATEGORIES OF FUND-RAISING/EXPENDITURES BY 1992
PRESIDENTIAL CANDIDATES (IN MILLIONS OF DOLLARS)

	Bush	Clinton	Perot
Campaign committees			
Public funding	55.2	55.2	—
Legal and accounting	3.0	4.4	—
Privately raised, unrestricted	—	—	69.0
Party committees			
Spent "on behalf of" the presidential candidates	10.3	10.3	—
"Soft money"	111.0	86.0	—
Totals	179.5	155.9	69.0

NOTE: Except for the "soft money" amounts, these figures are based on year-end reports filed with the Federal Election Commission. The "soft money" figures comprise the sums spent only through 23 October 1992; they include the parties' spending for all federal candidates, that is, the amounts spent on behalf of Senate, House, and presidential candidates are not differentiated. The tabulated amounts do not include administrative costs and institutional ads paid for by the two major parties.

USING THE NEWS MEDIA

National News: Charge and Countercharge.—If the Bush campaign was mesmerized by what had been accomplished in 1988 by focusing a personal attack on its opponent, the Clinton campaign was determined not to repeat the mistakes of Michael Dukakis. By 1992, the Democrats had assimilated the folklore of the 1988 campaign that a charge left unrefuted is a charge the public will believe. They were, in short, well prepared for the strategy the Bush campaign threw against them. In particular, George Stephanopoulos, who had headed Dukakis's rapid-response team and had seen his advice largely ignored, resolved not to let Clinton be put on the defensive in news reporting.[22]

When journalists pressed for the campaign's reaction to charges leveled by the president in a speech or by his campaign staff in their daily "fax attack," the Clinton response team would sift through their computerized data banks to develop a rebuttal based on contrary information. Press releases designed to discredit a Bush campaign charge were assembled and faxed to journalists from campaign headquarters in an effort to arrest a detrimental story within one news cycle. That is, the Clinton response team endeavored to reach journalists with their side of the story before the daily deadlines passed. They hoped to either kill the story or at least to ensure that the news reports would contain both the charge and their rebuttal. They wanted to keep a story from building into a two-day event.

In this game, the Republican campaign worked at something of a disadvantage of its own making. The 1988 campaign came back to haunt it, because many journalists and others believed that the aggressive attacks from the Republicans had trivialized the election choice. Since Bush opted for an attack strategy again in 1992, his campaign was constantly operating against the presumptions of a press corps watchful for distortions. Bush did not help his case when, almost before the campaign had begun, he commented in an interview with David Frost, "I'll do whatever I have to get elected." The statement was a good deal milder in context than the Clinton campaign made it seem. Bush was referring to the rigors of campaigning, but the quote quickly became twisted into evidence that Bush saw no ethical limits in the conduct of a campaign.

If rebutting Republican attacks at the staff level failed, or if the Clinton campaign saw a means of turning the story, then Clinton or Gore might respond directly. On 3 August, for example, Clinton changed his plans for a day free from public appearances and called a press conference to respond to Bush's charge that Clinton's health-care proposals would combine "the efficiency of the House post office with the compassion of the KGB." Arguing that his proposals had been successfully implemented in other nations, Clinton called Bush's attack "an act of desperation by an Administration that for twelve years has ignored the health-care needs of the American people." Noting that polls documented widespread concern about rising costs, one reporter observed, "Given a fat target, Mr. Clinton devoted a good 10 minutes to knocking Mr. Bush around on health care." His remarks were laden with data on rising health-care costs, as well as the fact dug up by the Clinton opposition research team that Bush had once referred to Medicare as "socialized medicine."[23] After that performance—so very different from Dukakis's reactions in 1988—the president did not return to health care again; an avenue of attack had been foreclosed.

Clinton clearly underestimated how severely he could be hurt by the draft issue. His maneuverings to avoid the draft in the late 1960s began to emerge just before the New Hampshire primary and just after sensational headlines involving Gennifer Flowers. His candidacy barely survived, and then only through the tenacity and grit of the candidate.[24] Once the general election campaign began, President Bush, his campaign officials, and numerous Republican surrogates took up the chorus, hammering away at Clinton's draft record as a means of dramatizing his untrustworthiness. Clinton was nothing more than a contrived politician trying to have it all; "Slick Willie" was not telling the full story about his efforts to avoid the draft. In the third presidential debate, Ross Perot came to Clinton's rescue, citing the common-sense proposition that a person's actions as a young man were less relevant than what he had done recently in public office. Perot went on to cite George Bush's role as vice-president in the decision to arrange to trade arms to Iran in return for its assistance in securing release of American hostages in Lebanon.

At critical points, overzealousness weakened the tactical effectiveness of Bush's attack. In early August, deputy campaign manager Mary Matalin composed a "fax attack" entitled "Sniveling Hypocritical Democrats: Stand Up and Be Counted" that was so personally caustic that the president himself felt compelled to disavow the attack and pledge that he would "keep this campaign out of the sleaze business."[25] Bush himself overstepped the draft issue when he insinuated that Clinton might have met with Soviet intelligence agents during a vacation trip to Moscow as a student. News reports of the State Department's zeal in searching the passport files of Clinton's mother allowed the Democrat to ridicule Republican dirty tricks. Finally, while stumping during the last weeks, Bush got carried away and referred to the Democratic ticket as "two Bozos."

Clinton's efforts to blunt the Republican assault were aided by a good deal of luck. Overall, his biggest break came in the form of the economic indicators that stayed just bad enough to perpetuate voter concern. Similarly, he was fortunate when Lawrence Walsh, special prosecutor in the Iran-contra affair, released documentary evidence late in October contradicting Bush's claim that, as vice-president, he had been "out of the loop" of decision making. Clinton quickly seized the opportunity to apply political jujitsu, questioning Bush's trustworthiness in a direct quote, which was widely covered on the evening news. The Democrat immediately jumped five points in the polls and his lead widened during the last critical days of the campaign.[26] In sum, though we can recognize that Clinton ran a strong campaign on the tactical level, we should not overlook the role that providence played.

Local News: The Campaign Schedule.—Where a campaign's dealings with the national media involve influencing the agenda of the election, contact with local reporters, which comes about mainly through travel, is devoted to securing exposure in critical media markets. To be sure, the campaign staff is careful that every event and appearance fits into its designs for the running national news story, yet it does make a difference where the candidate travels. Each foray produces so much coverage from local newspapers and television stations that it makes good sense to allocate travel according to a rational plan. According to Clinton's national campaign manager, David Wilhelm: "One thing that has struck all of us in this campaign is the importance of a candidate trip into a state. There's an immediate effect, two points, maybe even three points in some cases."[27]

The Clinton campaign used a sophisticated data-mapping operation to systematize its scheduling, media-buying, and get-out-the-vote operations. It began by superimposing media markets on the map of the United States. Week by week, each media market was ranked in terms of the number of persuadable voters in the market weighted by the Electoral College votes and the perceived strategic importance of the states reached in that market. The resulting map, in which the media markets were arrayed on an eight-point, color-coded scale, quickly revealed where the campaign needed to place its emphasis in travel, field organization, and media buys.

Strategically, the poll data and estimates of the "persuasion value of media markets" led the Clinton campaign to focus its energies on thirty-two states with 376 electoral votes.[28] It did, however, make exceptions. The campaign decided to schedule bus tours in two states that its maps indicated it had little chance of winning: Florida and Texas. Clinton's advisers felt it was worthwhile to make President Bush defend his own territory. The week after the Democrats visited Texas, for example, Clinton's maps showed that the Bush campaign responded with a heavy run of television ad time in seven large Texas media markets, a significant expenditure for the last week of September in the president's home state.

When the dust cleared on 4 November, Clinton had won thirty-three states with 370 electoral votes.[29] Of the thirty-two states on which his campaign had concentrated, the Democrat lost only North Carolina. That loss was partially offset by victories in Montana and Nevada.

Telephones and Computers. —For over a decade, journalists and scholars have been predicting the arrival of a new era in campaigning driven by access to an expanding array of communication technologies. That era clearly began in the 1992 presidential campaign, even though we cannot yet conclude that campaigning through the new media has significantly changed electoral organizing. Computers, nationwide WATS telephone numbers, fax machines, satellites, and VCRs all offered tactical applications that the candidates avidly seized upon. Innovation in the tactics of campaigning is always propelled by necessity. Much credit for exploring new ways of relating to citizens belongs to Ross Perot, whose inventiveness derived from a combination of circumstance and philosophy.

Perot, a committed, anti-Washington populist, drew abundant strength from an upsurge of citizen dissatisfaction directed toward both governance in Washington and the conduct of contemporary election politics.[30] Molding a populist, rejectionist movement into an effective political organization proved, however, to be a difficult tactical problem. The lack of an existing party organization was an enormous disadvantage in the fall campaign. Though party organizations have declined precipitously in recent decades, Bush and Clinton could still draw substantial help by running so-called combined campaigns with the organizations of candidates running on the same party slate.

Perot relied heavily on the latest in communication technology to master the problems of mobilizing a grass-roots insurgency. The resulting campaign structure differed fundamentally from the traditional pyramid employed by the major-party nominees. Instead of many layers intervening between the campaign's strategic decision-making circles and the grass roots, Perot's campaign was two-tiered: lots of troops and very few commanders.

Freed from the need to raise funds, the candidate asked citizens to give of their time by volunteering to help place his name on the ballot in all fifty states. Perot took a page from Democrat Jerry Brown and established a toll-free "800 number" to encourage direct contact with voters. A deluge of calls poured into his Dallas headquarters. In late March, for example, Perot's appearance on Phil Donahue's show reportedly resulted in over a quarter of a million calls, which overwhelmed the system.

Not surprisingly, given that Perot had made his money in computers, the campaign quickly turned to computer technology to manage the growing roster of volunteers. According to Tom Steinert-Threlkeld of the *Dallas Morning News,* the Perot Committee used a caller-recognition system to capture the telephone numbers of incoming calls. These numbers were then sent to a data matching service that provided the campaign with the names and addresses of callers, plus demographic information that described the communities toward which the Perot campaign could turn to enlist other supporters.[31]

The Talk-Show Campaign. — Since in Perot's mind the national news media were as much part of the system as his competitors, the two major parties, and the Congress, in both phases of his crusade Perot sought instinctively to bypass the national political reporters. In effect, Perot was the first candidate to discover that the structure of the news media had become so fragmented that it was possible to find alternative means of communicating with voters using channels in which he, as a candidate, would have greater control over the message. Rather than communicate through conduits mediated by journalists—that is, the three evening news shows on network television and stories reported by the major newspapers and news services—Perot wanted to carry his message directly to voters.

In fact, the Perot campaign began on a cable television interview show. Prodded by John Jay Hooker, an enthusiastic supporter from Tennessee, Perot agreed to go on CNN's "Larry King Live" two days after the New Hampshire primary (20 February).[32] Not leaving anything to chance, Hooker specifically prepped King to push Perot hard on whether he would run. After asking this question directly and receiving a flat "no," King turned to the many difficulties facing the country and then moved the conversation into speculation about scenarios under which Perot might be moved to address these problems by becoming a candidate. Thus was born the notion that if volunteers put him on the ballot, Perot would run. During the year, Perot appeared on the King show a total of six times.

When he resumed campaigning in October, Perot's unorthodoxy continued. Notably, he dispensed with the most visible part of presidential campaigns, the traveling roadshow. While Clinton-Gore turned to that most humble form of public transportation, the bus, and George Bush boarded a train, Perot hardly traveled at all. Instead, he relied on debates, talk-show interviews, and extensive purchased television time. Other than flying to the three national debates, in the course of a month Perot made campaign appearances only in New Jersey, Florida, Missouri, California, New York, and Washington, D.C.[33]

To a large extent, Perot, followed by Clinton and Bush, was driven to innovate by the inadequacies they perceived in normal news processes as a means of communicating with voters. Given the reality that television remains the primary source of news for many voters, two trends in the conduct of network journalism impelled this shift of tactics. First, as a number of studies have shown, the length of "sound bites" used by television networks, in which politicians actually appear on the screen explaining their views, has been shrinking. By the 1988 campaign, the average direct quote from a presidential candidate lasted only 8.9 seconds, down from 43.1 seconds during the 1968 campaign.[34] As a result, politicians are not able to communicate very much information directly through the news process.[35] Second, their ideas are truncated and embedded in commentary from both anchormen and correspondents, which inevitably puts their quotes into contexts not of the candidates' choosing. That context often works to the politician's disadvantage because the fundamental orientation of "hard" news reporting of political advocacy has become increasingly characterized by hostility.[36] The trend that began in the Watergate experience in the mid-1970s culminated in encounters during the 1988 cycle that led to the withdrawal of Senators Joseph Biden and Gary Hart. By 1992, this dominant style in news reporting by television networks had gone so far that media critics had named the syndrome "attack journalism."[37] In May and June, Perot learned firsthand how critical reporting could snowball to his detriment.[38] And, of course, earlier in 1992, Bill Clinton barely survived a one-two punch when revelations about his avoidance of the draft quickly followed the charges made by Gennifer Flowers.

Instead, the candidates searched for ways to avoid the intense scrutiny of their issue positions and political troubles that constitute what the pols and the critics also call "got-cha" journalism. They quickly found that appearances on regularly scheduled television shows that could loosely be termed "public affairs programming" provided them with more camera time and a softer format. The principal expansion occurred on the morning news hour shows. The campaigns discovered that the networks were willing to negotiate live, half-hour (or even longer) segments just to entice the candidates to their breakfast-hour programming.[39] ABC's "Nightline" also functioned as a means for the candidates and their staff members to talk about the "inside baseball" of the campaign. Over the year, the prime time network shows "60 Minutes," "Prime Time Live," and "20/20" also played a notable, though infrequent, role. For example, on a Sunday night in January, just after the Super Bowl, many viewers got their first look at Bill and Hillary Clinton as they discussed their marriage in the context of Gennifer Flowers' exposé.

Howard Kurtz of the *Washington Post* eventually coined a term for the entire election when he referred to this trend as "The Talk-Show Campaign of 1992."[40] According to Ted Savaglio, executive producer of the "CBS This Morning" program, the sudden mushrooming of candidate appearances in these formats started with a decision by the Clinton campaign to put their candidate on television as much as possible.[41] This decision was part strategy and part tactics. Their internal research, conducted mainly with focus groups, showed that by the end of the primaries, many voters had closed their minds on the Clinton candidacy. In May and June, voters were not prepared to hear Clinton's message of change—his argument that a new direction, a new generation, could redirect the economy. Blocking this message was the widespread public perception that Bill Clinton was just another politician.[42] Many voters did not know basic facts about his life and his career, believing, for example, that his background was typically "yuppie." The campaign concluded that it had to reposition Clinton by bringing the facts of his early life to light and by showing him off in settings that would display his personal warmth.

The effort to cure Clinton's image as a typical politician ultimately led to a sharp increase in candidates on non-news television programming. Talk shows tend to focus more on "lifestyle" programming than they do on the hard news of rough-and-tumble politics. And, as already noted, the questioning is usually of a softer tone than in those formats in which a candidate appears with veteran political reporters. They were perfect vehicles for communicating a message about Clinton the person rather than Clinton the politician.

Confidential documents released after the campaign describe the need to exploit the "counterpolitical" media, that is, the talk shows. In June, the presumptive Democratic nominee hit all three network breakfast shows and followed Perot onto Larry King's show. That same month, Stephanopoulos booked his candidate onto MTV, where he would reach a younger audience. And, in perhaps the most distinctive effort to move away from the image of a slick candidate, Clinton broke new ground by appearing on the late-night Arsenio Hall show, complete with saxophone and sun glasses.

At first, President Bush resisted the trend, sniping at Perot's willingness to appear on "weird talk shows." But when his opponents' appearances exploded in June, Bush joined the crowd. He invited CBS to broadcast its program "CBS This Morning" directly from the White House lawn.[43] Political reporters who normally host the "hard news" interview shows, such as Tim Russert from NBC's "Meet the Press," started to grumble that they could not get the candidates to appear on their shows.[44] By the fall campaign, things had only gotten worse for Mr. Russert. Near the end of October, the competing morning shows produced a plethora of appearances by the six presidential and vice-presidential candidates. In addition to appearances on talk shows, the candidates began turning up on the many cable channels: beyond CNN and C-SPAN, the highly segmented audiences watching MTV, ESPN, and the Nashville networks all had their chance to see the candidates.

Video by Satellite.—The Clinton campaign found other ways to use the new media to improve its control over the messages delivered to voters. In the

New Hampshire primary, during its time of troubles, the Clinton campaign prepared a videocassette of the candidate's issue stands that they reportedly distributed to undecided voters in 30,000 homes. Later in the fall campaign, the Clinton staff produced and distributed cassette copies in the hundreds of thousands of Clinton's bio, "The Man from Hope." Throughout the campaign year, both Clinton and Bush often used closed-circuit videoconferencing to appear simultaneously in scattered locations for events such as fund raisers or rallies of committed supporters.

During the fall campaign, strategists from both campaigns developed another, and probably more consequential, use of new media by providing frequent satellite feeds that allowed the news departments of local television stations to have direct access to the candidate.[45] Thus, as a service of the campaign, Clinton himself could be available for personal interviews by television anchors in pivotal media markets. From one location, the candidate could do five or six interviews live during the evening news hours. Interviews conducted at other times could be taped by stations for use in their news shows. More frequently, the campaign would try to interest the stations in access to key members of the campaign staff.

The Bush campaign was doing essentially the same thing. The two campaigns used technology to allow local stations to stage their own versions of spontaneous news, such as the confrontations of live interviews produced on ABC's "Nightline." Because journalists at the local level are not normally as involved in the minutiae of evolving stories about the candidate, however, this vehicle provided the campaigns with one more way of communicating with voters in critical areas while bypassing the pool of national journalists traveling with the candidate.

At major rallies or events, Clinton's operatives also set up cameras alongside those of the networks. Clinton's speeches could then be "pulled down off the bird" by any station interested in using a clip for its evening news. At Clinton headquarters, where the satellite signal was also received, a media producer monitored essentially the same picture that the networks were shooting. If the camera angle showed a sparse crowd, or if a garishly clad spectator distracted the viewer's eye, or if the signs down front blocked the candidate's tie, or if the opposition's signs began showing up in the background, a quick call from Little Rock to the cellular phone of the on-site advance staff could correct the offending blemish. Thus the campaign could improve the picture of the event in progress. By 1992 the local campaign appearance had become a video show produced by the candidates' staffs.

Extensive and instantaneous communication by video, cellular phone, and data exchange among computers allowed the Clinton organization to manage both the campaign and the message from headquarters. The traveling party was never out of touch with the rest of the campaign. In prior years, presidential candidates felt that when they traveled from state to state, they had to take their top-level staff with them. This allowed strategy and tactics to be debated continually as campaigners and journalists flew about in "the silver womb."[46] The downside of this arrangement was that the traveling community could become highly incestuous and isolated from a broader perspective. In contrast, by 1992 the Democrats had learned that modern communication media enabled them to function effectively with much of the strategic layer of the campaign staff back home in Little Rock. Presumably, this allowed James Carville to maintain the focus on the larger picture that the voters were receiving and specifically to concentrate its message upon the sign in Clinton's headquarters.

THE DEBATES

During the 1992 fall campaign, the presidential candidates debated three times—on 11, 15, and 19 October—while the vice-presidential candidates debated on 13 October. In every election since 1976, the two major-party nominees have debated each other on live television. The candidates and their staffs always view these events as highly significant. For one thing, presidential debates often prove to be exceptions to the well-established fact that the public is not interested in public affairs programming. Huge numbers of potential voters watch these events, particularly the first debate in a series. Given the size of the audience for debates, presidential campaigners are convinced that these events can have a significant impact of the election outcome.[47]

Political managers have spawned a folklore relating to debate strategy and tactics. Normally, incumbent presidents have been reluctant to debate. Ever since the Nixon-Kennedy debates of 1960, in which the vice-president debated a relatively unknown, upstart senator, incumbents have feared that the main effect of such meetings will be to legitimize their opponents. Simply appearing on the same stage bestows equality on the contestants, allowing the challenger to close what James Baker referred to as the "stature gap."[48] At the same time, a candidate who is leading in the polls usually concludes that a debate can only enhance the standing of his opponent.

In 1992 these pressures worked at cross-purposes. As the incumbent, Bush was less than enthusiastic about the impending debates. His opponent, moreover, was generally conceded to be more articulate and practiced than Bush, in part because of an extensive series of debates among Democratic candidates during the primaries. Nevertheless, Bush was running behind in the polls and uphill against the presumption that debates are now institutionalized as part of the general election contest.

Bush's strategists knew all along they would have to agree to debate Clinton, but they sought to delay the inevitable. Reportedly, James A. Baker, the White House chief of staff, believed that the debates could throw off the campaign's effort to focus its message.[49] He argued that once the debates were scheduled, the voters would suspend their decision making and the race would become "frozen" while voters awaited the televised confrontation.[50] Delaying agreement on the debates would, he hoped, allow Bush to move closer to Clinton in the polls.

Throughout September, the candidates circled one another. Bush's forces cited a difference over the format of debates in refusing to show up at prearranged sites. The Commission on Presidential Debates had suggested that the public would benefit from a looser format in which the candidates responded to questions from a single moderator and had an opportunity to question each other. Clinton agreed to these arrangements; Bush reportedly preferred the traditional format of a panel of reporters asking questions of each candidate in turn.[51] In the short run, Bush's strategists were willing to absorb the unavoidable criticism that they were refusing to debate.

Toward the end of September, however, Clinton found a device to turn up the heat. On 21 September, he traveled to East Lansing, Michigan, the site of the first scheduled debate and delivered a massive attack on Bush's refusal to participate. His speech, extensively covered by the networks, included the taunt, "I guess I don't blame him. If I had the worst record of any president in fifty years, I wouldn't want to debate that either." Clinton's opposition research team produced a triumph when they unearthed a 1980 quote from Bush that simultaneously allowed Clinton to attack Bush and keep to his own essential message. Clinton quoted George Bush speaking about then President Jimmy Carter:

"I believe he wants to avoid debate because he wants to avoid talking about his economic record. I mean, how do you debate the merits of an economic policy that put 1.9 million people out of work? " [Clinton continued:] This is 1992. The figure is not 1.9 million. There are 3 million more Americans out of work than when he [Bush] took office.[52]

After this experience, and as the second prearranged date drew near, the Bush campaign came to the table and the two sides quickly agreed to the three presidential debates and one vice-presidential debate. The two campaigns also agreed to pack the debates into eight days. The brief period resulted from the late agreement and from the desire on both sides for an opportunity to recover before election day from a possibly poor debate performance.

In the predebate negotiations, the Clinton side won some concessions that ultimately proved helpful to his candicacy. First, the candidates reached their agreement just as Ross Perot was reentering the race. Both sides went along with including him: Bush because he wanted Perot to cut into Clinton's support, Clinton because he hoped Perot would attack the president's economic leadership. Clinton's guess proved more accurate. Second, as to format, the candidates agreed to three different approaches: questioning by a panel of journalists, a sole moderator leading the discussion, and questioning by a group of ordinary citizens.[53] For the second presidential debate, which was held on 15 October in Richmond, Virginia, Clinton found a format that showcased his talents ideally. The Gallup Organization selected a random sample of uncommitted voters to make up the audience to whom the moderator, ABC's Carole Simpson, turned for questions. The Democrat candidate had been holding "electronic town halls" regularly and liked interacting directly with voters.

Citizens, it turns out, have a range of concerns that leads them to ask candidates different questions than those normally posed by political reporters. Compare these questions drawn from the first and second debates:

From reporters (debate 1):

Can you lock in a level here tonight on where middle income families can be guaranteed a tax cut or an income level where there will be no tax raise?

Would you go along with a plan to make the Federal Reserve Board more accountable to elected officials?

Even if you have the guts to make unpopular changes—cutting medicare—people say you haven't a prayer of getting anything passed. Since a president isn't a Lone Ranger in Washington, how in the world can you make such unpopular changes?

From citizens (debate 2):

Crime is rampant in the cities, twelve-year-olds are carrying guns to school. Where do you stand on gun control and what do you plan to do about the problem?

We've talked about creating jobs, but we have high school seniors who cannot fill out a job application. How can we create high paying jobs with the education we have, and what do you plan to do about it?

The social security program, the pension guarantee funds, and Medicare are all predicted to go bankrupt in the near future. What is your specific response of what you plan to do about retirees, considering each of these issues?

In *The Untapped Power of the Press,* journalism professor Louis Wolfson points out that all too frequently contemporary journalism does not provide citizens with the information necessary for informed participation in politics.[54] Here we find a graphic illustration. In the second debate, citizens wanted to know the candidate's programs, policies, and promises. Most political reporters, meanwhile, wished to explore the unexplicated details or inconsistencies in the candidates' stands; they saw political rhetoric as ambiguous and designed to mislead. As Helen Thomas of UPI observed, "A reporter, if given the chance, can try to pin the candidate down."[55]

As the debates unfolded, however, they proved mostly anticlimactic in terms of the final vote, even though the audience numbers were up substantially from 1988.[56] Clinton held on to a lead in most polls of somewhere between seven and ten points. The debates did, however, help legitimize the second Perot campaign. They were, in effect, his second debut, coming less than two weeks after his reentry. Perot's poll ratings had sunk, and his negative evaluations had increased considerably when he dropped out in July. So focused was his attack on the current drift of the United States in economic policy during the debates, however, that his standing improved dramatically.

THE ADVERTISING CAMPAIGNS

The advertising of all three presidential contenders reflected their strategies in terms of ideas to be communicated and audiences targeted for persuasion even more directly than their daily speeches and travel. Particularly on the presidential level, where they can obtain adequate funding, campaigners have complete command over the content of their messages and nearly absolute control over placement.

In the past fifteen years, political advertising on television has increased in both velocity and interactivity. Where campaign strategists used to map out a careful advertising program well in advance, now, in the midst of the campaign, they are constantly redesigning their commercials overnight to respond to events or to an opponent's ads. Purchasing advertising time has also become a highly fluid process in which campaigns must react continually to slight changes in the polls and in the opponent's media buy.

Advertising purchases can telegraph strategy to the other side. Since television stations must offer each candidate equal time, they have a duty to inform the competitors of the reservations of time made by their opponents. If one candidate starts advertising in a state in which he has been weak, his internal polling probably indicates that he might be able to win there. If surveys indicate that a candidate is slipping in his stronghold, the first sign to his opponents may come in a stepped-up ad buy. Conversely, if a candidate stops advertising in a pivotal state, it may mean he has conceded it. The opponent will also want to redirect his scarce money rapidly to other states that remain marginal.

Once a candidate sends the ads out to the stations, it is almost inevitable that the other side will see them. In the world of attack advertising, fearing that voters will believe any charge they leave unrefuted, campaign strategists react rapidly with counterads. For example, the Clinton campaign, reportedly, was able to peek at the Bush ads before they aired and ready their response.[57] In one instance, Frank Greer, Clinton's media consultant, went so far as to prepare his own version of a Bush ad for which he had only the script. Greer wanted to put the ad and several possible responses before a focus group session. The Bush ad depicted Arkansas as a barren wasteland of dead trees presided over by a buzzard. When the ad finally ran, the Clinton response was on the air within twenty-four hours.

In this highly interactive world, the mechanism of placing ads can also be used to deceive opponents. Reserving time and sending a reel of commercials to the station, a candidate can keep his opponent guessing as to his true intentions until an electronic fund transfer completes the deal at the last possible minute. If the funds never arrive, the ads do not run. While the opponent is concentrating on this diversion, the real attack can be mounted elsewhere. Preparing ads that never actually run is yet another way of throwing your opponent off guard and making him prepare for an attack that never materializes. All three campaigns produced numerous ads that never ran, often because of disagreements within the campaign staff due to a change of strategy, or simply as a ploy in tactical maneuvering.

We can discuss as illustrations only a few of the many ads that were produced in the course of the 1992 campaign. Many critics viewed the Bush advertising campaign as consisting of little more than attack ads directed against Clinton. The president was up to his old tricks from 1988. Yet this view is unfair inasmuch as the November Company, Bush's media team, did produce and air a number of positive commercials, and Clinton's campaign also used attack ads extensively.

In September, for example, coinciding with the Detroit economic speech, the November Company produced a five-minute "Agenda for American Renewal" in which the president discussed his plan and invited viewers to call his toll-free "800 number" for a copy. A similar ad presented Bush's economic plan while it tried to show him concerned for the impact of a poor economy on the nation. Bush boasted that the nation was not at war but acknowledged that shifting to a peacetime economy brought fear and uncertainty. He concluded, "We changed the world around us. Together we must do the same at home."[58]

In addition to advancing proposals, Bush's positive commercials often used a mixture of positive appeal and subtle put-down. For example, an ad produced in October shifted from scenes of the Gulf war with Bush's voice-over to an empty chair in the Oval Office while an announcer asked, "Who do you trust to be sitting in this chair?"[59]

Nevertheless, the Bush advertising program will be recalled mostly for its direct attacks on Clinton. Three ads stand out. In the first major assault, the Bush campaign calculated the costs of programs that Clinton had proposed and then estimated the impact of those in terms of income taxes. The ad featured three average Americans and flashed the Bush calculations of tax increases on the screen—$1088 for a steamfitter, and so on. The ad, produced in early October, met with such criticism from journalists and opponents that it was pulled from the air. For example, on "CBS This Morning," Bob Garfield of *Advertising Age* declared, "The President has used voodoo arithmetic to come up with these numbers."[60]

While it may be said that Bush made his point, nonetheless, the tone had been set, and collecting quotes from newspaper ad watchers, Clinton had all the ammunition he needed to denounce Bush's ads. His rejoinder ad complained, "George Bush is running attack ads.... 'Misleading' says the *Washington Post....*"[61]

Less than a week later, as the debates opened, the Bush campaign ran an ad that pulled back from a photographic negative of Clinton on the cover of *Time* magazine under the headline, *Why Voters Don't Trust Clinton*. The announcer rehearsed Clinton's shifting story about his efforts to avoid the draft and concluded, "Now, for Bill Clinton, it's a question of avoiding the truth."[62] *Time* threatened to sue Bush/Quayle for infringement of its copyrighted logo.[63]

Finally, toward the end of October, the Bush campaign ran an ad that Susan Spencer of CBS called "The Night of the Living Dead." Over black-and-white footage featuring a buzzard sitting on a dead tree overlooking a wasteland, an announcer recited dismal statistics about Clinton's record in Arkansas. "And now, Bill Clinton wants to do for America what he has done for Arkansas. America can't take that risk."[64] Again, many of the ad watchers screamed foul.

As noted earlier, the Clinton campaign had advance notice about this ad. Within twenty-four hours they were on with a rebuttal. An announcer intoned while the same text crawled up the screen,

CBS, CNN and newspapers across the country call George Bush's ads misleading and wrong. The fact is, under Bill Clinton Arkansas leads the nation in job growth.... No wonder the *Washington Post* says George Bush is lying about Bill Clinton's record, and why the *Oregonian* concluded, "Frankly, we no longer trust George Bush."[65]

For its part, the Clinton campaign also produced a mix of positive and negative commercials. The most directly positive video proved to be the biography used at the Democratic convention to present Clinton's childhood to a skeptical audience. Before the convention opened, the campaign previewed the film, "The Man from Hope," for reporters, a maneuver that resulted in lengthy feature stories in many of the major news outlets presenting the same favorable view of Clinton's past. In October, when Clinton was under heavy attack on the "trust issue," his campaign repackaged the same footage into a 60-second spot to remind viewers of Clinton's personal strengths.

As with the Bush campaign, however, most of the overtly positive commercials contained a hint of a criticism of the opponent. For example, in September the Clinton campaign released a thirty-second commercial that they titled "Make America Work." Seated in an office, facing the camera, wearing a suit, the candidate stated, "Government just isn't working for the hard-working families of America. We need fundamental change, not just more of the same. That's why I've offered a comprehensive plan...."[66]

One technique used by the Clinton campaign in their positive commercials sought to advance their proposals and simultaneously inoculate viewers against Bush's attacks. An ad released in early October, for example, featured pictures of both Clinton and Gore during their bus tours, while the announcer remarked, "They're a new generation of Democrats ... and they don't think the way the old Democratic party did." Then the screen shifted to the following phrase in black print on a white background, "Welfare Can Be a Second Chance, Not a Way of Life." The announcement continued: "They've called for an end to welfare as we know it...."[67] Clearly, the campaign was working hard to rebut the "tax-and-spend-liberal" tag line used by the Republicans at every opportunity.

Clinton's most effective attack commercials juxtaposed clips of George Bush at earlier points with an announcer's version of the facts.[68] In one of these, Bush opined, "I'm not prepared to say we are in recession." The narrator replied, "March 1992—jobless rate hits a six-year high.... If George Bush doesn't understand the problem, how can he solve it?" Another ad cited Bush's promise to create 30 million jobs in eight years, his claim to be an environmentalist, and his professed desire to be the education president. The announcer then reminded viewers that more private-sector jobs had been lost under the Bush administration than created, that the Sierra Club had accused

Bush of gutting the clean air regulations, and that Bush had tried to reduce college aid.

The so-called generic ads paid for by the Democratic National Committee (DNC) were even more blunt. A fifteen-second spot featured Bush saying, "You will be better off four years from now than you are today," to which the narrator replied, "Well, it's four years later.... How're you doing?"[69] In another, an ominous "odometer" clicked away, tallying the number of jobs lost as a result "of years of Republican neglect." This ad was roundly criticized by journalists as misleading.[70] Still another DNC ad reminded elderly voters, "Every year for the past twelve years, the Republicans tried to cut Medicare...."[71]

Perot's advertising team produced a number of highly professional, even slick, thirty- and sixty-second ads. In one that a New York audience rated most highly, the viewer saw faces of children, while an announcer asked, "What will they say if we tell them that by the year 2000, we will have left them with a national debt of $8 trillion?"[72]

Most of Perot's spot ads used a "crawl" in which the announcer's text scrolled up the screen, reinforcing the audio message. In one, on health care, the visual background was an EKG line, while the sound of a heartbeat grew stronger. The announcer commented: "Health care in America is in critical condition. We are pumping more money into it than any other nation, yet 3 million Americans have no coverage...."[73] Many of these ads stressed Perot's economic plans. Toward the end of the campaign, Perot's ads urged voters not to waste their votes on "politics as usual."

But the campaign's real mark became the long infomercials in which viewers were exposed to Ross Perot speaking directly to the camera. These ads deliberately took on a certain amateur quality, as Perot often used detailed charts and graphs to make his points. The series began with a broadcast that contained Perot's indictment of present economic policies. Another presented his proposals for restoring economic health. In an effort to soften the picture that emerged of Perot from the infomercials heavy with economic analysis, two others sought to give viewers a picture of Perot the person. A thirty-minute conversation with Ross Perot was entitled "Business Success, Leadership and His Life." In another, Perot introduced each member of his family.

Reactions from Journalists and Viewers.—The advertising of all three campaigns brought reactions from many news organizations, which have instituted programs to monitor and report on political advertising. At first, these beats seemed justified if only because so much of the action in campaigns occurred on the airwaves. But, as politicians have turned increasingly to attack advertising, ad reporting has inevitably taken on the tasks of a "truth squad."[74]

In 1992 most of this reporting was highly critical of the ads produced by both Bush and Clinton. In part, the criticism resulted from the fact that the advocacy of politicians inherently involves political perspective, a lens that colors facts and arguments. To reporters, this slant smacks of misleading distortion. In addition, reporters are, by instinct, inclined to demonstrate their objectivity by being critical of both sides. Thus, if many ad watchers were taking on the Bush campaign, they were also likely to balance that reporting with criticism of Clinton's advertising.

In general, the ad-watch reports may be less effective in giving voters a sense of perspective in viewing ads than they are in causing the politicians to stop and contemplate the veracity of their claims. In the 1992 campaign, both sides knew they would be challenged on the accuracy of their ads, and both tried to document the basis of their ads. They may still have been highly selective in picking out facts and figures, but at least they thought about documentation. This need sometimes spilled directly into the content of the ads themselves. For example, in a summary article, Richard L. Berke wrote in the *New York Times:* "The advertising this year is just as tough, but it seeks to appear more credible by giving the impression that it depends on documentation and third-party sources."[75]

During October, the Times-Mirror Center for the People and the Press conducted a series of national surveys of voters' reactions to the ads. These measurements recorded a worrisome picture for George Bush that was evident as early as 6 October. The first survey found that voters who had been exposed to the commercials were more likely to rate Clinton's ads as "more truthful and convincing." Fifty-one percent said the Democrat's ads were basically truthful versus 35 percent who said they were not. Meanwhile, 50 percent thought Bush's ads were *not* truthful and 38 percent said they were.[76] Worse yet, the survey concluded that voters were tuning Bush out: Only 18 percent said they had heard most about Bush among the candidates, while 33 percent each said they had heard most about Clinton and Perot. It is pertinent to point out that this question refers to domination of the news media as well as the visibility of the ads. In any case, subsequent surveys by the Times-Mirror show that these two trends—the greater credibility for Clinton's advertising and the lower visibility of the incumbent's campaign —continued throughout October.

Conclusions

The tasks of a presidential campaign are so complicated that welding them into a coherent design and managing them on a national basis can be a nightmare. After the campaign is over, however, armchair pundits lionize the victors and condemn the defeated, often without much recognition of how difficult the job really is.[77] Campaigns that lose seem to fly apart; participants provide journalists with colorful quotes, usually not for attribution, that document exactly how incompetent their coworkers were.

At the outset of the 1992 campaign, many observers pointed out that the Republicans had built a effective management team through three successive elections, while the Democratic candidate in each cycle seemed to assemble a new group of essentially untried amateurs. As we now know, Campaign '92 did not turn out that way. Postelection commentary followed the utterly predictable pattern of ridiculing the collapse of the much-vaunted Republican machine and praising the astute management of Clinton's campaign.[78] Neither view contains much judgment.

Clearly, Bill Clinton ran a campaign that was tactically superior to those of other recent Democrats. Even so, he took a considerable strategic risk in not throwing resources into energizing traditional elements of the Democratic party vote. Instead, the Clinton campaign went after the marginal votes in the center. Near the end of the campaign, Clinton's national field director reflected the strategy in a quote aired by National Public Radio: "They've basically conceded us states with 170 electoral votes, while we're fighting them everywhere. We're fighting them in Florida; we're fighting them in Kansas; ... We've got them pinned down between their 20 and their goal line, and that's where we want to keep them."[79]

The evidence that Clinton took his base for granted is fragmentary, but suggestive. Dukakis had won ten states in 1988. Considering that Dukakis did not do so well nationally, these ten states, constituting 109 electoral votes, might be taken as a starting point for the 1992 Democratic campaign, a base on which the candidate could expand. While Clinton also carried these states in 1992, he received fewer votes in each of them than Dukakis piled up in 1988. This shortfall is especially noticeable in that approximately 10 million more Americans went to the polls in 1992 than in 1988. Meanwhile, in the forty states that Dukakis lost in 1988, Clinton garnered more votes than Dukakis in thirty of them, even though he ran in a three-way contest.[80] Consider, as another example, that African Americans, a group with extremely high rates of voting for Democratic presidential candidates, voted in smaller numbers in 1992 than in earlier election years. In 1988, an estimated 8.3 million African Americans voted, constituting 10.5 percent of the national electorate; in 1992, these figures dropped to 8.1 million, or 8 percent of the electorate.[81]

From this perspective, one might argue that additional votes could have been awakened by a focused campaign. If George Bush had continued the march that began about twelve days out but stalled on the last weekend before election day, Clinton could certainly have used those extra votes.

Of course, there is an opposing view. The message and targeting components of strategy are obviously interwoven; one cannot construct one without affecting the other. Consider, therefore, the implications for Clinton's message that going after these traditional Democratic votes would have entailed. As it turns out, the positions that Clinton would have had to take in order to shore up those votes might have put Clinton and Gore into the same position as earlier Democratic tickets. In energizing those elements, Clinton might have moved too far and alienated the moderate voters who, in five of the last six elections, have supported Republican candidates in droves. In short, there is more than one way to lose an election.

While debating strategy with the first Democrat to win the White House in sixteen years seems rather foolish, we should avoid the temptation to view Clinton's strategy and tactical achievements as flawless. Clinton did, of course, demonstrate some considerable strengths, but the Democratic team took some risks and caught some lucky breaks. The Bush campaign, meanwhile, made some mistakes but hardly warrants our scorn. Though the election results were far from a foregone conclusion, the Republican campaign did have the disadvantage of running an incumbent in the midst of an economic downturn. Moreover, at two points in the fall, in mid-September and again in the third week of October, the Bush strategists succeeded in coordinating his message, audience, and tactical delivery with measurable results.

The 1992 campaign did not produce a "60–40 landslide" in which one side obliterated the other. Rather, the popular vote given to the two major-party nominees divided 53 to 47 percent, which just about parallels an impressionistic balance of the strategic and tactical successes of these two competing campaigns.

Notes

1. For an early discussion of competition over the perceptual environment within which presidential contests are fought, see F. Christopher Arterton, *Media Politics: The News Strategies of Presidential Campaigns* (Lexington, Mass.: Lexington Books, 1984).

2. National Public Radio, "Weekend Edition," 14 November 1992.

3. Remarks of Samuel L. Popkin at a panel discussion sponsored by the Graduate School of Political Management and the House Legislative Assistants' Association, 11 October 1992, cablecast on C-SPAN.

4. For a discussion of the development of message through campaign advertising, see F. Christopher Arterton, "The Persuasive Art in Politics: The Role of Paid Advertising in Presidential Campaigns," in *Under the Watchful Eye: Managing Presidential Campaigns in the Television Era,* edited by Mathew D. McCubbins (Washington, D.C.: CQ Press, 1992), 83–126.

5. Among the numerous econometric studies, see Edward Tufte, *Political Control of the Economy* (Princeton: Princeton University Press, 1980); and Steven Rosenstone, *Forecasting Presidential Elections* (New Haven: Yale University Press, 1983). For theories of retrospective voting, see Morris P. Fiorina, *Retrospective Voting in American National Elections* (New Haven: Yale University Press, 1979); and Samuel L. Popkin, *The Reasoning Voter* (Chicago: University of Chicago Press, 1991).

6. In the aftermath of the race, many Republicans would argue that the media were overwhelmingly biased against the incumbent, an analysis buoyed by data from the Center for Media and Public Affairs in *The Media Monitor*. In fact, much of this adverse reporting concerned the state of the economy, which, as Ted Smith has argued, normally tends to overstate bad news and underreport good news. See Ted J. Smith III, "The Vanishing Economy: Television Coverage of Economic Affairs, 1982–87," in *The Media Monitor,* edited by S. Robert Lichter and Linda Lichter (Washington, D.C.: The Media Institute, 1988).

7. See, for example, Peter Goldman and Tom Mathews, "America Changes the Guard: Part II. The Republicans: Unhappy Warrior," *Newsweek,* Election Special Issue, November/December 1992, 58–61; and Michael Wines, "Crippled by Chaos and Lack of Strategy, Bush Campaign Stumbled to Defeat," *New York Times,* 29 November 1992, 26.

8. See the resulting "point-and-counterpoint" reporting in Joel Brinkley, "Truth's Several Sides: Bush's Attack on the Clinton Record Is Accurate, at Least as Far as It Goes," *New York Times,* 23 September 1992, A20.

9. A set of four Times-Mirror surveys conducted in October found that Ross Perot commanded more voter attention than George Bush or Bill Clinton. In the last full week of Campaign '92, for example, "39 percent of voters said they had heard the most about Perot in the news media, 26 percent named Clinton, and only 22 percent named George Bush." See "The People, the Press and Politics, Campaign '92: Air Wars, Air Wars II, Air Wars III, and Air Wars IV," Times-Mirror Center for the People and the Press, Washington, D.C., October 1992.

10. Quotes taken from Ann Devroy and Dan Balz, "For Bush Aides, Positive Tack Isn't a Winner," *Washington Post,* 16 September 1992, A1, A12.

11. See, for example, the report commissioned by the Kettering Foundation, "Citizens and Politics: A View from Main Street" (Dayton, Ohio: Kettering Foundation, 1991).

12. William Safire wrote that George Bush's central problem on the right was this: Republicans assume that in his heart Bush is a moderate, a centrist—words that fall gently on the ears of independent voters, but which to even the reasonable right mean "weaseling pragmatist devoid of all principle." "Bush's Gamble," *New York Times Magazine,* 12 October 1992, 33.

13. Wines, "Crippled by Chaos and Lack of Strategy," 26.

14. Frank I. Luntz, who provided opinion data to the Perot campaign, reported that his role was to conduct "market research." Remarks at a panel discussion sponsored by the Graduate School of Political Management and the House Legislative Assistants' Association, 11 October 1992, cablecast on C-SPAN.

15. I am greatly indebted to Ms. Carol Darr for her help in describing all the various vehicles through which campaigns can spend money. The credit belongs to her; any errors here are mine. Personal interview, 1 August 1992.

16. I concentrate here on funding for the general election campaigns. The nomination phase of the presidential contest has an entirely different set of rules, which are, if anything, even more complicated. See Herbert Alexander, *Financing the 1988 Elections* (Boulder, Colo.: Westview Press, 1991).

17. This money is sometimes referred to as "441a(d) money" after the provision of the act that makes it possible.

18. For a mid-campaign description of how this fund raising was going, see Stephen Labaton, "Democrats Awash in Money While G.O.P. Coffers Suffer," *New York Times,* 13 September 1992, 38; or Ann Devroy and Charles R. Babcock, "GOP Fund-Raising Trouble," *Washington Post,* 17 September 1992, A1, A15.

19. These figures are estimated on the basis of news reports in mid-September. This area of expenditure is extremely difficult to pin down. Public disclosure is not complete since both parties have an interest in channeling money through state party committees. A month after the election, the Federal Election Commission reported soft money expenditures of $47.7 million for the Republicans and $32.2 million for the Democrats. But these figures include money that could have been used to support candidates for the U.S. Senate and House of Representatives. Meanwhile, the "off-the-record word on the street" is that the Democrats raised around $80 million and the Republicans around $60 million. These figures opt for the conservative estimates on the public record.

20. Ross Perot's campaign received contributions of $4.0 million from other persons according to his year-end report filed with the Federal Election Commission.

21. The finding is notable even though Perot suspended his campaign for two and a half months during a time when the other campaigns were piling up significant expenditures. We should also note that Perot's expenditures are for the entire election year, while those for Bush and Clinton do not include the money they spent in pursuit of their nominations.

22. See Jeffrey H. Birnbaum, "Youthful George Stephanopoulos Poised to Leap from Clinton Bandwagon to White House Perch," *Wall Street Journal,* 18 November 1992, A18.

23. The details of this event and the quotations are from Michael Kelly, "Clinton Moves Swiftly Against Bush," *New York Times,* 4 August 1992, A13.

24. Postelection commentary almost uniformly credited Clinton's determination as the sole factor that allowed his campaign to survive this storm. See, for example, Goldman and Mathews, "Inside the Campaign," 32–36.

25. Robin Toner, "Renouncing an Attack on Clinton, Bush Vows to Stay Above 'Sleaze,'" *New York Times,* 4 August 1992, A1, A12.

26. Wines, "Crippled by Chaos and Lack of Strategy," 26.

27. Remarks of David Wilhelm on an ABC "Nightline" Special, "72 Hours to Victory: Behind the Scenes with Bill Clinton," 5 November 1992.

28. Gwen Ifill, "Clinton: Forging Discipline, Vision, and Luck into the Road to Victory," *New York Times*, 5 November 1992, A1 and B3.

29. These figures count the District of Columbia with three electoral votes as if it were a state.

30. An expanded discussion of the material in this section was published in *Campaign Magazine*, June 1992, 1, 17.

31. Tom Steinert-Threlkeld, "High-tech Tactics by Perot Could Reshape Politics, Experts Say," *Dallas Morning News*, 3 May 1992, 1, 15.

32. For excerpts from Perot's early interviews, see "King and Perot," *Campaign Magazine*, June 1992, 31–41. Details of the early behind-the-scenes debate among Perot's supporters can be found in Goldman and Mathews, "The Inside Story," 70–77.

33. Travel schedules for the candidates were taken from *Campaign HOTLINE*, a daily electronic news service of the American Political Network.

34. John Tierney, "Sound Bites Become Smaller Mouthfuls," *New York Times*, 23 January 1992, A1, A18. Though some analysts have quibbled with the precise measurements, see Daniel Hallin, "Sound Bite News: Television Coverage of Elections, 1969–1988" (Washington, D.C.: Woodrow Wilson International Center for Scholars, 1991); and Kiku Adatto, "The Incredible Shrinking Soundbite," Research Paper no. 2, June 1990, Joan Shorenstein Barone Center, John F. Kennedy School of Government, Harvard University.

35. The initial criticism of truncated sound bites and the movement of candidates toward interview formats caused some rethinking at the network news organizations. See Richard L. Berke, "Ever-Shrinking Sound Bites Prompt Edict at CBS News," *New York Times*, 3 July 1992, A18. However, data compiled by *Campaign HOTLINE* in September showed little improvement. See the reporting of Richard Harms, "Checking the Bites," *New York Newsday*, 17 September 1992, 21.

36. For an analysis, see Ted J. Smith III, "The Watchdog's Bite," *American Enterprise* 1, no. 1 (January/February 1990): 62–70.

37. See, for example, Larry J. Sabato, *Feeding Frenzy: How Attack Journalism Has Transformed American Politics* (New York: Free Press, 1991).

38. Perot's press secretary, Jim Squires, himself a journalist with years of experience, likened the treatment as akin to the savage police beating of Rodney King in "How the Press Savaged Perot," *Neiman Reports*, Fall 1992, 3–5.

39. See, for example, the discussion in Elizabeth Kolbert, "Talk Shows Wrangling to Book the Candidates," *New York Times*, 6 July 1992, A10.

40. Howard Kurtz, "The Talk Show Campaign: TV Interviews Emerge as Preferred Forum," *Washington Post*, 28 October 1992, A1, A14.

41. Kolbert, "Talk Shows Wrangling," A10.

42. See the extensive reporting by Goldman and Mathews on the efforts to revitalize the public perception of Clinton, dubbed the "Manhattan Project" by the campaign staff. "The Inside Story," 40–56.

43. See Andrew Rosenthal, "Focus Is Elusive for Bush," *New York Times*, 2

July 1992, A1, A14; and in the same edition, Elizabeth Kolbert, "From the Rose Garden, the Bush TV Show," A14.

44. Kolbert, "Talk Show Wrangling," A10.

45. Richard L. Berke, "Satellite Technology Allows Campaigns to Deliver the Messages Unfiltered," *New York Times,* 23 October 1992, A18.

46. For a discussion of how campaigners used constant travel to influence news reporting by isolating journalists from external information sources, see Arterton, *Media Politics,* 98–101.

47. Academics, meanwhile, are less sure, believing that, at most, debates serve to reinforce the leanings of voters but rarely change any minds. See George F. Bishop et al., eds., *The Presidential Debates* (New York: Praeger, 1978).

48. Quoted by Thomas B. Edsall, "Bush Rejects Rescheduling of Debate," *Washington Post,* 23 September 1992, A1, A14.

49. B. Drummond Ayers, "Bush Rejects Panel's Plan for Three Debates," *New York Times,* 4 September 1992, A13.

50. Edsall, "Bush Rejects Rescheduling," A14.

51. See Ayers, "Bush Rejects Panel's Plan," for a discussion of these maneuverings.

52. Quotes from Edsall, "Bush Rejects Rescheduling," A1 and A14.

53. Richard L. Berke points out that in negotiating the debates, both major candidates had strong preferences about the format they liked best, but by the end of the debates, both had changed their minds. See "Which Debate System Worked Best? It's a Debate," *New York Times,* 21 October 1992, A13.

54. Louis Wolfson, *The Untapped Power of the Press: Explaining Government to the People* (New York: Praeger, 1986).

55. Quoted in Berke, "Which Debate System Worked Best?" A13.

56. Ratings by the A.C. Nielsen Company recorded higher levels in 1992 than four years earlier; 34.4 million homes watched the first presidential debate on the three major networks combined and 33.6 million homes watched the vice-presidential debate. Their figures for the last two debates included the audience on Fox Broadcasting: 40.4 and 41.5 million homes respectively. ABC estimated that 88 million viewers watched the last debate. None of these figures includes the smaller audiences on CNN, PBS, or C-SPAN, which also carried the debates. See the box scores in *New York Times,* 15 October 1992, A23, and 21 October 1992, A13.

57. Howard Kurtz, "Sneaking a Peek at the Deck: The Clinton Campaign Previewed Bush's Ads," *Washington Post National Weekly Edition,* 16–22 November 1992.

58. Renee Loth, "Ad Watch: Bush-Quayle Campaign," *Boston Sunday Globe,* 25 October 1992, 19.

59. Howard Kurtz, "Ad Watch," *Washington Post,* 24 October 1992, A7.

60. Quote in American Political Network, *Campaign HOTLINE,* 5 October 1992, para. 3.

61. Richard L. Berke, "Ad Campaign," *New York Times,* 3 October 1992.

62. American Political Network, *Campaign HOTLINE,* 12 October 1992, para. 10.

63. American Political Network, *Campaign HOTLINE,* 14 October 1992, para. 6.

64. American Political Network, *Campaign HOTLINE,* 29 October 1992, para. 5.

65. American Political Network, *Campaign HOTLINE,* 30 October 1992, para. 4.

66. Richard L. Berke, "Ad Campaign," *New York Times,* 17 September 1992, A13.

67. American Political Network, *Campaign HOTLINE,* 8 October 1992, para. 4.

68. A focus group conducted among New York voters by *New York Newsday* found that this was the only negative ad that viewers liked and believed. See William Bunch and Harry Berkowitz, "Bush Blitz Bombs," 18 October 1992, 20–21.

69. American Political Network, *Campaign HOTLINE,* 23 October 1992, para. 7.

70. Howard Kurtz, "Thirty-Second Politics," *Washington Post,* 8 October 1992, A24.

71. American Political Network, *Campaign HOTLINE,* 29 October 1992, para. 6.

72. Bunch and Berkowitz, "Bush Blitz Bombs," 21.

73. American Political Network, *Campaign HOTLINE,* 23 October 1992, para. 5.

74. For a discussion of why journalists have difficulty fulfilling this role, see Arterton, "The Persuasive Art in Politics," 111–13.

75. Richard L. Berke, "Volley of Data Replace Blatant Attacks of 1988," *New York Times,* 29 October 1992.

76. Times-Mirror Center for the People and the Press, "The People, the Press and Politics, Campaign '92: Air Wars," 8 October 1992, 2.

77. See Marjorie Hershey, "The Constructed Explanation: Interpreting Election Results in the 1984 Presidential Race," *Journal of Politics* 54 (November 1992): 943–76.

78. See, for example, the postelection reporting by Peter Goldman and Tom Mathews, "The Inside Story," *Newsweek,* Special Election Issue, November/December 1992, 20–95.

79. Craig Smith, National Public Radio, "Weekend Edition," 31 October 1992.

80. In the ten states carried by the Democrat in both elections, overall turnout increased by an average of only 3.5 percent; whereas in those twenty-one states carried by Bush in 1988 and by Clinton in 1992, turnout increased by 5.8 percent. In the nineteen remaining states carried by Bush in both years, turnout increased by an average of 5.6 percent. These data will require more analysis as final returns become available, at which point it will be worthwhile computing the overall increased levels of turnout rather than relying upon these estimates computed by averaging the surge in the states within a category. These data also ignore the special case of the District of Columbia, which voted overwhelmingly for

the Democrat in both 1988 and 1992 and where 1992 turnout surged by 11.7 percent over the 1988 election turnout.

81. These data, which are based on initial figures reported from exit polls by the *New York Times,* will require more study before they can be considered conclusive. See the chart published both years, entitled "Portrait of the Electorate," 5 November 1992, B9–10, November 1988, B6. Note that, due to rounding, the national figures in 1988 placed black voters as 10 percent of the electorate, while those for different age brackets summed to 11 percent. Consequently, the computation here used 10.5 percent. See also Katherine Tate, "Black Political Participation in the 1984 and 1988 Presidential Elections," *American Political Science Review* 85 (December 1991): 1159–76.

4

Public Opinion in the
1992 Campaign

KATHLEEN A. FRANKOVIC

It's but little good you'll do a-watering the last
year's crops.
— George Eliot, *Adam Bede*

President George Bush, and many analysts, thought 1992 would be a rerun
of 1988 because they believed in some conventional wisdom about public
opinion. In retrospect, they proved to be wrong.

There were four salient attributes of public opinion in the 1992 presidential campaign. This chapter examines each of the following themes in relation to the final election outcome:

1. *Transient events and short-term changes in electoral mood and issues
often masked underlying continuities.* Public concern about the national
economy overwhelmed the high but short-lived approval that Bush had won
in the Persian Gulf war, driving down his popularity and altering the "terrain" on which the campaign would be fought.

2. *Variations in public evaluation of the candidates reflected real changes
in voters' awareness, not fickle "volatility."* Many of these changes came after
the candidates took advantage of "windows of opportunity" to define, even
to redefine, their images.

3. *Voters assessed new standards of "character."* These criteria differed
from familiar yardsticks of policy, background, and image. Moreover, voters'
assessments of character differed from many analysts' predictions.

4. *The 1992 campaigns changed the American public itself, as an electorate.* Voters changed not so much in their attitudes toward the candidates as in the way they viewed themselves and the political process. Voters appeared happier and more interested in the election than they had for many years.

The Political Landscape

By November 1991, a full year before the general election, the political landscape had already settled into place; some essential contours could not be reshaped by the campaigners. The boost in popularity that President Bush enjoyed from successfully waging the Gulf war earlier in the year had been completely dissipated.[1] His great popularity alone, even at its all-time high, could not turn the American people away from their chief concern: the economy. Before Iraq's invasion of Kuwait, Americans said the economy was the country's biggest problem. As early as three days after the war ended, foreign affairs had faded from the public's mind and was replaced again by economic issues.

The presidential campaign would be fought domestically, on terrain that was becoming increasingly uncomfortable for the incumbent. But Bush did not appear to be worried; his approval rating had dropped before, to a bare majority just before the midterm congressional election. In a CBS News/*New York Times* poll conducted 28–31 October 1990, 52 percent of the public approved of the way the president was handling his job, while 37 percent disapproved (see figure 2.1). That decline was attributed to his budget agreement with Congress which was perceived as breaking his "no new taxes" pledge. Then he reverted to his earlier level of popularity. But six months after the war ended, it seemed as if the war had never occurred. In the CBS News/*New York Times* poll of 18–22 November 1991, 51 percent approved and 37 percent disapproved (see table 4.1).[2]

Bush's foreign policy approval ratings also slipped back to their prewar levels, while public evaluation of his economic performance was actually lower in November 1991 than it had been one year before. The president's economic performance was always rated lower than his overall job performance and his handling of foreign policy. Even during the war, his economic ratings never matched the levels reached before the 1990 budget agreement. After December 1990, there would always be more Americans who disapproved of the president's economic performance than approved of it.

The precampaign rise and fall of Bush's approval rating meant that the war alone was not going to reelect the president. Even worse for him, Americans were less likely to say they judged the Persian Gulf conflict a complete success. Three in four thought the United States was wrong to stop when it

TABLE 4.1
GEORGE BUSH: PREWAR AND POSTWAR

	Prewar	1991	
	October 1990	March	November
Overall			
Approve	52%	88%	51%
Disapprove	37	8	37
Foreign policy			
Approve	58	83	57
Disapprove	32	11	32
Economy			
Approve	34	42	25
Disapprove	55	43	66

Questions: Do you approve or disapprove of the way George Bush is handling his job as President? Foreign policy? The economy?

did; that is, they felt that the United States should have continued fighting until Saddam Hussein was removed from power.

But the national economy clearly was Bush's weakest suit. Despite his assertion that the United States was pulling out of the recession (later shown to be technically correct), the American public viewed the economy as in poor shape and not getting better. At the beginning of 1992, 82 percent said the economy was in bad shape, and only 8 percent thought it was getting better. By the end of the campaign, those results had hardly changed. A full 75 percent said the economy was in bad shape, and despite the release of some favorable economic indicators in the last days of the campaign, only 18 percent said the economy was improving.

Reading the entrails of those early polls *now* raises the question, Could President Bush *ever* have won the election? The Bush campaign team looked to the 1984 Reagan campaign for its model, but the 1992 contest was really more like the reelection bid of Jimmy Carter in 1980. In both campaigns, whether accurately or not, the public felt deeply that the economy was in crisis and that it, rather than any global concerns, should be the president's main focus. Carter's candidacy had been boosted by the hostage crisis in Iran, but his improved standing lasted even less time than Bush's Gulf war rise. Ultimately, both presidents had to respond to the voters' demand that they face the nation's economic concerns.

Campaigns in which a president runs for reelection traditionally turn into referenda on their performance.[3] True, Bush was significantly more popular in late 1991 than Jimmy Carter had been in the fall of 1979, but barely half the public approved of Bush's performance one year before the 1992 vote, and that figure would decline during the campaign.

By the beginning of the 1992 Republican convention, the public's evaluation of how Bush was managing the economy had actually fallen below Carter's all-time low.

Candidate Popularity: "Volatility" and "Windows"

The public's evaluations of the 1992 candidates changed considerably over time. These changes were not random responses by a fickle electorate; they reflected serious and explicable thought.[4]

The word volatile was tossed around throughout the campaign when it was said that the electorate was "volatile." This notion may have arisen because poll results often confounded the pundits. But in the light of the outcome, volatility appears to be the wrong word, and an exaggeration of reality. There was *movement* in the public's evaluation of candidates, but the progressions were logical and resulted from events in the campaign; they were not whims, as though voters were paying little heed to the news.

Voters assess candidates in two different ways. First, voters begin to pay attention, to become aware of names and faces, as those running for president gain visibility on television screens and in print. Figure 4.1 shows that voter awareness of President Bush was always high; Clinton and Perot had to gain awareness. Second, voters assess a candidate by asking in effect, Is this person good enough to be president of the United States? Later evaluations involve both awareness *and* assessment, and there was a lot of evaluation and reevaluation during 1992. That caused the *movement,* not the *volatility,* that occurred in public perceptions of the major presidential candidates.[5]

The candidates' changing popularity is charted in figure 4.2, which shows the ratio of favorable to unfavorable impressions of each man.[6] The most dramatic changes in this figure correspond to those moments when new information was being channeled to the voters—the campaign's "windows of opportunity." Those "windows" were limited, but there were at least three, more than most observers originally expected.

The first "window" came in the early primary states when the appearances of both the unknown Clinton and the president set the tone for their evaluations by the public. The second "window" came with the major candidates' respective conventions. Perot had "windows" too, and they were also limited, but they occurred at different times due to the radically differ-

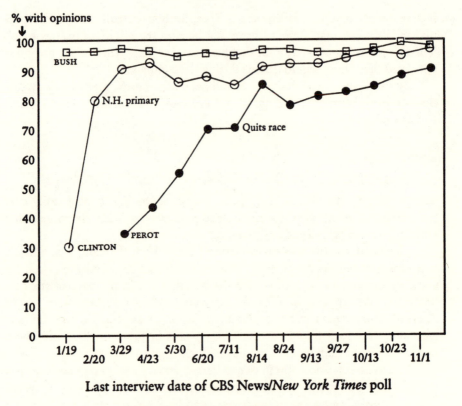

% with opinions

Last interview date of CBS News/*New York Times* poll

Key: □ = Bush; ○ = Clinton; ● = Perot

FIGURE 4.1
PUBLIC AWARENESS OF THE CANDIDATES

ent nature of his campaign. Perot's return to the campaign, ironically, opened another "window" for voters to reassess Bush and Clinton, as well as the independent candidate.

EARLY PRIMARIES: CLINTON AND BUSH

Public awareness of Bill Clinton at the beginning of 1992 changed to a degree that must be called astonishing. In late fall 1991, four out of five registered voters said they had not heard enough about Clinton to form an opinion. By early January, as seen in figure 4.1, seven in ten admitted ignorance. But *one month later,* only 19 percent of all registered voters said they had not heard enough about Clinton to form an opinion. In the space of five weeks, half the

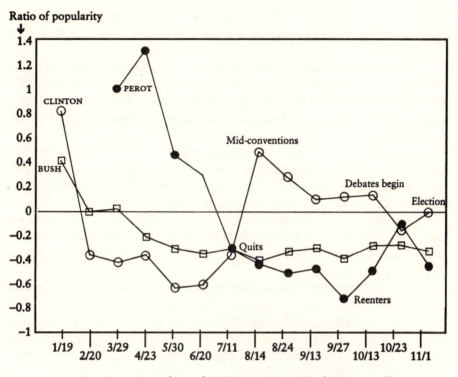

Last interview date of CBS News/*New York Times* poll

Key: □ = Bush; ○ = Clinton; ● = Perot

FIGURE 4.2
THE CANDIDATES' CHANGING POPULARITY

voting public had become aware of the Arkansas governor. Such a change would have been phenomenal for any candidate. In 1988 candidate Michael Dukakis (another Democratic governor) moved from obscurity to public awareness with what was then thought to be unusual speed. In November 1987, more than half the voters claimed not to know enough about Dukakis to express an opinion. In March 1988 almost one-third said they still had not heard enough about Dukakis to offer an evaluation. Only after he had clinched the Democratic nomination did public awareness of Dukakis reach 80 percent. In contrast, by March 1992, fewer than one in ten people had formed no opinion of Bill Clinton. Not until his nomination did Dukakis have the visibility among voters that Clinton had *before the first primary of 1992 was held.*

This rapid movement in public awareness of Clinton, it must be noted, came in the wake of accusations of sexual impropriety and draft evasion. The developing evaluations were overwhelmingly negative, and they continued in that direction throughout the spring, even as the Clinton campaign steamrollered its way to the Democratic nomination.

By late March, 40 percent of all registered voters held unfavorable views of Clinton. That was, historically, a watershed in candidate polling; such high unfavorable ratings tended to predict electoral defeat. Once a candidate was shown to be so unpopular, he or she rarely regained public confidence.

For Clinton, the ratio of favorable to unfavorable evaluations would decline *even further* as the spring primary season progressed, reaching its low point (−0.6) in May. At that time, there were twice as many negative as positive evaluations of Clinton.

President Bush, by contrast, never had to overcome a lack of public awareness; he had long been familiar to the electorate. In October 1991, only 5 percent felt ill equipped to judge the president. Even in the 1988 campaign season four years earlier, only *once* did more than one in ten potential voters feel that they did not know enough about the then vice-president to reach a judgment.

Nevertheless, as mentioned earlier, "awareness" is not the only factor in candidate evaluation. Bush faced a more serious problem, the declining public assessment of his presidency. Until the campaign, personal evaluations of the president remained generally positive. In January, 47 percent of the voters held a favorable view of the president, 33 percent were unfavorable. Once the campaign began, however, Bush came under attack not only by Democrats but by a challenger within his own political party. His positive balance would decrease and finally disappear. By April it turned negative, and it continued steadily downward until stabilizing at the Republican National Convention in August.

THE PEROT ENTRY: CHANNELING NEGATIVE FEELINGS

Ross Perot took advantage of the public's continuing and increasing dissatisfaction with the two major-party nominees. Images of Perot would never be as fully formed as impressions of the two major candidates, but his prominence during the late primary period would lead not only inexperienced supporters but expert political handlers, such as Ed Rollins and Hamilton Jordan, to believe that Perot could win. Even by early May, which is late in the primary season, more than half the voters admitted they did not know enough about Perot to have an opinion about him, but those who *had* formed opinions were overwhelmingly positive.

Everything changed in early July, as the Democratic convention drew near. The favorable-to-unfavorable ratios for the candidates were now at approximately the same point: *negative* for all three. This marked the second "window of opportunity" for them, the point at which all three candidates were being evaluated in comparison to one another. Opinions about George Bush had stabilized, but Perot's positive opinions had declined sharply from their unrealistic high of early spring; voters now took the opportunity to reassess Clinton. The governor's favorable-to-unfavorable ratio matched Bush's and surpassed Perot's, setting the stage for Clinton's emergence as the front-runner after the convention.

The pattern of 1992 evaluations resembles earlier trends in one respect. Opinions about candidates are *always* formed in opposition to someone or something. In the early primaries, Clinton was measured against charges of infidelity and draft evasion. He was compared not only to Bush but to a Democratic war hero, Senator Bob Kerrey of Nebraska; to Paul Tsongas, who told Democrats what he called "hard truths"; and later to Ross Perot, whom the public perceived as a "can-do" businessman.

The president was set in opposition too: against the idealized image that he had generated with Desert Storm. Democrats would be able to counter this image by promoting one of a weak, out-of-touch, economic failure of a president. Bush was also compared with Ross Perot, who had an image of economic competence and an ability to identify and solve problems.

THE IMPACT OF THE CONVENTIONS

The Democratic convention came at this crucial point in the movement of public opinion. The president's overall approval rating was stuck in the mid-30s, and doubts about Ross Perot were increasing. By early July, a plurality of voters held an unfavorable view of Ross Perot, and he was viewed increasingly as something of a "traditional politician." Voters were now equally likely to think Perot was telling them what they wanted to hear, rather than what he really believed.

In the two weeks before and during the Democratic convention, voters *did* reassess the Clinton candidacy. They were willing to listen, as indicated by the slight increase in the percentage who said they did not know enough about Clinton to form an opinion. Several events apparently affected voters: Jesse Jackson's endorsement of Clinton, the selection of Tennessee Senator Al Gore as Clinton's running mate, and some generally positive media exposure for the Democratic nominees. The change in public evaluation was already under way on the day that Clinton accepted the nomination and Ross Perot withdrew from the race. Perot's departure apparently enhanced the favorable mood toward Clinton. Clinton left the convention with positive ratings and a 23-point lead over George Bush (see figure 5.2).

For the president, the timing of his convention was by no means as fortunate as the Democrats' convention had been. Clinton had dominated the news coverage before his nomination; even before the Democratic convention began, he had pulled even with the president in a head-to-head race. By the time the Republicans met, Bush was running far behind Clinton. Clinton's postconvention lead of 23 points had continued during the interconvention period. The president was still 18 points behind his challenger on the day the Republican convention began.

Conventions typically improve the image of their party's nominee and cast doubt on the other party's candidate.[7] This effect comes largely by consolidating support from one's partisans and reaching out to Independents. The Democratic convention performed these functions well. Improvement in Clinton's evaluations came mainly from consolidation among Democrats: Their favorable images of Clinton rose from 34 percent before the convention to 64 percent afterward. There were also small gains from Independents.

For Democrats, Clinton was no longer battling Paul Tsongas, Bob Kerrey, or even Jerry Brown; he was battling a disliked Republican president. Also, Clinton had more room for gain from his own partisans, many of whom had expressed a neutral or negative feeling toward him before the convention. There were smaller gains among Independents, and no change in his image as perceived by Republicans. By midweek, the image of the Democratic party itself had also improved. Before the convention, only 49 percent of voters were favorable, 42 percent were not. After the convention began, 58 percent were favorable, and only 32 percent were critical.

In addition, Clinton and Gore managed to convince many voters of the things they *wanted* the voters to believe. More than four in ten voters said Clinton and Gore were different from previous Democratic nominees. Most voters (including a plurality of Republicans) thought the two men understood the problems of the average voter. Even before Ross Perot withdrew, Clinton was named as the candidate who could both bring about change *and* handle the economy. Furthermore, by three to one, voters said they would choose Gore for vice-president over incumbent Republican Dan Quayle. The Democrats were also successful in raising negative evaluations of George Bush.

The Republicans were unable to claim comparable success after their convention. There were only marginal improvements in the president's favorable-to-unfavorable ratio. Unlike Clinton's improvement among Democrats, the president, already rated positively by Republican voters, could make no further gain among his partisans. Like Clinton, however, Bush generated a marginal improvement among Independents. The public's view of the Republican party changed from mixed to positive. The public's impression of Dan Quayle, however, improved only marginally.

The Republicans were more successful in creating doubts about Clinton. In midconvention, there were nearly as many voters with negative as positive views of the Arkansan. But three days after the Republican convention ended, the Clinton ratings bounced back nearly to their preconvention levels. The Republicans had convinced no more voters that Clinton deserved what they considered the negative label of "liberal" than had felt that way before the convention. And while most voters expected that, as president, Clinton would raise their taxes, they thought a reelected President Bush would do the same.

Evaluations of the Republican convention itself were surprisingly negative, given the party's control of its proceedings. Voters viewed the president as spending more time attacking the Democrat than explaining what he would do if reelected; they disapproved of spending campaign time on issues concerning homosexuals; and 76 percent said that criticism of Hillary Clinton was going too far.

The one area where the president *gained* popular support from his convention was the same area in which he had always scored well: his management of foreign policy. Not since the early months of 1992 had a majority of Americans approved of the way George Bush handled foreign policy. After the Republican convention, 55 percent did, and that figure would change little for the rest of the campaign.

THE FALL DEBATES AND THE FINAL CAMPAIGN

Candidate debates may provide a fresh opportunity for voters' evaluation. Most of the time, however, they are said to reinforce what voters already think.[8] In 1980, the debates served to calm voters' worries about the presidential abilities of Ronald Reagan. In 1988, the debates confirmed the public's doubts about Michael Dukakis. But in 1992, the debates seemed to turn around voters' evaluations of the third candidate, Ross Perot.

Before the first debate, and on his reentry into the race, Perot was viewed favorably by only 7 percent of the voters. By the time the debates ended, that percentage had more than quadrupled. By the end of the debates, too, voters had regained confidence in Perot's ability to deal with the economy and viewed him as the most trustworthy of the three candidates. Although Perot's poll support never rose above the mid-teens throughout the late fall, Perot was as likely as Clinton to be viewed as the candidate who would do the best job handling the economy.

TABLE 4.2
WHO WON THE DEBATE?

	First	Second	Third
Clinton	30%	54%	30%
Bush	16	25	23
Perot	33	20	30

Question: Which candidate do you think did the best job—or won—tonight's debate? (Asked of those who had watched or listened to each debate.)

For voters, the presidential debates became a showcase for Perot. Just as they had reassessed their opinion of Clinton during his party's convention, and had agreed that Bush could manage foreign policy (though not the economy) during *his* convention, they saw the debates as "Perot's convention." For him, it meant more than consolidating his narrow base. In each debate, as seen in table 4.2, the percentage of viewers who thought that Perot had "won" the debate exceeded the percentage committed to voting for him. Perot was getting his chance at reevaluation.[9] After the debates were over, Perot's favorable ratings improved.

Perot's opportunity for reevaluation unsettled the campaign and reduced Clinton's margin significantly. There were now *two* candidates of change and one incumbent. This new lineup gave Bush the chance to divide the opposition and present himself as an experienced leader.

The final weeks of the campaign took a toll on all three contenders. Perot, who had raised his favorable-to-unfavorable ratio close to even (and marginally better than Clinton's) after the last debate, fell back in the last two weeks. The president's ratio stubbornly refused to rise, hovering at the level it had sustained for most of the year. His campaign's relentlessness in raising doubts about Clinton's honesty and trustworthiness, however, finally affected the voters, but only in that the Democrat's ratios turned negative. For that matter, after the debates, so did they all. Eventually, Clinton rebounded and ended the campaign close to even in public evaluation.

In the past, campaign analysts have tended to view a candidate's image as fixed. Once that image is formed, the common wisdom asserts, it is hard to shake except as a result of some extreme or extraordinary event. Certainly conventional wisdom has held that once an image turns negative, it can never change.

But the 1992 campaign showed just the opposite to be true: Americans *do* change their minds.[10] Perhaps they now recognize that their first impressions may be based on insufficient knowledge. When new information becomes available, voters change evaluations, and both Clinton and Perot evidently succeeded, where Bush did not, in making the voters change their minds.[11]

The Voters Decide: "Character" and Other Issues

In making up their minds, voters consistently applied relevant yardsticks to the candidates. Many of these involved "character"—but with a political, not personal, meaning.

CHARACTER AND LEADERSHIP

Perot illustrates the traits sought by voters. His early rise capitalized on weaknesses—as the public perceived them—in the major parties' nominees: strength of character and trustworthiness. In June, by a three-to-one margin (54 percent to 18 percent), those with opinions described Perot as having strong qualities of leadership. By comparison, and by overwhelming margins, both Bush and Clinton were viewed as most often using a strictly political tactic, pandering to the voters. As with the other candidates, negative impressions grew as the Perot candidacy became more and more of a possibility; yet, through mid-June, more voters with opinions held favorable than unfavorable impressions.

Doubts about their credibility arose from more than just a perception that Bush and Clinton were "typical politicians." For much of Bush's administration, majorities had believed the president was lying about his involvement in the Iran-contra affair. Voters were also evenly divided about Clinton's honesty in answering questions about his efforts to avoid the draft.

While Bush was viewed as a strong leader (by something less than two to one), Clinton was not viewed that way. But Clinton's evaluations on all issues improved after the Democratic convention, paralleling the rise in his popularity.

At the end of the campaign, as different issues emerged, Bush contrasted himself with both challengers, and by election day he could claim advantages from his foreign policy experience and the strength and knowledge of an incumbent. In fact, Bush eventually scored better than his challengers *only* on those characteristics that could be thought of as "presidential." As shown in table 4.3, voters were more likely to view Bush as capable of dealing with presidential problems. Though he clearly led on that, voters were very unlikely to view him as capable of bringing about change. And nearly half doubted the president's overall trustworthiness.

TABLE 4.3
CANDIDATE EVALUATIONS IN THE CAMPAIGN'S LAST WEEK

	Clinton	Bush	Perot
Could bring change country needs	41%	26%	29%
Have doubts about trustworthiness	60	47	44
Can be trusted to deal with presidential problems	38	47	25
Overall opinion:			
Favorable	40	35	24
Unfavorable	41	48	43

Questions: Do you think electing [CANDIDATE] in November would bring about the kind of change the country needs, or not? Regardless of how you intend to vote, do you have any doubts about [CANDIDATE]'s trustworthiness? Do you think [CANDIDATE] can be trusted to deal with all the problems a president has to deal with, or are you concerned he might make serious mistakes? Is your opinion of [CANDIDATE] favorable, not favorable, undecided, or haven't you heard enough about [CANDIDATE] yet to have an opinion?

REDEFINING ISSUES FOR BABY BOOMERS

Bush asked voters point-blank, "Who do you trust?" In his attack on Clinton, "trust" involved charges of extramarital affairs and draft evasion during the Vietnam war. In raising these questions, the president set his own generation's traditional standards of morality against those of Clinton's postwar, baby-boom generation.

The issue of marital infidelity resurfaced in modern presidential campaigns in 1987, forcing Democrat Gary Hart from the nomination race. Such charges also threatened to cut short the Clinton campaign. But, as the "boomers" grew up, voting and running for office in greater numbers, their relative tolerance for what had once been "immoral" behavior may have affected their political judgments. Voters consistently claimed that marital fidelity was not something on which they would base a voting judgment. Those voters who said it did matter exhibited political and demographic characteristics (e.g., Republican loyalists and white fundamentalist Christians) that suggested they would not support a Democrat under any circumstances.

When voters were given the opportunity to establish their own criteria, to ask questions, to say what *they* wanted to learn about the candidates, their queries were overwhelmingly issue oriented and were not about "character," at least not in the sense of marital fidelity. On election day, only 12 percent of all voters cited marital fidelity as a important reason for their vote. Women over the age of forty-five, those born before the "boom," were the most likely to cite this criterion, but even they put the subject well behind concerns about the economy.[12]

Doubts surrounding Clinton's avoidance of military service during the Vietnam war loomed more important than marital fidelity to voters, both in the early primary states and on election day, when 20 percent of voters cited it as very important to their vote. The draft issue was an ongoing problem for Clinton, but it had differing impacts on different kinds of voters. On election day, women expressed less concern than men, and younger women (those of Clinton's generation and younger) expressed the least concern of all groups. The varying emphases on the draft went beyond generational and gender differences. Voters who had lived through World War II but did not fight in it were the least concerned group of men; war veterans themselves (of World War II and subsequent wars) were divided in their vote, as seen in table 4.4. Two groups of men—white veterans over age forty-five and *all* white men under forty-five—said the draft issue was very important to them. While veterans in both age groups were less likely than nonveterans in their cohort to support Clinton, George Bush was not always the beneficiary. In fact, Bush did better with nonveterans under the age of forty-five than he did with veterans.

If anything, it was Clinton's repeated problems in explaining his past that contributed to the "Slick Willie" label, a characterization that inherently questioned his honesty and made these charges relevant to the presidential race. The most frequently cited poll measurement of Clinton's honesty was this query: "Do you think Bill Clinton has the honesty and integrity to serve effectively as president?"[13]

In each primary, the percentage answering yes consistently matched Clinton's percentage of the vote in that state's primary. Not until the primary field had narrowed to two candidates did majorities of Democratic primary voters say Clinton did have the honesty and integrity to serve as president. In three-way contests that Clinton won with a plurality, usually less than half the voters expressed confidence in Clinton's integrity.[14]

TABLE 4.4

THE IMPACT OF CLINTON'S DRAFT RECORD

ON THE VOTE

	White men under 45		*White men over 45*	
	Veterans	*Nonveterans*	*Veterans*	*Nonveterans*
Clinton	33%	36%	39%	45%
Bush	34	41	42	38
Perot	33	24	19	18

SOURCE: Voter Research and Surveys Election Day Exit Poll, 3 November 1992.

Voters are perhaps most polarized when they make their final election decisions. At that time, they may take any opportunity to criticize the person they reject. Among Democrats, Republicans, and Independents nationally, views of Clinton's honesty in the summer and fall varied directly with his electoral support. Before the convention, and Perot's withdrawal, only 56 percent said Clinton had the honesty and integrity to serve as president. By August, after Clinton's nomination, 70 percent did. The percentage fell to just 52 percent in late October, after the debates and the Republican barrage of negative advertising (as voters were preparing to cast their real votes), but the percentage rose again after the election to 69 percent.[15]

After the final debate, 56 percent of registered voters admitted they had some doubts about Clinton's trustworthiness, suggesting that the "character" issues had not gone away completely. But while voters were not entirely satisfied with Clinton's integrity, most judged it high enough for him to be president.

The Real Issue: The Economy

George Bush's problem stemmed from the voters' belief that the economy was the country's most important problem and that the president was managing it badly. When voters were asked what one question they would pose to a candidate, economic concerns always dominated. On election day, supporters of all three presidential candidates ranked the economy first on their lists of issues that mattered.

Voter assessment of the candidates' capabilities in handling the economy oscillated within very restrictive parameters. Bush was *never* viewed as the candidate best able to handle the economy. He could not even make voters believe in a traditional strength of Republican candidates, keeping taxes low. The percentage of registered voters who thought it was likely Bush would raise their taxes if he were reelected was never lower than 61 percent. At times, it was as high as 77 percent. While the percentages saying that Clinton and Perot would raise their taxes was usually somewhat higher than the percentage that thought Bush would, the differences were surprisingly small. Breaking his "no new taxes" pledge did great damage to the president's credibility. On election day, more voters cited the breaking of that pledge than cited the "character" questions of marital fidelity and draft avoidance as an important factor in their votes.

The competition for economic leadership came down to a race between Bill Clinton and Ross Perot, as seen in table 4.5. Clinton had maintained a narrow lead over Perot on this issue from the time of the Democratic convention. Even when Perot's favorable ratings sagged, he held a clear lead over Bush on economic management. After Perot's rehabilitation in the candidate

TABLE 4.5
BEST AT HANDLING THE ECONOMY

	Clinton	Perot	Bush
July	36%	28%	17%
12–14 October	37	29	23
16–17 October	36	30	21
31 October–2 November	35	33	25

Question: Regardless of how you intend to vote, which candidate do you think would do the best job solving the country's economic problems?

debates, he was named as best to handle the economy by nearly as many voters as cited the eventual winner. Despite all the Republican attempts to recast the election, the economy remained the dominant cause of the Republican incumbent's downfall.

Voters: The Real Change

There was one major opinion change during the election campaign, quite different from the pundits' predictions. It was a change not in voters' attitudes about the candidates, but toward themselves and their role in the electoral process.

VOTER SATISFACTION

In the spring of 1992, *Time* magazine produced a cover story on "The Angry Voter," centering on voters' unhappiness with the available choices and their desire for someone new. The implication was that voters were turned off by politics. But 1992 became the first election year since 1960 where voter turnout *increased.*[16] American voters took every opportunity to examine and enhance their role in the democratic process.[17]

The voters' role in politics is twofold: the public decision-making role, in which voters judge the candidates, and that of critics at a play, in which voters judge the way the election proceeds. Evaluations that voters make in these two roles may coincide, or they may conflict.

After both the 1980 and 1988 elections, voters judged the candidates in much the same way: About two in five voters claimed they voted the way they did mainly to vote against the other choices. But the public assessment of the *process* in each year was very different. After the 1980 election, the "reviews" were generally good. About 54 percent of the voters reported having paid a lot of attention to what was happening. In 1988, the voters (as critics) were turned off by the election itself: Only 43 percent said they had paid a lot of attention to the campaign; 54 percent of them said that campaign itself was dull, not interesting. By comparison, 1984 was a year when voters generally *liked* both their choices and the process; only 35 percent described the 1984 campaign as dull.

In 1992, voters ended up both liking their candidates and feeling good about the process. Although they often despaired over the available choices, by election day they were both more intrigued and more satisfied than in any recent election year. Only 19 percent of the public thought the 1992 campaign was dull.

Early in the campaign, voters expressed dissatisfaction with the choice of candidates. This discontent diminished when Ross Perot was available. But even Perot failed to satisfy a desire for more choices. By October, about half the voters said they wanted still more candidates. This desire, as seen in table 4.6, was not unusual. It was about the same percentage who had wanted more choices in September 1980 and September 1984, but it was significantly lower than the percentage of voters who had wanted more choices in October 1988.

Despite the prediction of "anger," the voters of 1992 were much like those of 1984 and 1980 in their eventual satisfaction with the existing choices. It may be that voters always want more choices. Even when Ross Perot was popular (and was leading the major-party candidates in some polls), 36 percent of all registered voters wanted additional candidates. Again, the 1988 campaign had been the exception.

Voters were increasingly *content* with their favorite candidates. At the end of the campaign, more than half of those who had decided to vote for Bill Clinton described themselves as strongly favoring their choice, and nearly half the Bush voters felt the same way about the president. Just over one in four voters in 1992 said they were mainly voting against a candidate. Each candidate's share of committed supporters increased as election day neared, and more voters were committed to Bush or Clinton than had been committed to Bush or Dukakis at the end of the 1988 campaign. Perot support-

TABLE 4.6

VOTER SATISFACTION WITH THE CHOICES

	Oct. '92	Oct. '88	Oct. '84	Oct. '80
Satisfied with choices	49%	34%	47%	50%
Want more	48	64	48	45

Question: Are you satisfied in choosing among [LIST OF CANDIDATES], or do you wish there had been other choices?

ers were somewhat less strongly committed: Only 38 percent of the Perot voters said they were strong supporters of their candidate.

Voter interest rose sharply in 1992, far beyond the levels of earlier campaigns. The percentage of registered voters who said they were paying a lot of attention to the campaign was higher by the summer of 1992 than it had been at any time in the 1988 election. By mid-August, 45 percent said they were paying a lot of attention to the campaign. (That level of interest certainly helped the Democrats focus attention on their convention, opening up that "window of opportunity" for Clinton.) In November 1988, only 38 percent were paying a lot of attention. By the end of the 1992 campaign, nearly seven in ten voters reported paying a lot of attention.

Figure 4.3 shows the increase in interest through the 1992 campaign. There was a distinct relationship, at least at first, between voters' candidate preferences and their interest in the campaign. New and different candidates (Perot and Clinton) spurred attention more often than the known alternative, Bush. While Perot was a fresh face in politics, his candidacy was not the only reason for high voter interest. When he left the race in July, interest *stayed* high and continued to climb.

In the first wave of a panel survey conducted for the Times-Mirror Center for the People and the Press in late May, Perot supporters expressed more interest in the campaign than did supporters of either Bush or Clinton. After his withdrawal, former Perot supporters who switched to Clinton were more interested than Perot supporters who switched to Bush. And while former Perot supporters were less likely to be satisfied having only two choices, 46 percent of the Clinton converts were satisfied while only 26 percent of the Bush converts were.

The net result of having a happier and more interested electorate was that turnout increased for the first time since 1960. On election day, 11 percent of the voters said they were voting in a presidential election for the first time. To most voters, this election really mattered; nearly three in four Americans of voting age said they thought the 1992 election was more important than previous presidential elections.

CAMPAIGN INNOVATIONS

One reason for voter attention in 1992 may have been that some innovations appeared in this campaign, opening new doors of access for both candidates and voters. Political advertising was different. It always matters in campaigns,[18] and one in four voters admitted that a political ad had made a difference in their votes, twice as many as in 1984 and more than in 1988. But the ads that moved voters in 1992 were the ones that appeared to be the most straightforward and the least manipulative (see chapter 3). Voters who

Interest in the campaign (%)

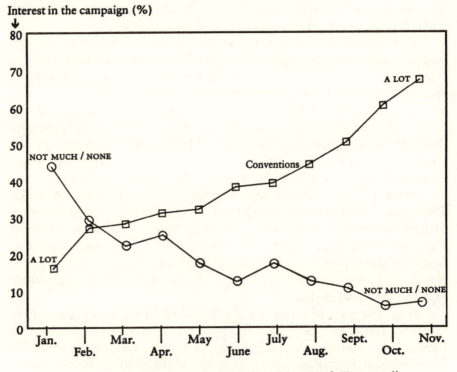

Last interview date of CBS News/*New York Times* poll

Key: □ = "A lot"; ○ = "Not much/none"

SOURCE: CBS News/*New York Times* poll.
NOTE: Responses of "some" interest omitted.

FIGURE 4.3
VOTER INTEREST IN THE CAMPAIGN

saw television ads (see table 4.7) said they paid the most attention to Perot's. They rated his ads as the most truthful and said the ads made them most likely to vote for Perot. His half-hour "infomercials" also received highly positive evaluations (and viewership). That worked to the advantage of Ross Perot and to the disadvantage of the president. Voters also obtained information in 1992 from improbable and yet highly accessible media formats. "Infomercials" and television talk or interview shows were more likely than political ads to affect decision making. Nearly half the voters on Election Day said that the candidates' appearances on television talk shows helped them

TABLE 4.7
CANDIDATES' TELEVISION ADS

Ad viewers	Bush	Clinton	Perot
Paid a lot of attention to	30%	36%	43%
Almost all truthful	28	27	55
Made you more likely to vote for the candidate	6	14	20

SOURCE: CBS News/*New York Times* poll, 20–23 October 1992.
Questions: How much attention have you paid to these commercials for [CANDIDATE]? Of the commercials you've seen for [CANDIDATE], have almost all of them been truthful, or have some of them been truthful and some false, or have almost all of them been false? Have [CANDIDATE]'s commercials made a difference in how you will vote in November? (IF YES) Have they made you more likely to vote for (Bush/Clinton/Perot) or less likely to vote for (Bush/Clinton/Perot)?

decide how to vote. The talk shows especially influenced less-frequent voters, those who (it developed) were more likely to vote for Perot and Clinton.

Talk shows often had a call-in component. In early January, 15 percent of Americans said that at some time in the past year they had called in to a television or radio talk show. When CBS News conducted a post–State of the Union "call-in," the phone company registered 24 million attempts at dialing the 800 number. That total was abnormally high, but each time a candidate appeared on a program with the capacity to take phoned-in questions, it was not unusual for more than a million attempts to be registered. Such "participatory" voters were generally younger, more likely to live in urban areas, and better educated. Younger voters may have found these formats a comfortable, and hence appealing, sort of socialization to politics, further encouraging their participation.

Younger voters in particular took advantage of even the most unlikely sources of information. MTV covered the campaign and invited the candidates to appear in young adult forums. Humorists did more than make people laugh. Although fewer than one out of five members of the general public said they learned something new about the presidential campaign or the candidates from late-night comedians, 30 percent of those under the age of thirty said they *did* learn new things from these comics. Younger voters who first encountered politics as a spectator sport turned into participants. They were more likely than their elders, for example, to report wearing a campaign button, and more likely to say they had volunteered in a campaign.

The sources of information in 1992 were not completely new, but they were more disparate and more all-encompassing in 1992 than they had been in the past. But two of the candidates also were novel: a saxophone-playing Democrat who had avoided the draft and a tough-talking billionaire from Texas. So voters felt no stigma in learning more about them from alternative sources. These media formats helped dilute the sourness and feelings of manipulation that had permeated the 1988 campaign and may have helped voters feel better about both the process and their choices. Many voters did feel positive about the process, and while there was still an ongoing desire for more choices, most voters said they were content with, if not overwhelmingly thrilled about, their options.

Conclusion

Voters in the 1992 election were different but straightforward. The degree to which they engaged in the process put an end to decades of decline in electoral attention and turnout. The voters were in control. They sorted out which "character" issues were important from those the candidates *said* were important. They defined the campaign landscape and set the ground rules for the next presidential election.

Yet, despite the unusual formats, the multiple "windows" of informational opportunity, the generational changes in the issues, and the relatively high level of voter contentment, 1992 turned out to be a very simple election. It was a referendum on the incumbent president—and George Bush lost.

Acknowledgments

The author would like to thank Hal Glatzer, who provided help with style and grace.

Notes

1. This phenomenon was originally investigated in John E. Mueller, *War, Presidents and Public Opinion* (New York: Wiley, 1973).

2. Unless otherwise specified, all data come from CBS News/*New York Times* polls.

3. See Martin P. Wattenberg, *The Rise of Candidate-Centered Politics* (Cambridge, Mass.: Harvard University Press, 1991), chap. 6.

4. Two recent books provide accounts of a sensible public. See Samuel L. Popkin, *The Reasoning Voter: Communication and Persuasion in Presidential Campaigns* (Chicago: University of Chicago Press, 1991); and Benjamin I. Page and Robert Y. Shapiro, *The Rational Public: Fifty Years of Trends in Americans' Policy Preferences* (Chicago: University of Chicago Press, 1992).

5. For analysis of how voters assess candidates, see Arthur Miller et al., "Schematic Assessments of Presidential Candidates," *American Political Science Review* 80 (June 1986): 521–40, and "Throwing the Rascals Out," *American Political Science Review* 79 (June 1985): 359–72.

6. The ratio is calculated by dividing the percentage of registered voters who express a favorable impression of each candidate by the percentage expressing an unfavorable opinion. For ease of presentation, 1 is subtracted from the result. A ratio greater than zero indicates a net favorable evaluation; a ratio less than zero a net *unfavorable* impression.

7. See John Kessel, *Presidential Campaign Politics*, 4th ed. (Pacific Grove, Calif.: Brooks/Cole, 1992), chap. 2.

8. An early analysis of television debates can be found in Sidney Kraus, *The Great Debates* (Bloomington: Indiana University Press, 1977).

9. Polls by other news organizations, while reporting somewhat different results, all indicate that many voters who were not then currently supporting Perot nonetheless viewed him as performing the best of the three men in the debate.

10. For some support of the notion of possible change during primaries, see Larry Bartels, *Presidential Primaries and the Dynamics of Public Choice* (Princeton, N.J.: Princeton University Press, 1988), chap. 4.

11. This pattern is consistent with that described in Morris Fiorina, *Retrospective Voting in American National Elections* (New Haven: Yale University Press, 1981).

12. CBS News asked voters twice during the campaign what one question they would ask a candidate. Both times, in early June and mid-October, questions about the economy ranked first.

13. There were various wordings of this item, and changes were made not so much because results varied, but to make the language of the question clearer. For example, the first version began, "Are you *satisfied that* Bill Clinton has the honesty and integrity ...?" (Later, the adverb "effectively" was dropped.) These changes in wording appeared to have had little effect on the results.

14. Only in the South Dakota primary, before Clinton had emerged as the front-runner for the nomination, were voters rejecting Clinton the candidate yet affirming him as an honest man.

15. CNN/*USA Today*/Gallup national polls.

16. The reasons for the earlier decline are discussed in Ruy Teixeira, *Why Americans Don't Vote* (Westport, Conn.: Greenwood Press, 1987), chap. 4.

17. Voters tend to be examined by political analysts, not to analyze themselves. In most cases, the public is found wanting. One of the more extreme statements of this belief is found in Walter Lippmann, *The Phantom Public* (New Brunswick, N.J.: Transaction, 1992).

18. See Edwin Diamond and Stephen Bates, *The Spot*, 3d ed. (Cambridge, Mass.: MIT Press, 1993); and Kathleen Hall Jamieson, *Packaging the President* (New York: Oxford University Press, 1984).

5

The Presidential Election

GERALD M. POMPER

There is a tide in the affairs of men,
Which taken at the flood, leads on to fortune;
Omitted, all the voyage of their life
Is bound in shallows and in miseries.

— *Julius Caesar* (IV, iii)

On 3 November, the floodtides of American politics elected Governor Bill Clinton president of the United States and Senator Al Gore vice-president. On a secondary wave, Ross Perot roiled the electoral waters. Submerged in the political wake were President George Bush and a corps of timid or inexpert Democratic politicians.

The presidential election tides carved sharp changes in the contours of the American political landscape. Clinton gained the first Democratic win in sixteen years and only the second convincing party victory (including 1964) since World War II. Clinton and Gore personified change—as explicit revisionists within their party, as the only successful all-southern ticket since 1828, and as the first of their generation to assume power.

Perot demonstrated the openness, even the vulnerable porousness, of the American political system. After an eccentric and lavish self-financed campaign, he won more votes than all but one independent candidate (Theodore Roosevelt in 1912) in American history. Without any party organization, he won a place on the ballot in every state, topped his publicly subsidized rivals in direct campaign spending, and raised the possibility of a constitutional crisis, the election of the president by the House of Representatives.

Most astonishing was the defeat of the incumbent president. George

Bush had been easily elected in 1988 as the heir of a popular and innovative leader, Ronald Reagan.[1] He had led the United States to its overwhelming military victory in the Persian Gulf, the only clear national triumph of arms in nearly fifty years. He had presided over the even more astounding fulfillment of American strategic goals—the end of the cold war and the dissolution of the Soviet Union. By March 1991, nearly 90 percent of the public commended Bush's performance in office, the highest level ever recorded in opinion polls (see figure 2.1, p. 42).

Ironically, these very successes were the root causes of Bush's defeat in the 1992 election. Inheriting the Reagan legacy, as Burnham writes in chapter 1, Bush confined himself to the role of understudy, dismissing what he ridiculed as "the vision thing." The end of the cold war allowed voters to concentrate on domestic problems, even as it opened fissures within the Republican party. Bush's unprecedented standing in opinion polls made him complacent, as he ignored the growing economic distress at home.

President Bush appropriately characterized the events occurring during his administration as changes of biblical proportions. Scripture also provides an explanation of his failure to win reelection. Like the mighty pharaoh of ancient Egypt, Bush failed to hear the distress of his people, leading eventually to the drowning of his legions.

The Democratic Victory

The election results present a bundle of anomalies. The Democratic tide swept across a nation that had become habituated to Republican presidents. The Democrats won decisively, yet gained a smaller share of the vote than in their stunning defeat in 1988. Social alignments resembled the established party cleavages, but new patterns emerged. An electorate disillusioned with politicians paid rapt attention to the political process. An independent candidate captured nearly a fifth of the vote, yet had no direct impact on the outcome.

THE ELECTORAL MAP

Clinton's victory was national, encompassing 370 of the 538 total electoral votes. As seen on the electoral map (see inside front cover), the Arkansas governor carried states in all regions of the country: all of the Northeast (eleven states plus the District of Columbia), six of the fourteen states of his native South and the border region, seven of the twelve Midwest and Plains states, and eight of the thirteen mountain and Pacific states.

Although Clinton won only a minority of the popular vote, his margin of 5.6 percentage points over George Bush was comfortable—almost identical, on a two-party basis, to the Republican's own victory in 1988. Even on a three-party basis, Clinton did better than his Democratic ancestor Woodrow Wilson in 1912. He also did as well as Richard Nixon in 1968, the most recent race with a major independent candidate in the running.

The victory of 1992 was the culmination of previous growth in Democratic electoral strength. Capturing thirty-two states, Clinton carried the ten won and all but one of the states narrowly lost by Michael Dukakis in 1988, while adding new strength, particularly in the South and the border region. The Arkansas governor extended the Democratic coalition; he did not transform the political map. George Bush's support, in contrast, shrank. Of the forty states he had carried four years earlier, fewer than half remained loyal in 1992. Table 5.1 (pp. 136–37) provides details.

Continuity in the parties' geographical support is demonstrated by some simple statistics. The average change in the states' (two-party) vote was only 6.8 percentage points, and most states clustered around this average.[2] The shift reached ten points only in nine states: the Democratic candidates' home states, the northern tier of New England, and four other scattered locales (California, Delaware, Georgia, Nevada). Consequently, there was a very close relationship between the vote in 1992 and that in 1988, as well as between 1992 and the four previous elections (a correlation of .89 in both cases).[3]

The Clinton victory potentially had a deeper impact on the parties' futures. In their victories in the 1980s, Reagan and Bush appeared to have created a new majority coalition, which held a "lock" on the Electoral College. This presumed dominance was based on Republican strength in the South and West. There the party had won six straight elections in twenty-one states having 191 electoral votes; its strength was reinforced by seventeen additional states, casting 217 electoral votes consistently Republican during the 1980s.[4]

The asserted Republican "lock" had always been somewhat of a statistical artifact, ignoring the popular vote breakdown within states. Even while consistently losing California, for example, the Democrats had remained within striking distance, averaging 45 percent of the vote since 1976. In 1992, the Democrats successfully scaled the walls of Republican strongholds. On the map on the inside back cover, the states are classified into three equal groups, on the basis of the shift in their 1992 vote from the average Democratic proportion in the four previous presidential contests. The greatest changes came in the areas of previous party weakness, particularly the West, with other significant gains in the South and industrial states. These shifts provide reasons for Democratic optimism in future elections—and for caution in future electoral analyses.

An important effect of the election results was to demonstrate the virtues of the Electoral College. The system has been frequently condemned as antiquated and antidemocratic. Throughout American history, many have sought to replace the Constitutional mechanism with direct election of the president or other schemes.[5] In 1992, these alternatives could have led to serious problems. The direct election of a president without a popular majority would have undermined the legitimacy of the office or forced a second, and wearisome, runoff between Clinton and Bush. A proportional division of electoral votes would probably have meant a deadlock or even corrupt bargaining in the Electoral College and uncertain selection of the president by the House of Representatives. The existing system, while hard to justify in democratic philosophy, gave the nation a clear, immediate, and legitimate verdict.

SOCIAL GROUPS AND THE VOTE

The Clinton-Gore appeal becomes clearer when we examine the vote of social groups, as detailed in table 5.2 (p. 138). The large vote for Perot complicates the picture, but the general outline of the vote is still clear.

The core Democratic constituency since the New Deal of the 1930s has been the less advantaged in society: those of lower income and education, urban residents, nonwhites, and ethnic minorities. Combined with votes from the South and the lower middle class, this coalition became a dominant majority during the presidency of Franklin Delano Roosevelt.

In more recent elections, the Democratic coalition has been fractured, particularly by issues associated with race. As the Edsalls put it, "Race has crystallized and provided a focus for value conflicts—conflicts over subjects as diverse as social welfare spending, neighborhood schooling, the distribution of the tax burden, criminal violence, sexual conduct, family structure, political competition, and union membership."[6] Exploiting these newer issues, Republicans had won all but one presidential election in the past quarter of a century, making particularly notable gains among whites, men, southerners, and Catholics.

In 1992, the Democratic core was maintained, with its fractures repaired, and then expanded.[7] Clinton's support is greatest among the previous bulwarks of the party, with clear majorities among America's disadvantaged: blacks, Hispanics, the unemployed, the poor, and those with only a high school education. There is a clear class-based gradient in the ballots: Clinton won three of every five votes from those below the poverty level, with decreasing proportions up the income ladder, and only about one of three votes from the wealthy. Jews, as in the past, were an exception; although relatively high in social position, they gave Clinton a higher proportion of their vote

TABLE 5.1

THE 1992 PRESIDENTIAL VOTE

State	Electoral vote		Popular vote			Percentage, 3-party vote			Percentage, 2-party vote	
	Clinton	Bush	Clinton	Bush	Perot	Clinton	Bush	Perot	Clinton	Bush
Alabama		9	690,080	804,283	183,109	41.1	47.9	10.9	46.2	53.8
Alaska		3	78,294	102,000	73,481	30.9	40.2	29.0	43.4	56.6
Arizona		8	543,050	572,086	353,741	37.0	38.9	24.1	48.7	51.3
Arkansas	6		505,823	337,324	99,132	53.7	35.8	10.5	60.0	40.0
California	54		5,121,325	3,630,575	2,296,006	46.4	32.9	20.8	58.5	41.5
Colorado	8		629,681	562,850	366,010	40.4	36.1	23.5	52.8	47.2
Connecticut	8		682,318	578,313	348,771	42.4	35.9	21.7	54.1	45.9
Delaware	3		126,054	102,313	59,213	43.8	35.6	20.6	55.2	44.8
District of Columbia	3*		192,619	20,698	9,681	86.4	9.3	4.3	90.3	9.7
Florida		25	2,071,651	2,171,781	1,052,481	39.1	41.0	19.9	48.8	51.2
Georgia	13		1,008,966	995,252	309,657	43.6	43.0	13.4	50.3	49.7
Hawaii	4*		179,310	136,822	53,003	48.6	37.1	14.4	56.7	43.3
Idaho		4	137,013	202,645	130,395	29.1	43.1	27.7	40.3	59.7
Illinois	22		2,453,350	1,734,096	840,515	48.8	34.5	16.7	58.6	41.4
Indiana		12	848,420	989,375	455,934	37.0	43.1	19.9	46.2	53.8
Iowa	7*		586,353	504,891	253,468	43.6	37.5	18.8	53.7	46.3
Kansas		6	390,434	449,951	312,358	33.9	39.0	27.1	46.5	53.5
Kentucky	8		665,104	617,178	203,944	44.8	41.5	13.7	51.9	48.1
Louisiana	9		815,971	733,386	211,478	46.3	41.6	12.0	52.7	47.3
Maine	4		263,420	206,504	206,820	38.9	30.5	30.6	56.1	43.9
Maryland	10		988,571	707,094	281,414	50.0	35.8	14.2	58.3	41.7
Massachusetts	12*		1,318,639	805,039	630,731	47.9	29.2	22.9	62.1	37.9
Michigan	18		1,871,182	1,554,940	824,813	44.0	36.6	19.4	54.6	45.4
Minnesota	10*		1,020,997	747,841	562,506	43.8	32.1	24.1	57.7	42.3
Mississippi		7	400,258	487,793	85,626	41.1	50.1	8.8	45.1	54.9

Missouri	11		1,053,873	811,159	518,741	44.2	34.0	21.8	56.5	43.5
Montana	3		154,507	144,207	107,225	38.1	35.5	26.4	51.7	48.3
Nebraska		5	216,864	343,678	174,104	29.5	46.8	23.7	38.7	61.3
Nevada	4		189,148	175,828	132,580	38.0	35.3	26.6	51.8	48.2
New Hampshire	4		209,040	202,484	121,337	39.2	38.0	22.8	50.8	49.2
New Jersey	15		1,436,206	1,356,865	521,829	43.3	40.9	15.7	51.4	48.6
New Mexico	5		261,617	212,824	91,895	46.2	37.6	16.2	55.1	44.9
New York	33*		3,444,450	2,346,649	1,090,721	50.1	34.1	15.8	59.5	40.5
North Carolina		14	1,114,042	1,134,661	357,864	42.7	43.5	13.7	49.5	50.5
North Dakota		3	99,168	136,244	71,084	32.4	44.5	23.2	42.1	57.9
Ohio	21		1,984,919	1,894,248	1,036,403	40.4	38.5	21.1	51.2	48.8
Oklahoma		8	473,066	592,929	319,878	34.1	42.8	23.1	44.4	55.6
Oregon	7*		621,314	475,757	354,091	42.8	32.8	24.4	56.6	43.4
Pennsylvania	23		2,239,164	1,791,841	902,667	45.4	36.3	18.3	55.5	44.5
Rhode Island	4*		213,299	131,601	105,045	47.4	29.2	23.3	61.8	38.2
South Carolina		8	479,514	577,507	138,872	40.1	48.3	11.6	45.4	54.6
South Dakota		3	124,888	136,718	73,295	37.3	40.8	21.9	47.7	52.3
Tennessee	11		933,521	841,300	199,968	47.3	42.6	10.1	52.6	47.4
Texas		32	2,281,815	2,496,071	1,354,781	37.2	40.7	22.1	47.8	52.2
Utah		5	183,429	322,632	203,400	25.9	45.5	28.7	36.2	63.8
Vermont	3		133,592	88,122	65,991	46.4	30.6	22.9	60.3	39.7
Virginia		13	1,038,650	1,150,517	348,639	40.9	45.3	13.7	47.4	52.6
Washington	11*		993,037	731,234	541,780	43.8	32.3	23.9	57.6	42.4
West Virginia	5*		331,001	241,974	108,829	48.5	35.5	16.0	57.8	42.2
Wisconsin	11*		1,041,066	930,855	544,479	41.4	37.0	21.6	52.8	47.2
Wyoming		3	68,160	79,347	51,263	34.3	39.9	25.8	46.2	53.8
Total	370	168	44,908,233	39,102,282	19,741,048	43.3	37.7	19.0	53.5	46.5

SOURCE: *Congressional Quarterly Weekly Report* 51 (23 January 1993): 190.

* = States voting Democratic in 1988; total electoral vote = 112 under 1980 apportionment.

The total popular vote officially reported by secretaries of state for the fifty states and the District of Columbia was 104,420,887. The above table omits 0.6 percent of the total, votes that were cast for candidates other than Clinton, Bush, and Perot. Of the total popular vote, Clinton received 43.0 percent, Bush 37.4 percent, and Perot 18.9 percent.

TABLE 5.2

THE PRESIDENTIAL VOTE IN SOCIAL GROUPS

(IN PERCENTAGES)

% of 1992 total		1992			1992 two-party		1988	
		Clinton	Bush	Perot	Clinton	Bush	Bush	Dukakis
	Party and ideology							
17	Republican liberals/moderates	15	62	22	20	80	85	14
18	Republican conservatives	5	82	14	6	94	95	4
5	Independent liberals	54	16	30	77	23	26	71
14	Independent moderates	42	28	30	60	40	51	47
7	Independent conservatives	18	54	28	25	75	77	20
13	Democratic liberals	85	4	11	96	4	6	93
20	Democratic moderates	76	10	14	88	12	18	81
6	Democratic conservatives	60	24	16	71	29	34	65
	Sex and marital status							
30	Married men	38	40	21	48	52	60	39
35	Married women	42	39	19	52	48	54	46
15	Unmarried men	45	32	22	58	42	51	47
19	Unmarried women	51	34	15	60	40	42	57
	Age							
22	18-29 years old	44	34	22	56	44	52	47
38	30-44 years old	42	38	20	52	48	54	45
24	45-59 years old	41	40	19	51	49	57	42
16	60 and older	50	38	12	57	43	50	49
	Education							
6	Not a high school graduate	55	28	17	66	34	43	56
25	High school graduate	43	36	20	54	46	50	49
29	Some college education	42	37	21	43	47	57	42
24	College graduate	40	41	19	49	51	62	37
16	Post graduate education	49	36	15	58	42	50	48

Continued ...

than any other white ethnic or religious group. To this extent, previous patterns held. The voting also showed the persistence of a more recent division between the parties, a "gender gap" between the votes of men for the Republicans and of women for the Democrats. In 1992, women did provide about 5 percent more support for Clinton than men, a Democratic advantage similar to that in 1988. But in 1992, men were not particularly drawn to Bush; instead, they showed greater attraction than women to Perot.

Sex, however, is not a major explanation of this vote; on a two-party basis, the gap is only about half that in 1988, a consequence of a male move away from Bush. Women's remaining distinctive support for the Democrats is a consequence of economics, not gender. Their support for Clinton is par-

TABLE 5.2 –*Continued*

% of 1992 total		1992			1992 two-party		1988	
		Clinton	Bush	Perot	Clinton	Bush	Bush	Dukakis
	Race and region							
21	Whites in the East	45	36	19	56	44	54	45
25	Whites in the Midwest	39	39	22	50	50	57	42
24	Whites in the South	34	48	18	41	59	67	32
16	Whites in the West	39	37	24	51	49	58	41
8	Blacks	82	11	7	88	12	12	88
3	Latinos	62	25	14	72	28	30	69
	Religion							
49	White Protestant	33	46	21	42	58	66	33
27	Catholic	44	36	20	55	45	52	47
4	Jewish	78	12	10	87	13	35	64
17	White born-again Christian	23	61	15	27	73	81	18
	Family income							
14	Under $15,000	59	23	18	72	28	37	62
24	$15,000–$29,999	45	35	20	56	44	49	50
30	$30,000–$49,999	41	38	21	52	48	56	44
20	$50,000–$74,999	40	42	18	49	51	56	42
13	$75,000 and over	36	48	16	42	58	62	37
	Community size							
11	Large cities	52	33	15	61	39	40	58
55	Suburbs/small cities	44	37	19	54	46	54	44
34	Town/rural	41	39	20	51	49	56	42

ticularly high among those disadvantaged in the marketplace—those who are unmarried, working outside the home, or black. By contrast, homemakers supported Bush.

But 1992 is obviously different—the Democrats won a victory that came from shifts within these previous patterns. If we look at the two-party vote, as in the right-hand columns of table 5.2, there is an overall net change of 7 percent from Bush toward Clinton. Nationally, including the vote for Perot, the shift amounted to a massive loss of support by Bush (–16 percent) and a small Democratic net loss when comparing Dukakis to Clinton (–3 percent).

For the most part, this same degree of change is evident among all social groups. There are telltale signs of significantly higher change, however, in some categories. In these categories, the Democratic vote held steady, even in the face of the Perot candidacy, or rose more than nationally in the two-party comparisons.

One set of Clinton enthusiasts comprises the oft-derided "Bubba vote": white male southerners and born-again Christians, who overlap the economically poor and less educated. Clinton had an obvious personal appeal here, supplemented by Gore, by dint of his southern roots, his accent, and his history of family poverty.

More important, the Arkansan could step over the fractures in the old Democratic coalition. His acceptance, indeed implementation, of the death penalty made him invulnerable to the typical attack on Democrats (e.g., Dukakis in 1988) as "soft on crime." On the more fundamental division, race, Clinton engendered support by his emphasis on the commonalities of blacks and whites, and by deliberately distancing himself from the most unpopular (to whites) black leaders, such as Jesse Jackson. Economic concerns became predominant over racial anxieties. "Now, for every voter who has a relative or friend who lost out on a job opportunity or promotion because of affirmative action (blamed, rightly or wrongly, on the Democrats and liberalism) there are voters who know someone, maybe themselves, who lost a job—period."[8]

The other groups showing a distinctive turn toward Clinton are quite different, composed of the most wealthy Americans, male college graduates, those over forty-five years old, and suburban residents. They are typified by the insecure professional, the engineer or computer programmer affected by the poor state of the economy. Clinton's campaign focus on jobs and economic security was critical in winning these votes.

PARTIES, PRINCIPLES, AND PEROT

Party and ideology also affected the vote. Past loyalties largely held, Clinton winning the overwhelming proportion of Democrats and liberals, Bush gaining the bulk of Republicans and conservatives. Between these two factors, party was the greater influence; Clinton won a majority even among conservative Democrats, just as Bush did among liberal Republicans. More important than these typical, overall patterns were the shifts in the vote from 1988.

Here Clinton was notably more successful in holding past support and adding new voters to his cause. Even in the face of the Perot candidacy, Clinton was able to keep the Democratic vote close to the levels reached by Dukakis. Particularly important were the ideological moderates, the largest bloc, who showed a large shift, on a two-party basis, toward the Arkansan. Bush, by contrast, lost in all groups, and most substantially among moderate Republicans and both moderate and conservative Independents. These losses came despite a Republican campaign aimed at winning votes on grounds of "traditional values" considered important by these constituencies.

The partisan flow of the vote since 1988 is pictured in figure 5.1. Bush's vote was almost totally composed of persons who had voted for him four years earlier.[9] Clinton had a much broader appeal, holding almost all of those who reported a 1988 vote for Dukakis ("loyalists" in the graph) and winning converts from previous Bush voters, as well as a large proportion of those "recruits" who did not vote four years earlier. Perot drew far more heavily from those who had once supported the president than from the Dukakis vote, and gained about a fourth of the new entrants to the polling booths.

The vote for Ross Perot was large, but hazy in character. Typically, a third-party or independent candidate will draw strong support from particular groups, such as the southern segregationists who supported George Wallace in 1968 or the liberal Republicans drawn to John Anderson in 1980. Perot, by contrast, drew his fraction of the vote from almost all groups. He gained at least a tenth of the ballots in every state but Mississippi, and similar percentages in every region. His steady vote denied Clinton a popular majority in every state but Arkansas, even as he deprived Bush of a majority in

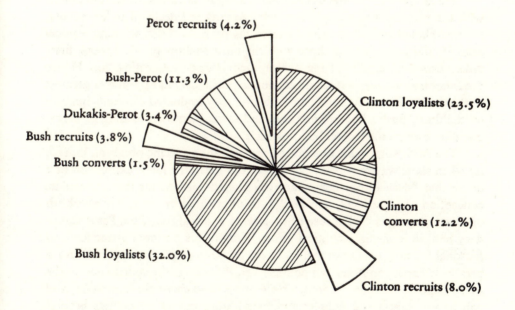

FIGURE 5.1
DYNAMICS OF THE PRESIDENTIAL VOTE.
REPORTED CHANGE IN 1988 VOTES

every state but Mississippi. But by running a consistent third everywhere but Maine and Utah, Perot was completely shut out in the Electoral College.[10]

In a two-man race, the Perot vote would have divided evenly, 38 percent each to Clinton and Bush, with the rest choosing minor candidates or abstaining. No state's electoral vote was obviously affected.[11] His backers also equally divided their congressional ballots between Republican and Democratic candidates. Perot took votes from Bush in the South, but the president still carried the region. The independent took votes from Clinton in the Northeast, but the governor still won all these states. In the other regions, Perot equally affected the two major candidates. With or without the billionaire, Clinton and Gore would have won the election.

Moreover, the Texan independent's support was fairly similar among most social groups, approximating his national share of 19 percent. Only some ethnic minorities—African Americans and Jews—clearly resisted his appeal, while some reservations were evident among the retired elderly, unmarried women, and Hispanics. Just as there was no clear Perot platform, there was no discernible ideological base to his vote; he drew about the same among liberals, moderates, and conservatives.

Threading through the quilt of Perot support is an unfocused discontent with the political and economic system. Among self-declared Independents, the unaffiliated candidate came close to his partisan rivals, winning 30 percent. He did better among those with the most shallow political roots; first-time voters, especially young white men; those not voting for House candidates; and those in insecure economic positions. His appeal was greatest to those who distrusted politicians, whether they evaluated Clinton's honesty on the draft, Bush's honesty on taxes and secret payments to Iran, or everyone's honesty on the federal budget deficit.

The Perot vote was a generalized protest, not a specific program. Indeed, it was in some ways a protest against politics itself, the latest expression of a desire that "deep in our democracy has always yearned for the immaculate conception of a president, delivered to us unsmeared by the messy afterbirth of most campaigns."[12] Because of its lack of political roots, the Perot candidacy had no immediate political effect. Without his personal attraction and personal fortune, his movement lacks the social or organizational basis for a persistent impact on American politics. Yet, Perot certainly contributed to the sharp increase in voter turnout, affected the conduct of the campaign, and will have a substantial indirect and long-lasting impact on politics beyond 1992.

Using innovative techniques, Perot's campaign hastened the continuing change in American politics toward a plebiscitarian democracy, where voters communicate directly to politicians, without the help or hindrance of intermediaries such as political parties, mass media, or opinion leaders. He evidenced the vulnerabilities of unmediated politics in his unregulated spending, authoritarian conduct, and disregard for representative institutions. At the same time, he helped make the election a more serious discussion of national problems, particularly jobs and the federal deficit.

The Issues and the Candidates

The election results must be placed in a broader context of immense change in the environment of American politics. For fifty years, the lifetime of most voters, the predominant national policy concern had been international affairs. Suddenly, the fixed stars of the cold war had disappeared, requiring new guides for political navigation. Even in the midst of international triumph, Americans were troubled. Four-fifths of them thought the nation was "on the wrong track," and consumer confidence hit record lows. Even a year before the election, there was a pervasive "sense that things have gone awry in America, that the country that once was No. 1 in the world, that organized and led Operation Desert Storm only 10 months ago, has nonetheless lost control of its destiny."[13]

The president's foreign successes did not make him invulnerable to these concerns. Indeed, they may have hurt him, creating a false confidence that his achievements abroad would easily bring him the deserved reward of reelection. Democrats implicitly shared this belief, as almost all possible contenders for the party nomination declined the contest.[14] Yet, although few saw the signs, trouble lay ahead. A year before the election, polls showed the president actually losing the contest to an unnamed "Democratic candidate."[15] Although Bush beat every particular Democrat in a direct match-up, defeat was possible. National conditions eventually provided Clinton with an opportunity.

THE CAMPAIGN

The 1992 election was certainly different. New techniques of direct and individualized campaigning emerged, aided by innovative technology, such as facsimile communication, cable television, satellite broadcasting, and computer bulletin boards. Voter interest soared, as reflected in the large audience for the national conventions and in the intense popular concentration on the television debates. Turnout on election day rose 14 percent, bringing 104 million citizens to the polls.

The campaign was also serious. In reaching their decisions, voters focused on issues, severely criticizing negative personal attacks. They cast troubled ballots, evidencing only limited approval for the candidates as individuals. For most of the campaign, voters' evaluations were unfavorable to the candidates. "In many ways," wrote a *New York Times* correspondent, "the election is cruel. It has highlighted the country's problems, persuaded voters action must be taken, then left them with candidates they don't think are up to the job."[16] This reserved attitude is reflected in the ratio of popularity graphed in figure 4.2.[17]

Even as the candidates worked heroically but often futilely to improve their ratings, voters showed a persistence in their preferences.[18] Once the major contenders had been named, Clinton maintained a steady two-party lead over Bush that changed little until voters came to a final resolution in the last week. Perot's standing, by contrast, varied enormously. The course of the campaign is shown in figure 5.2. The upper portion of the graph pictures the direct contest between Bush and Clinton, displaying voter preferences in a two-man race, excluding Perot. The bottom portion separately displays the support for Perot.[19]

Economics, Politics, and Principles

As voters decided, they also explained their decisions. In table 5.3 (p. 146), we examine responses to two questions asked in exit polls, the most important issues and the most important personal qualities. For each question, in the last set of columns, we calculate the contribution made by each issue or characteristic to the vote for each candidate.[20]

The responses demonstrate a focus on the economy that was obvious in public opinion during the campaign (see chapter 4). The famous sign in Clinton headquarters reminded the staff, "It's the economy, stupid." Democratic television advertisements insistently reminded the voters of George Bush's economic failures—in some cases not even mentioning Clinton's candidacy. Voters both heard and sent that message: about two of three cited national economic concerns (jobs, the deficit, taxes) as the most important issue.

Political humor made the same point. Cartoonist Ted Rall imagined an outrageous scenario in which Republicans found that Clinton had made a human sacrifice of his college roommate to the ancient pagan god Baal. Clinton is pictured as excusing his action in various ways: "It was the Sixties! Everyone was doing it! ... Sure, I feel badly about my roomie, Eddie, but I owe everything I have today to Baal." The fictional electorate, however, put economics over morality: The average voter decided, "I'm voting for Clinton. Since he's got a direct line to Baal, maybe he can get me a job."

The real economic issue, however, was not *one* issue but a set of different, though related, concerns. At the simplest level, voters were reacting to present conditions, answering the self-centered question first posed by Ronald Reagan in 1980: "Are you better off today than you were four years ago?" In a familiar pattern, three-fifths of those who saw themselves as better

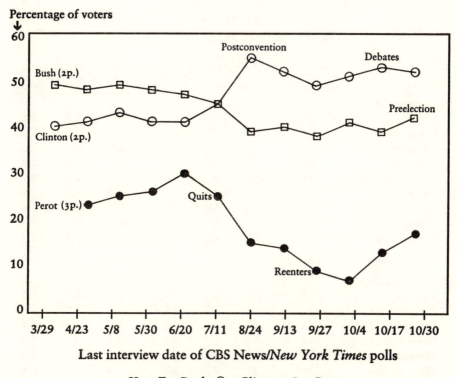

Percentage of voters

FIGURE 5.2
THE PRESIDENTIAL RACE IN THE POLLS

off voted for the incumbent, Bush; among those who saw themselves as worse off, the same proportion voted for the main challenger, Clinton. These ballots were pure examples of retrospective voting.[21]

But these sentiments alone did not guarantee Bush's defeat. A majority of voters actually thought their own economic situation was either improved or unchanged over the past four years and might have voted for Bush to maintain this stability. Voters went beyond their personal circumstances to a judgment on the president; Bush won fewer than one vote in five of the national plurality who disapproved of his economic management.

Instead of self-interest, the key element of the economic issue was a concern for the national welfare. In this respect, citizen perceptions were overwhelmingly negative. While only a third of the electorate saw itself as in personal economic trouble, 80 percent thought national economic conditions

TABLE 5.3
SOURCES OF THE PRESIDENTIAL VOTE

	Total	Percent voting for			Contribution to vote for		
	mentions	Clinton	Bush	Perot	Clinton	Bush	Perot
Issue priorities							
Health care	19	67	19	13	8.4	2.4	1.6
U.S. deficit	21	36	27	38	5.0	3.8	5.3
Abortion	12	36	56	8	2.9	4.5	0.6
Education	13	60	25	15	5.2	2.2	1.3
Economy/jobs	43	52	25	24	14.8	7.1	6.8
Environment	6	72	15	13	2.9	0.6	0.5
Taxes	14	26	57	17	2.4	5.3	1.6
Foreign policy	8	8	87	5	0.4	4.6	0.3
Family values	15	23	66	11	2.3	6.6	1.1
Totals	151				44.3	36.9	19.1
Personal qualities							
Experience	18	22	65	13	2.6	7.7	1.5
Bring change	37	58	20	23	14.2	4.9	5.6
My party	5	45	42	13	1.5	1.4	0.4
Cares about people	14	55	25	20	5.1	2.3	1.9
Honest	14	30	50	20	2.8	4.6	1.9
Best plan	25	51	27	22	8.4	4.5	3.6
Crisis judgment	16	25	64	11	2.6	6.8	1.2
Vice-president	8	64	24	11	3.4	1.3	0.6
Strong convictions	14	32	44	24	3.0	4.1	2.2
Totals	151				43.7	37.6	18.9

SOURCE: Voter Research and Surveys Exit Poll. For calculations see note 20.

were either "not so good" or "poor." Orienting their votes to social, not personal, problems,[22] those pessimistic on the national economy cast strong votes against the incumbent president.

The importance of these social orientations is seen in table 5.4, which presents the Clinton vote among groups of voters with various perceptions both of the national economy and their own financial situation. Certainly the two are related; people tend to think the nation is doing well or badly when they are individually prospering or suffering. Yet, even among those subjectively better off, only a 37 percent minority thought the national economy was excellent or good.

TABLE 5.4

ECONOMIC EFFECTS OF THE PRESIDENTIAL VOTE

(IN PERCENT VOTING FOR CLINTON) [a]

| View of national economy | Change in personal finances in past four years | | | | | |
	Better off (24%)		About the same (34%)		Worse off (41%)	
Excellent/good (20%)	7	(7)	11	(10)	40	(31)
Not so good (47%)	34	(29)	52	(42)	75	(56)
Poor (33%)	71	(55)	80	(63)	90	(67)

a. The first number is Clinton's percentage of the two-candidate vote; the number in parentheses is Clinton's percentage of the three-candidate vote.

Whatever their subjective situation, those who saw the national economy as poor voted largely for Clinton, including a majority of those doing well on their own. In contrast, Bush won a plurality among the few Panglossian optimists who were personally in economic distress but saw the national economy in good shape. The Perot vote is more closely tied to personal situations. All those who felt worse off gave him high support, regardless of their views of social conditions.

The significance of these concerns went still deeper. In objective terms, the national economy was not truly desperate. Indeed, models of the vote based on economic data actually forecast a Bush victory.[23] The peak unemployment level of 7.6 percent was considerably below the 10 percent of 1982, not to mention the 25 percent of the Great Depression. In those earlier and worse circumstances, persuasive leaders such as Ronald Reagan and Franklin Roosevelt could convince the citizens to endure hardships, which they assured the nation would be only temporary. The difference in the Bush administration was that the economic travails of the present were tied to a much deeper fear of the future, but the president provided no solace.

The Bush recession, if not as deep as past downturns, persisted far longer than a normal turn of the business cycle. As a result, private-sector jobs actually declined during his tenure, and the economic growth rate was the lowest since Herbert Hoover's administration. Unlike previous downturns, moreover, this recession did not only mean that autoworkers lost their jobs; it affected the long-term life chances of the middle and professional classes. Americans "were battered not by a shallow recession in incomes but by a deep recession in wealth that since 1990 has seen home and business owners lose $842 billion in the value of their assets."[24]

As a result, ordinary Americans came to fear "not only that they have failed to achieve the comfort they expected in life, but that they are never going to achieve it.... What most experts took forever to realize is that for many of these people, 1992 is the political equivalent of 1932."[25] Social science data confirmed their disquiet, rating the "social health" of the nation at the lowest level in twenty years of evaluation.[26]

These realities deeply troubled the electorate. Popular concern was evident throughout the nominating contests. Candidates with grim messages rapidly won support, then rapidly fell from favor. This "School of Savonarolas," castigating the national decline, included Paul Tsongas, Jerry Brown, Pat Buchanan, and the two incarnations of Perot. "Lord, people anguished, trying to do the right thing, confused as shoppers hunting for the healthiest breakfast cereal. Back and forth they went, lifting the products from the shelf, peering at the labels, deciding to buy, then hastily changing their minds."[27]

By election day, two-thirds of the voters feared that the next generation of Americans would find their lives no better than "life today." The incumbent president was, of course, the most likely target of this pessimism, but not its inevitable victim. Americans, after all, have shown a capacity for sacrifice and patience when their leaders assert these civic virtues. Bush himself had successfully rallied the nation to war in the Persian Gulf and had invoked the symbols of patriotism in his 1988 election race.

But in 1992 Bush could not plausibly issue a call for civic action. His administration's economic program was no more than a justification of private gain. In 1988 his most famous promise—"Read my lips: no new taxes" —was a pledge he knew to be deceptive at the moment it was uttered.[28] After acting responsibly to renounce that impossible promise, he then renounced his own responsibility, blamed everyone from Congress to Saddam Hussein for his act of statesmanship, and even briefly ventured into new promises of tax reduction. "At the end," wrote his 1988 speechwriter, "voters thought he wasn't serious. Serious people in public life stand for things and fight for them.... Mr. Bush seemed embarrassed to believe. It left those who felt sympathy for him embarrassed to support him."[29]

By these actions, Bush lost his positive appeal to the electorate. Relatively few voters considered his broken tax pledge, or taxes themselves, to be the most important issue. Of greater significance were other qualities—his perceived lack of leadership and his perceived lack of compassion. The president had failed to provide leadership. Missing many opportunities in the previous two years to develop new economic programs, he did little more than inappropriately repeat his strong language on the Iraqi invasion of Kuwait, "This will not stand."

These perceptions made even small incidents damaging to the president.

At a grocers' convention, Bush was reported to be unfamiliar with electronic scanners used at check-out counters. The facts of the story were probably garbled, but the report seemed at least metaphorically true. Similarly, during the second presidential debate, Bush was unable to give a convincing answer to a heartfelt, if unclear, question, "How can you honestly find a cure for the economic problems of the common people if you have no experience in what's ailing them?"[30] If the president did not know how ordinary people lived, how then could he call on them to change their nation?

In the final balloting, the economic issue turned from a judgment on the past to a bet on the future. The electorate's dim view of the economy was not simply the cause of their decisions, but evidence of their worrisome prospects. Even before the campaign, the public mood had shifted in favor of more active government.[31] Now the reality of a damaged economy reinforced the need for action. This turn toward activism is further evidenced by the personal qualities cited by voters. The most decisive factors were whether a candidate "will bring about needed change" and "has the best plan for the country." Clinton, along with Perot, was preferred on these criteria, which provided half of the Democrat's vote.

The voting decision in 1992 confirmed the leading academic models of electoral behavior: "Future expectations count and count very heavily among contemporary American voters."[32] The citizenry evinced concern with future government action, not only on general economic policy but on more specific questions. In addition to the financial concerns, a third of the voters focused on domestic problems of health, education, and the environment. On each of these concerns, Clinton was the preferred candidate, providing policy emphases for his future government.

George Bush did have some strengths in the voters' minds. The Republican campaign had been a search for a winning argument, as analyzed in chapter 3. At different times, the Bush forces attempted to consolidate conservative support for moralistic "traditional" or "family" values, to raise doubts about the character and honesty of Clinton or the mental health of Perot, to denigrate the quality of life in Arkansas, to criticize the Congress, to present a changed economic program, to attack Hillary Clinton, and even to stress the positive experience and judgment of the president.

Nothing worked. The Republican loss was the bitter fruit of the party's effort to harvest the limited vote of conservatives, an effort evident from the Bush primary campaign to the Republican national convention, as analyzed in chapter 2. Retaining Dan Quayle on the ticket was another bid for right-wing support, but the Indianan remained a drag on the president, although less severely than in 1988. By contrast, Democratic nominee Gore won more favorable comments from the electorate than any of the six national candidates. Preferred over Quayle by margins of 3–1, Gore made a distinct contribution to the Democratic victory. James Stockdale, Perot's running mate, was never a serious political figure; eventually he was an embarrassment to the independent ticket.

The lack of consistent focus in the Bush campaign was not a mistake; given the poor economic conditions, it was a futile necessity to try to change the subject of national attention. The effort achieved some, but insufficient, success. Fractions of the electorate did stress such issues as "family values" (14 percent) or foreign affairs (8 percent), and voted Republican. Personal qualities of experience and crisis judgment also were considered important by a third of the voters, again to Bush's advantage.

The president also gained, surprisingly, on the abortion issue. Although a strong 2–1 majority favored the "right-to-choice" position, the pro-Bush minority favoring "right-to-life" was more likely to cast ballots on the basis of this issue. Ultimately, however, the Bush appeal was too diffuse and too restricted to win a second term. Nothing worked because the Bush administration was too broke to fix.

The Effects of the Election

What's next? Clinton and Gore did not capture the hearts of the nation, or even the votes of a majority of Americans. They did speak their country's mind with sufficient precision to claim a mandate for change. The electoral decision in 1992 was not only a choice among candidates; it was also a judgment on the basic philosophical and policy differences between the major parties. Beyond a Democratic victory, it provides a Democratic opportunity.

THE PARTIES' FUTURES

There is no party realignment evident in the election, but there is an opportunity to consolidate Democratic gains and to move beyond their 1992 electoral minority. No new party coalition emerges from the vote, but rather a shift among all groups, based on discontent with existing conditions and uncertain expectations for the future. Partisan identification is virtually unchanged since 1988 (38 percent Democratic, 35 percent Republican), although there are glimmers of change among the youngest voters. Democratic party prospects will rise or fall with the achievements or failures of the Clinton administration.

Even without realignment, however, the major parties face vital challenges. The Perot vote clearly underlines voters' willingness to abandon partisan loyalties and receptivity to new appeals. The new campaign technologies of the 1992 election, by circumventing the party organizations, cast new doubt on their role in the political process and even raise the question of their viability in an era of direct communication between candidates and voters.

The major parties did remain important in 1992 as organizational shells and financial conduits for the candidates. Including their direct spending and "soft money" contributions, they each outspent Perot by a 2-to-1 margin. Viable parties, however, need more; they must have heads and hearts, not only deep pockets in empty clothes. Both Democrats and Republicans need to foster loyalties by clarifying their beliefs.

The Democratic party has been riven for decades on issues of international involvement, social liberalism, and the competing claims of economic redistribution and economic growth. That debate was muted in 1992 by the year's unique circumstances. With a limited field, Clinton's Democratic moderates could capture the party nomination quickly and without major damage. The end of the cold war cast foreign policy issues aside. Social liberals were willing to dampen their demands in order to forestall the final conservative capture of the judiciary. Given the economic failures of the Bush administration, the pacified Democrats achieved victory.

The rifts remain and may become evident as Clinton seeks support of his programs from a Democratic Congress. He will have advantages: the power of the presidency, his political skills, and the Democrats' need to prove their competence in government. Yet he must also deal with entrenched interests in and near the Capitol and with a party structure that facilitates factional conflict. As president, assured of renomination, he may be able to move his party toward both organizational and policy coherence.

Republicans face similar problems of ideological incohesion, and now without leaders in office to give direction. Factions within the party will debate "Who lost the White House?" with the fervor of cold-war controversies over "Who lost China?" Social conservatives and abortion rights advocates will battle within state and local organizations, as others argue economic theories. The resulting debate will be contentious yet helpful in marking the underlying ideologies within and between the major parties.

PRINCIPLES AND PARTIES

The basic party difference, at least since the New Deal, has been in the two parties' attitudes toward government. Republicans distrust government, even when they control it. They rely on the private sector, and particularly the accumulation of private capital, to meet social needs. It was not by whim that Ronald Reagan put Calvin Coolidge's portrait in a place of honor in the White House. Reagan often declared his party's basic philosophy, that government itself was the problem and could not be the solution to the nation's problems.

The Democratic party since the New Deal, by contrast, has looked on government as a potentially benign force, which can take action—at the very least to stimulate the private sector and, more ambitiously, to redistribute the national wealth. When Franklin Roosevelt, in his first Inaugural Address, found one-third of the nation "ill-fed, ill-clothed, ill-housed," he sought the remedy in government programs, not in the invisible beneficence of the marketplace.

That basic philosophical distinction was evident in this election campaign, in the party platforms and television debates, and in the contrasting programs offered by Bush and Clinton. They often acknowledged the same national needs, but they presented different solutions. Each candidate pointed, for example, to the need to provide basic health care, particularly for the 37 million Americans without medical insurance. President Bush showed the consistent Republican aversion to government in his plan to give tax benefits to businesses providing insurance for their employees and to individuals buying private health plans. President Clinton will be using the power of government to require some degree of universal coverage.

The same distinction is evident on other issues. In regard to family leave, Bush again wanted to give tax breaks to businesses that allowed new parents to take time off from their jobs without losing their positions; Clinton promised to sign legislation requiring most employers to provide unpaid leaves. Bush would stimulate the economy by reducing capital gains taxation; Clinton proposed to prime the economic pump through government spending on infrastructure. Bush expected to improve education by giving parents vouchers to "buy" better schools in a competitive educational marketplace; Clinton preferred to set national goals and provide federal financial aid.

To be sure, the differences are not absolute or always consistent. Bush and most Republicans do support the basic elements of the welfare state, such as social security, just as Democrats are increasingly willing to use market incentives, as in Clinton's endorsement of urban enterprise zones. Neither party has ever come close to socialist programs of government ownership. Both use the language of American individualism, whether in Quayle's simplistic analysis of the evils of single parenthood or in Clinton's rhetorical emphasis on personal responsibility in his welfare-reform program.

Nevertheless, the basic distinction remains. America has a complex political belief system, which tries to balance a commitment to individual liberty with a commitment to social equality, to balance the pursuit of our private interests with our search for a public community. We engage in a perpetual personal and national debate asking, to paraphrase John Kennedy, *both* what we can do for ourselves and what we can do for others in our country. In that debate, Republicans are more likely to raise the banner of individualism:

Pursuit of individual goals will add up to the common good. Democrats are more likely to raise the banner of community: Pursuing the social good will be better for each of us individually.[33]

PROSPECTS FOR THE FUTURE

Clinton and Gore's success is built on a revival of Democratic commitments, not their replacement. Their program accepts much of the social liberalism of their own young years, the 1960s, most notably women's liberation. Yet, in an important sense, it also returns to earlier values, seeking the votes of those erstwhile Democrats who "came to see the party as indifferent, if not hostile, to their moral sentiments and not much interested in their economic struggles."[34] From the Madison Square Garden convention to the Old State House victory celebration, Clinton stressed this new and old appeal to "those who do the work, pay the taxes, raise the kids and play by the rules ... the hard-working Americans who make up our forgotten middle class."[35]

The party's predominance had been based on its commitment to governmental action aimed at economic growth and the interests of those at risk in the private marketplace. Previously, that commitment focused on the poor and industrial working class and was effective when these groups were a majority of the electorate. Clinton did not change the appeal; he modernized it for a nation with higher average incomes and higher expectations.

The United States is now a middle-class, suburban nation with a service-oriented economy, but differences in wealth and opportunity are as evident today as in the industrial age. Clinton's campaign can be seen as a rhetorical echo of FDR, with an upscale appeal, speaking of a nation ill educated, ill healed, ill transported. By renewing the traditional Democratic stress on economic disadvantages, he brought his party back to power.

It remains to be seen if he can keep it there. Voters are still skeptical of government—proposals to limit the terms of senators and representatives passed in all fourteen states considering the issue. At the same time, voters retain some trust in their government—all but 6 of 116 Congressmen were re-elected in these same states. Despite their discontent, as analyzed in the next chapter, voters returned most incumbents to office. The Clinton victory was clear, but tentative, an electoral plurality within a possible majority. He won not a personal mandate but a chance to prove himself. Clinton differed from Bush more in his potential than his popularity; the distinction was "that one man has exhausted the possibilities of office ... while the other has hardly begun."[36]

Politics in a democracy, wrote Emerson, is always a contest between "the party of memory" and "the party of hope." The Democrats had become too committed to their memories, too dependent on the waning coalition established in earlier, New Deal generations, and too committed to statist programs. Now the Democrats have full control of the national government, but also full responsibility for the public welfare. With a leader appropriately born in "a place called Hope," they have the chance to rebuild confidence in their party—and in their nation's future.

Notes

1. See the analysis in Gerald M. Pomper et al., *The Election of 1988* (Chatham, N.J.: Chatham House, 1989), chap. 5; and Martin Wattenberg, *The Rise of Candidate-Centered Politics* (Cambridge, Mass.: Harvard University Press, 1991), chaps. 5, 6.

2. The standard deviation is 3.80. If the three-party vote is used, the average change is even less, −3.35, but the spread is greater, a standard deviation of 4.79.

3. By comparison, the correlation of the votes in 1984 and 1988, the highest of any paired elections in U.S. history, is .94. The correlations for the three-party vote in 1992 are .83 with 1988 alone, and .94 with the four-election average. The election returns used in preparing the map on the inside back cover are those reported in *Congressional Quarterly Weekly Report* 50 (7 November 1992): 3552.

4. Rhodes Cook, "Clinton Win Would Redraw Electoral College Map," *Congressional Quarterly Weekly Report,* 50 (24 October 1992): 3333–38.

5. See Neal Peirce, *The People's President* (New York: Simon and Schuster, 1968); and Judith Best, *The Case against Direct Election of the President* (Ithaca, N.Y.: Cornell University Press, 1975).

6. Thomas Edsall with Mary Edsall, *Chain Reaction* (New York: Norton, 1992), 5. For an academic treatment of the same process, see Edward Carmines and James Stimson, *Issue Evolution* (Princeton: Princeton University Press, 1989).

7. All opinion data, if not specifically identified, are from the exit poll conducted by Voter Research and Surveys, provided by CBS News, or from the pre-election surveys of CBS News and the *New York Times*. I deeply appreciate the help of coauthor Kathleen Frankovic, director of surveys for CBS News. 8. Thomas Edsall, "Bloc Busting: The Demise of the GOP Quest for a Majority," *Washington Post National Weekly,* 19–25 October 1992, 23.

9. More precisely, these are persons who *report* that they voted for Bush in 1988. These reports are grossly exaggerated, as persons forget their vote or rationalize that they voted for the winner. Of all respondents, including previous nonvoters, 53 percent said they voted for Bush and only 26 percent for Dukakis. The actual results in the 1988 exit polls were 53 percent Bush, 45 percent Dukakis.

10. In Maine, however, he came close to winning a single electoral vote. Unlike every other state but Nebraska, Maine divides its electoral vote by congressional districts.

11. If state exit polls were completely accurate, Perot's absence from the race

would have shifted Georgia, New Hampshire, and Ohio to Bush. Nevertheless, the margin of error in individual state polls is too large to allow confident predictions.

12. Garry Wills, "Ross Perot and the Immaculate Election," *Washington Post National Weekly*, 1–7 June 1992, 23.

13. Dan Balz and Richard Marin, "An Electorate Ready to Revolt," *Washington Post National Weekly*, 11–17 November 1991, 6.

14. They did so contrary to the prescient advice of Jack Germond and Jules Witcover: "'Wait Until 1996' May Be Wrong Move," *National Journal* 23 (30 March 1991): 757.

15. *Los Angeles Times-Mirror*, "The People, The Press and Politics on the Eve of '92," 4 December 1991, 11.

16. Jeffrey Schmalz, "Voting Scared," *New York Times*, 1 November 1992, IV:E1.

17. As figure 4.2 shows, Bush's rating became steadily negative after the beginning of the year, Clinton barely achieved tepid support, and Perot regressed during the campaign from the most favorable to the most unfavorable evaluations of any candidate at any time.

18. Such stability is characteristic of opinion more generally, despite common assumptions of the manipulability of the public. See the major work of Benjamin Page and Robert Shapiro, *The Rational Public* (Chicago: University of Chicago Press, 1992), chaps. 2, 8.

18. Undecided voters are not included. In the final weeks, leaning voters are included in each candidate's percentage, and the base is likely voters, rather than all registered voters.

20. The contribution of each item is calculated by multiplying the proportion who mentioned the item by the proportion of that group voting for Clinton, Bush, or Perot. Since more than one response was permitted, the resulting figures are then normalized on a base of 100. Illustratively, 19 percent cited the health-care issue, and 67 percent of this group voted for Clinton. Total responses were 151 percent of all individuals. The contribution of health care to Clinton's 44 percent of the vote was then calculated as $.19 \times .67 + 1.51 = 8.4$ percent.

21. Anthony Downs, *An Economic Theory of Democracy* (New York: Harper, 1957), chap. 3.

22. Such "sociotropic" voting is more common than simple individualistic voting. See Donald Kinder and Roderick Kiewiet, "Sociotropic Politics: The American Case," *British Journal of Political Science* 11 (1981): 129–61.

23. See the critique by Nathaniel Beck, "Forecasting the 1992 Presidential Election," *Public Perspective* 3 (September/October 1992): 32–34.

24. Michael Barone, "The Cry for More Direction," *U.S. News & World Report* 113 (16 November 1992): 69.

25. Alan Ehrenhalt, "An Era Ends. Silently," *New York Times*, 1 November 1992, IV:E17.

26. *New York Times*, 5 October 1992, B6. This measure is a composite of sixteen indicators of social problems, such as unemployment, drug abuse, alcohol-related deaths on highways, child abuse, and teen-age suicide.

27. David Von Drehle, "Election '92: The Year of the Truly Weird," *Washington Post National Weekly,* 9–15 November 1992, 11.

28. Bob Woodward, "The Anatomy of a Decision," *Washington Post National Weekly,* 12–18 October 1992, 6–7.

29. Peggy Noonan, "Why Bush Failed," *The New York Times,* 5 November 1992, A35.

30. *New York Times,* 16 October 1992, A13.

31. William Mayer, *The Changing American Mind* (Ann Arbor: University of Michigan Press, 1992).

32. Morris Fiorina, *Retrospective Voting in American National Elections* (New Haven: Yale University Press, 1981), 197. See also Samuel Popkin, *The Reasoning Voter* (Chicago: University of Chicago Press, 1991).

33. See Orlando Patterson's insightful discussion, "Our History vs. Clinton's Covenant," *New York Times,* 13 November 1992, A29.

34. John Leo, "Stitching America Back Together," *U.S. News & World Report,* 16 November 1992, 26.

35. Acceptance speech, *Congressional Quarterly Weekly Report* 50 (18 July 1992): 2128.

36. "Time to Choose," *Economist,* 31 October 1992, 13.

6

The Congressional Elections

MARJORIE RANDON HERSHEY

> But 'tis a common proof,
> That lowliness is young ambition's ladder,
> Whereto the climber-upward turns his face;
> But when he once attains the upmost round,
> He then unto the ladder turns his back,
> Looks in the clouds, scorning the base degrees
> By which he did ascend.
>
> — *Julius Caesar* (II, i)

Congressional candidates in 1992 inevitably looked back to the recent past. The previous election, in 1990, had taken place in a year of congressional scandal. Members had voted themselves a stealth pay raise. Senators known as the "Keating Five" were accused of pressuring regulators to go easy on a big contributor. On election day, 76 percent of voters leaving the polls said they were dissatisfied with the way Congress was doing its job.[1] But before leaving the polls, they also reelected all but one of the incumbent senators who were running again and all but fifteen incumbent House candidates. Go figure.

W. Lance Bennett summed up the congressional elections of 1990 this way: "Most Americans blamed Congress for a large part of the trouble with America; most Americans also made an exception in the case of their own representatives; and for the third straight election, incumbents in the House of Representatives were returned to office at a stunning rate of 96 percent or higher. How long can this pressure and these contradictions build without exploding? Which election will bring on the voter eruption?"[2]

The eruption came in 1992—or did it? Both houses of Congress were dramatically changed. The 103rd Congress includes 110 new House members and 13 new senators, the largest number of new members since 1948. The numbers of women, black, and Hispanic representatives almost doubled. The newcomers' prevailing campaign theme was change: limits on incumbent "perks," limitations on congressional terms, reform of the institution itself.

Yet much of the change did not come from the voting booths. Challengers beat incumbents in only thirty-four races for the House—fifteen in primaries and nineteen in the general election—and in only five races for the Senate (including one in a primary). In most of the other districts, it was the incumbent's decision to retire (though many may have jumped overboard in advance of being pushed) that led to the election of a new member. Nor did the results bring much change in the party balance. Although Republicans had hoped to make big gains in the House, the 1992 election produced a smaller net change in party strength than in all but one other recent election.

Nevertheless, the big freshman class was the raw material for marked change, in particular because it accompanied an end to twelve years of divided government. The vote resulted in a Democratic president, a continued Democratic Senate majority, and only a ten-seat Democratic loss in the House of Representatives that did not threaten the party's control. Was this a genuine wave of change in American politics or a dramatic instance of the same forces that have driven congressional victories and defeats for decades? And what does it portend for the grinding challenges besetting the federal government in the early 1990s: legislative gridlock, stalemate between the legislative and executive branches, and too little cash to solve old and new problems?

To understand congressional campaigns, we start with the premise that they are candidate-centered. In an environment in which political party organizations are a variable rather than a constant, candidates must take the initiative to set up an effective campaign organization, to determine who their likely supporters are and what will motivate their votes, and to raise enough money to be able to reach those potential supporters. They must cope with an increasingly fragmented and perilous political world, consisting of voters less anchored by stable allegiances than in years past, aggressive interest groups and their political action committees (PACs), competing independent consultants ranging from pollsters and fund raisers to media and organization experts, and rapidly evolving technology that can be used against candidates as easily as for them.[3] The largest element of a candidate's ability to cope with this environment is incumbency.

Advantage: Incumbent

Observers of American politics may be tempted to conclude that in a typical election year, members of Congress have been much more likely to lose their dignity than to lose their seats. In House races from 1980 through 1990, an average of 95 percent of those seeking reelection won both their primary and general election races. That is a higher proportion than in earlier decades, but not much higher; from 1950 through 1990, the percentage of House incumbents defeated for reelection never topped 14 percent. There was a bigger turnover in the old Soviet Politburo.

Senate seats have been somewhat more competitive. The average reelection rate for senators was only 83 percent from 1980 through 1990 and ranged much more widely as well, from 55 percent in 1980 to 97 percent in 1990. But outside the South, senatorial elections became less competitive in the 1980s than they were before 1970.[4]

WHY INCUMBENTS WIN

Money is one of the primary culprits. Challengers' campaign spending has a major impact on congressional election results; if the challenger cannot spend enough to counteract the incumbent's advantage in name recognition and other factors, the incumbent wins.[5] In recent years, the cost of House campaigns has increased greatly, and House challengers are finding it more and more difficult to raise funds. Campaign spending by House incumbents has risen substantially in the past two decades, but challenger spending actually decreased from 1982 to 1990, in part because of the growing tendency of PACs to give to incumbents. The preponderance of poorly financed challengers, then, helps to explain why House incumbents win in such large numbers. In 1984 and 1986, for example, the few challengers who defeated incumbents spent an average of $541,000 on their races. But the *median* campaign expenditure for House challengers in those years was only $48,000.[6]

As if the financial advantage were not enough, campaign coverage in the media tends to treat incumbents and challengers differently, in ways that help the incumbent.[7] House incumbents, researchers find, do not receive a great deal of media attention, but the coverage they do receive is orchestrated by their offices because local media outlets tend to print incumbents' press releases. The coverage, then, gives readers and viewers a largely positive image of the incumbent. House challengers typically start their campaigns with minimal name recognition and get even less media attention than their opponents do.

Senators are more vulnerable than representatives at the polls, not necessarily because constituents identify them more closely with issues or because their campaigns are more heavily issue-laden,[8] but probably because they receive much more media scrutiny, as do their challengers. Senators are less likely to be both the objects *and* the orchestrators of their coverage by the media.

Another key to the puzzle is the challenger's previous political experience. People who have already held public office have many advantages when they run again. The contacts they have made in office, their fund-raising experience, the name recognition they have built, all make the experienced challenger a potent competitor. But in recent years, at least until 1992, House challengers have been less and less likely previously to have held elective office.[9] The political inexperience (or limited experience) of these challengers adds to their burden.

Institutional forces are also at work. Some view the Congress as almost perfectly designed to meet its members' reelection needs: a committee structure decentralized enough to let members concentrate on legislative concerns relevant to their own districts; congressional parties willing to let members vote against their party whenever necessary for reelection; and pork-barrel policies that provide a little something for every organized group.[10]

Thus a cycle builds. Because most House incumbents seem to be good bets for reelection, they normally attract big money and only beatable opponents, which in turn eases their way to a substantial victory. Only the few incumbents who seem vulnerable, and virtually all races with no incumbent, attract more experienced challengers, high spending, and intense competition. Senate seats, because they are fewer and more prestigious than House seats, are even more desired prizes; at least in the big states, they attract more experienced and better known challengers, who are better able to raise the campaign funds they need.

Interestingly, incumbents' victory margins do not seem to be expanded by the volume of services to constituents they perform, their visits to the district, or the numbers of grants and contracts awarded in their district.[11] It may be that the definitive test eludes us, given that incumbents who find themselves in electoral trouble are likely to work especially hard at servicing their districts. But it is clear that even apart from the favors they can bestow on constituents, incumbents carry a whole arsenal of advantages into a campaign, not the least of which is what they have learned from past victories.

YET INCUMBENTS OFTEN DO NOT FEEL SAFE

Given these trends, it would seem that most House members, in particular, would feel safe at election time—yet they rarely do. Although incumbents' vote margins look comfortably large (for instance, in both 1986 and 1988, more than 85 percent of House incumbents won by at least 20 percent),[12] these big winners are not necessarily safe the next time they run. Interelection vote swings have become larger in recent years.[13] And there has been a recent increase in the number of very close House races; in 1988, only twenty-one House incumbents were reelected with less than 55 percent of the vote, whereas in 1990, there were thirty-five. One interpretation of these findings is that House seats are no safer now than they used to be and that the chill of these occasional close calls seeps into the thinking of other incumbents, who then work ever harder to please their districts and fend off strong challengers.

Not everyone agrees. In contrast to the view that incumbents' defeats are often unpredictable and therefore likely to keep all incumbents on their toes, other researchers argue that these defeats are unusual and reasonably predictable. Redistricting and scandal, they suggest, are the primary causes for incumbents' losing; and the increase in both these factors during the early 1970s (the Watergate years) produced the swings noted in once-safe districts.[14] Taking account of these causes, big winners were no more likely to lose reelection in the 1970s and 1980s than were the big winners of earlier years. Further, all agree that incumbents in the 1980s who won by narrow margins (59 percent or less) were more proficient at holding their seats in the next election than were similarly marginal incumbents in the 1950s.[15] If so, then the electoral power of incumbency remains alive and well.

Why should we be concerned about the incumbency advantage? If incumbents *feel* safe, they may be less inclined to behave responsively toward their constituents. In fact, there is little evidence that representatives do feel very safe. But if electoral competition is unbalanced by incumbents' advantages, then there is the risk that voters' choices are being unduly limited. Moreover, a substantial incumbency advantage can weaken the political parties in Congress, or keep them from getting stronger, because representatives have little need of their parties in winning reelection.

THE TWO FACES OF INCUMBENCY

Well before the 1990 elections, however, it became apparent that incumbency had another face. Anyone who could make use of a congressional staff, resources for constituent service, pork-barrel projects, and respectful media attention was also close enough to be blamed for the perks, the scandals, and the gridlock that have dominated the public image of Congress in recent years. For some time, congressional insiders had been able to win reelection by running against Congress—by taking the pose of an outsider and criticizing the institution's excesses. Yet the possibility remained that if Congress's image as a place of ill repute grew strong enough, it could raise at least some voters' suspicions about the honor of their own representatives.

In 1990, voters flirted with the dark side. Although only 15 of 406 House incumbents lost the general election (and only a single senator), 110 incumbents—more than one-fourth of the House—recorded the lowest reelection percentages they had received since their first House election.[16] The average vote for House incumbents with major-party opposition was almost 5 percent below the incumbent average in 1986 and 1988,[17] the most dramatic drop since World War II, and it occurred among incumbents of both parties.

The incumbents' close shaves weren't caused by the high quality of their challengers. In a number of instances incumbents outspent their opponents by a ratio of at least 20–1. Because most of the challengers were little known and underfinanced, they could be considered equivalent to a "none of the above" choice.[18] Gary Jacobson, pointing out that the 1990 House challengers raised less money in real terms than had any class of challengers since 1974, and that only 10 percent had previously held elective office, termed them "the most unpromising group of challengers in any postwar election."[19] The continued high reelection rate, then, had less to do with voters' love for their incumbents than with the absence of an alternative.

AND THINGS GOT SUBSTANTIALLY WORSE

Scandal and disarray are not new to Congress, but they did seem to have been raised to a high art in the late 1980s. Through a process designed to leave no fingerprints, the House increased its own pay several times, from $77,400 in 1987 to $125,100 in 1991—something most Americans would love to be able to do, but rarely achieve. A former House Speaker and Democratic Whip resigned in 1989 after having been accused of unethical conduct. The savings-and-loan scandal seemed to show that Congress could find hundreds of billions of dollars to rescue financial institutions from the results of their own greed and bad judgment, but could not rescue common people from multitudes of other problems.

Then in 1991 came what House Speaker Tom Foley called "the Congress from Hell." The House Post Office was found to have been poorly administered, and there was evidence of embezzlement and drug dealing. Other investigators disclosed that members' campaign funds had been used for a variety of noncampaign purposes, such as country club memberships and luxury cars. During Senate hearings on the nomination of Clarence Thomas to the Supreme Court, centering on charges that he had sexually harassed one or more female employees, several senators appeared monumentally insensitive to women's concerns about sexual harassment. But the mother of all congressional scandals was yet to unfold.

THE OVERDRAFT STORY: FROM THE KEATING 5
TO THE HOUSE BANK 325

Since the early 1800s, House members had gotten their paychecks at the office of the House sergeant at arms. That office maintained a depository, termed by the media the "House bank," where members could keep their paychecks and other money in non-interest-paying checking accounts. This office routinely covered any member's checks, using other members' deposits, when his or her account did not have enough funds; the result amounted to interest-free loans. In practice, members could float overdrafts for up to a month as long as the total was less than their next paycheck, and sometimes when it was more. Commercial banks, of course, are less generous.

In September 1991 the General Accounting Office reported that the "bank" had made good 8331 bad checks in a recent one-year period. In fact, there are records of member overdrafts going back to 1830.[20] These overdrafts had been reported in yearly audits since 1947, but they were only noticed in a big way by the media in the fall of 1991. On 3 October the House voted to close the bank by year's end and asked the House Ethics Committee to determine whether those with a pattern of abuse should face penalties. The committee's investigation found that 267 current voting members and 58 former and nonvoting House members had each written at least one bad check. Although many of the checks were small and quickly covered, some were for amounts exceeding $40,000. In a few instances, members were found to have used overdrafts to rescue their dwindling campaign funds or to finance personal investments. One of the major offenders was the chairman of the House Ethics Committee.

After intense wrangling, the House voted to disclose the identity and the accounts of all members who had written overdrafts from 1988 to 1991. Disclosure came in April 1992. Some members complained that they were being unfairly accused because the sergeant at arms would normally cover overdrafts without notifying the member as long as the overdraft did not exceed the amount of the member's next paycheck. Moreover, the "bank's" recordkeeping was admittedly slipshod. Nevertheless, in the words of Ethics Committee member Fred Grandy (R-Iowa), "As of today, ... your talk show hosts have a topic, your opponent has an issue and your constituents have a reason to support term limits."[21]

For incumbents worried about the effect of this news on their reelection chances, the early soundings were not good. Soon after the story broke, one of the most flagrant check kiters (Democrat Charles Hayes of Illinois, who had written 716 bad checks), formerly a safe incumbent, lost his race for renomination. By late June, eleven other House members had been defeated in their primaries—equal to the largest number in more than four decades.

Congress made a hurried effort at the appearance of reform. On the House side, there were big price increases at the government-subsidized House barber shop (all the way up to $10 for a haircut) and the House gym, and a task force was appointed to consider management changes, including the appointment of a professional House administrator. The Senate had no such bank, but it weighed in with more limited hours at the Senate dining room.

The damage had been done, however. Public approval ratings of Congress, already in the ice-cold range, dropped even lower in March 1992. Even favorable ratings of the respondent's own representative, always substantially higher than ratings of the institution as a whole, began to edge closer to 50 percent (see figure 6.1).

Why was the House bank scandal so powerful a symbol of the "other face" of incumbency? The savings-and-loan crisis took a much bigger bite out of voters' pocketbooks. But the failure of S&Ls and the details of the complicated bailout were too intricate and abstract for most citizens to want to explore. In contrast, a bad check is a familiar and tangible sign whose

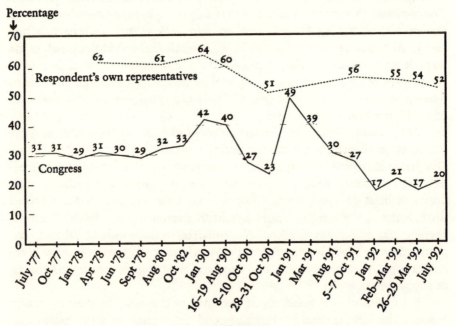

SOURCE: Reported in "Congress, My Congressman," *Public Perspective* 3 (May/June 1992): 102. July 1992 data from CBS/*New York Times* poll.

The questions are: "Do you approve or disapprove of the way Congress is handling its job? How about the representative in Congress from your district? Do you approve or disapprove of the way your representative is handling his or her job?"

FIGURE 6.1

APPROVAL OF CONGRESS

meaning is almost universally understood. The sheer volume of kited checks, and the casualness with which the practice was accepted by House administrators, contributed to the impression that members of Congress consider themselves persons of privilege who can thumb their noses at the conventions (even laws) that mere citizens must follow, and yet expect taxpayers to foot the bill for their extravagance. Ironically, many incumbents had laid the foundation for just such a conclusion by the anti-Washington rhetoric of their previous campaigns.

Redistricting added to the electoral woes of House incumbents. Because of population shifts documented by the 1990 census, nineteen House seats, mainly from the Northeast and the Midwest, were redistributed to eight rapidly growing Sunbelt states. The redrawing of district lines was further affected by the Voting Rights Act, which mandated that minorities—primarily blacks and Hispanics—receive a fair chance of obtaining representation in the process. In a few districts, including some redrawn for the sake of minority representation, the incumbent would be facing a population that was as much as 75 percent different from that of his or her previous race. In several more, two incumbents would have to compete for the same seat.

There were other reasons for incumbents to contemplate a career change. Congress had earlier amended campaign finance rules so that incumbents could keep leftover campaign money for their personal use as long as they had entered the House before 1980 and retired by the end of 1992. More than one-third of House members would be eligible to keep the cash—which totalled several hundred thousand dollars in some instances—if they left Congress by 1993 (although few thought it prudent to do so).

For many, even these incentives to leave would not have been enough if it had not been for the mounting frustrations of the job. The heavy burden of the $4 trillion national debt and ever-growing federal budget deficits meant that there was no money to fund new ideas or programs. Serious problems such as the rising cost and inequitable distribution of health care were not being addressed for lack of any national consensus as to what to do about them. As problems mounted, comity within the House suffered, no more clearly than in the remarks of Representative William E. Dannemeyer (R-Calif.) in his last House appearance before retiring: "I hate this process. The place is miserable. I only have an hour and a half left, and I'm going to cause as much damage as I can." Representative David Obey (D-Wisc.) responded, "Above all others I have ever served with, you have absolutely no redeeming social value."[22]

Soon, the biennial trickle of retirements began to look like a flood. During the past two decades, the number of House members leaving office voluntarily had been declining. An average of forty-two members retired in time for the election years 1972–82, but the average had dropped to only twenty-seven in the years 1984 through 1990.[23] Retirements had remained the primary source of turnover in the House, but only because of the very high re-election rate for those who remained. In 1992, however, with three-fifths of the House implicated in the bank scandal and many facing the necessity to get to know thousands of new constituents, all records were broken. Fifty-two House members and eight senators chose not to run again. Another thirteen House incumbents decided to take their chances on another office.

The number of retirements, which set a postwar high, was significant in itself. It was made more significant by the fact that the retirees included a large number of influential members. One who stepped down was the acting chairman of the Ethics Committee, widely respected New York Democrat Matthew McHugh. As Obey put it, "The banshees and monkeys are staying, and the sequoias are falling."[24]

The Primaries

For House members who chose to run for reelection, the big question was the likely impact of the bank scandal, not only on the voters but also on the decisions of potential challengers and contributors. Deadlines for filing to run for office had already passed in some states by the time the names of the House Bank 325 were released. In other states, there was still time for primary opponents to emerge. Because sizable numbers of Republican as well as Democratic House members were on the list, including three Bush cabinet members who had previously served in the House, the partisan ramifications of the scandal appeared to be less clear than the anti-incumbent impact.

It soon became apparent that incumbents had ample reason to worry. In the years since 1950, primary defeats had been uncommon. In 1988 and in 1990, only a single House member was defeated in the primaries, and in both instances the losing incumbent had been dogged by charges of significant ethical lapses. But in 1992, records came crashing down. More House members—nineteen of them—lost their primaries than in any congressional election since World War II—more, in fact, than in any *general* election since 1982 (see figure 6.2). And one senator, Alan J. Dixon (D-Ill.), also lost his race for renomination.

In addition to the nineteen incumbents who went down in flames, many of their surviving colleagues were singed. The proportion of House members who received less than 60 percent of the primary vote in 1992 was more than triple that of 1990. Fully fifty-four incumbents fell into this marginal category (including the nineteen who were defeated), compared with fifteen in 1990 and seven in 1988.

As in other recent elections, senior members were at greater risk than

Number of House members (total = 435)

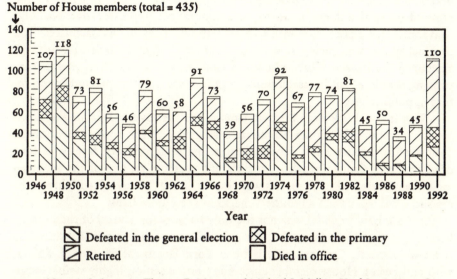

FIGURE 6.2

HOUSE TURNOVER. ELECTION DEFEATS AND
RETIREMENTS, 1946–92

SOURCE: Norman J. Ornstein, Thomas E. Mann, and Michael J. Malbin, *Vital Statistics on Congress, 1991–1992*, 58. Figures for 1992 were calculated from *Congressional Quarterly Weekly Report*, 7 November 1992, 3579.

were freshmen. One Congress watcher noted, "The prototypical incumbent who has lost a House primary this year is not a relatively inexperienced first- or second-termer who has trouble raising money. He is, on average, a 58-year-old Hill veteran with 14 years' seniority and a substantial financial advantage over his primary competition."[25] Even national name recognition did not protect some House members; the chair of the National Republican Congressional Committee, Michigan Representative Guy Vander Jagt, was defeated for renomination in August. Counting Vander Jagt's twenty-seven years in the House and the retirements of six other members of his state delegation, Michigan lost a total of 138 years of congressional experience before Labor Day.

The anti-incumbent effect was far from uniform, however. In the California primary, two months after the Ethics Committee released its list, only two House members had tough renomination races, and only one lost. Representative Barbara Boxer, who had been tarred with 143 House bank overdrafts, succeeded in focusing the campaign on other issues and won the Democratic nomination for a Senate seat with unexpected ease. In other areas, the taint of scandal did not seem to be a hindrance; Representative Nicholas Mavroules, for example, won his Democratic primary in Massachusetts at a time when he was facing seventeen criminal charges in federal court. (A sidebar in the *Boston Globe* discussing similar previous cases carried this intriguing headline: "In Massachusetts, prison doesn't always preclude one's future in politics."[26])

Was it the bank scandal that caused the turnover? Of the seventeen House members the Ethics Committee singled out for special mention as "abusers" of House bank privileges, five lost their primary races and four others retired. Considered from a different perspective, five of the nineteen incumbents defeated in primaries were on the list of "abusers" and three others had kited more than a hundred checks at the House bank.

But the bank scandal was not the only liability for several of these members. Nine of the nineteen who lost primaries were running in substantially redrawn districts. One example is New York Democrat Stephen J. Solarz, who had been a House member since 1975 and a senior, highly visible member of the Foreign Affairs Committee. His district was carved up in 1992 to create a majority Hispanic constituency; in fact, he was criticized for seeking reelection at all, instead of stepping down in favor of a Hispanic candidate. Similarly, Democrat Charles Hatcher sought renomination in a district that had been redrawn to produce a black majority. Solarz and Hatcher were both prominently featured on the Ethics Committee's "abusers" list, thanks to 819 and 743 bad checks, respectively; but although the bank scandal undoubtedly cost them votes, redistricting was a bigger handicap.

The large number of primary defeats, then, was not at all unpredictable. Although half of the declared "abusers" did win renomination, as did many incumbents facing redrawn districts—testimony to the advantage of incumbency—the combination of extensive redistricting and a highly publicized, easily understood scandal tied directly to specific House members put a substantial number at risk and took a big toll.

Had the voters' fury been spent, or was it just beginning to be expressed? Pessimists among the waiting incumbents could point to the reduced margins of victory in the primaries as evidence that a chill wind would blow across the Capitol in November. Optimists could argue that the primaries and the wave of retirements had culled the most vulnerable from their midst, so there was little left to fear in the general election. After all, most of the primary defeats had taken place before the end of June. That led some to speculate that the bank scandal had been most potent while it was current in the headlines and that it would be old news by November. Not, however, if their challengers could help it.

The Campaign

With all this fuel for change, as the fall campaign approached, observers who had seen minimal change in Congress for a decade were on the edge of their chairs. *Congressional Quarterly,* the bible of Congress watchers, concluded in mid-September that nearly half of all House districts had "serious competition" and that in 132 of these races, neither candidate had built more than a slim edge.[27] These were unprecedented numbers, at least in recent memory. An unusually large number of Senate races also looked genuinely competitive.

That was terrific news for House Republicans, whose minority status was so long-standing that a Republican House majority was only a distant memory; none of their number had ever served in one. The National Republican Congressional Committee (NRCC) normally targets about twenty House candidates on whom to "max out"—to give the maximum allowed party contributions of money and services. Its 1992 target list, issued in August, included 124 candidates; the lure of redistricting, retirements, and anti-incumbent sentiment led to the dream of big Republican gains in both the House and Senate.

The leading issue for these Republican challengers proved to be the same as that used by Democratic challengers. Campaign ads featuring bouncing checks, bouncing politicians, "perk monsters," and even jail doors clanging shut, hit television screens all over the nation between Labor Day and 3 November. In fact, the NRCC went so far as to mail election-eve letters to constituents of Democratic House members, supposedly signed by the incumbent, thanking voters for their pay raise, pensions, junkets, and other perks, and asking voters to remember them on election day. These deceitful mailings were carried out for willing Republican challengers in districts all over the nation.

Many of the nonincumbents, and even some incumbents, took this theme further by campaigning for limits on the number of terms members of the House and Senate could serve. It was, as Adam Clymer pointed out, "the simplest way to run for Congress and against it at the same time."[28] Frequent arguments were that unrestricted congressional service leaves incumbents too dependent on PAC money and thus hedged in by the fear of offending a variety of interests, or so captive of the Beltway that they become unable to relate to the lives and concerns of Americans who live outside the capital.

President Bush emphasized some of the same themes as these congressional challengers. As he promised during the Republican convention, Bush broke new ground by denouncing Democratic House and Senate incumbents by name in their districts. It was part of his strategy to counter Bill Clinton's appeal as an agent of change by identifying Congress as the real source of the stagnation in Washington—a Congress controlled by Clinton's Democratic colleagues. Many of the targeted Democrats commented hopefully that it was not working: The Bush attacks did not get much media play in their districts, they often generated a sympathetic backlash, and, most damning of all, as one targeted House Democrat put it, Bush "has a 37 percent approval in my district.... For him to come out and blast me doesn't resonate quite the way it would have if Ronald Reagan had done it in 1984."[29]

Indeed, the possibly negative impact of the presidential race on congressional campaigns was beginning to worry Republican candidates. Although Bush's approval rating had soared to 89 percent after the Persian Gulf war, by mid-summer of 1992 it had crashed to 29 percent. The tortoise pace of economic growth, a strikingly inept Bush campaign, and the nomination of a Democratic ticket with unexpected energy and appeal combined to drag the president more than 20 percent behind Bill Clinton after the Democratic convention. Party activists openly debated calls for dropping Vice-President Quayle from the Republican ticket; in fact, columnist George F. Will and a few other conservatives suggested dropping *Bush* from the ticket. Though all Republican senators and House members were invited to attend the party's national convention, fully half chose to stay home and campaign instead.

With the slide in Bush's appeal came a turnaround in voters' attitudes toward the two parties in Congress. Since 1986, voters' preference for Democrats in Congress had been eroding. But in early August 1992 the Gallup poll showed a sharp increase in preference for Democratic candidates, who now led Republicans 56 percent to 36 percent. In consequence, consultant David B. Hill noted, a number of Republican candidates who had agreed to run in the heady aftermath of the Gulf war, expecting to benefit from a coming Bush landslide, were now debating whether it was safe to invite the president into their districts.[30] In sharp contrast, Democratic Senate and House candidates were *not* running from the top of their ticket—headline news, given recent history. Clinton finished his race by campaigning for a number of congressional candidates who welcomed his help.

As always, there were elements of the bizarre. An underdog in a Republican primary in Indiana ran television spots showing graphic footage of the body parts of aborted fetuses to dramatize his fervent opposition to abortion. The ads attracted national news coverage, and when he won the primary, the gory footage was soon broadcast by at least sixteen other House challengers (none of whom won).[31]

Wisconsin Democratic Senate candidate Russell Feingold announced a mock endorsement from Elvis Presley, whose electoral clout must be impressive; Feingold won 70 percent of the vote against two much better-known primary opponents in a race that was widely interpreted as a vote against politics as usual. On election eve, however, Feingold and hundreds of other Senate and House challengers sweated out the possibility that politics as usual—overwhelming numbers of incumbent victories—was waiting just ahead.

The November Elections

Before the election, it was hard to imagine that the low turnover of 1990 could be repeated. There had been only twenty-eight open seats (those where no incumbent is running) in the House that year and three in the Senate; in 1992, counting the large number of retirements as well as primary defeats, there were eighty-six open House seats and nine in the Senate. In 1990, more than one in five House incumbents had no major-party opponent in the general election; neither did five senators. Not counting Louisiana (where it is possible to win a seat with a majority of the primary vote), not a single Senate incumbent and only 6 percent of the House members running in the general election went unopposed in 1992.

Yet when the smoke and mirrors cleared on election day, the great majority of incumbents were left standing. In the House, 325 members were reelected and 24 were defeated; in the Senate, 23 incumbents won and four lost (see table 6.1). Fully 93 percent of House incumbents on the general election ballot were reelected; including primary defeats (as in figure 6.3) brings the figure down to 88 percent. The Senate reelection rate was 85 percent (82 percent counting primary losses).

To an extent, interpreting these results is a matter of deciding whether the proverbial glass is half full or half empty. On the one hand, the House reelection rate was the lowest since 1974, and within two percentage points of the lowest rate in forty years. On the other hand, an election in which almost nine in ten incumbents are returned to office is something less than a massacre, and the Senate reelection rate was well within the range of the past ten years. Granted, the reelection rate of House incumbents in 1992 was built on a reduced base, reflecting the unusually large number who chose not to run again, and it is possible that a larger percentage of those retirees might have been defeated if they had run. But as Representative Dannemeyer's comments suggested, these retirements were not all caused by a fear of defeat at the polls.

The Congress that was sworn in on 5 January looked like a renovated institution. There were 110 new House members and 12 newly elected senators, with a thirteenth appointed to take the Senate seat of Vice-President Al Gore. For the first time since 1950, one-fourth of House members were freshmen. Yet these freshmen certainly could not be called antipoliticians; al-

TABLE 6.1

WINNERS, LOSERS, AND PARTY CHANGE, 1992

	House	Senate
Democratic incumbents reelected [a]	195	13
Republican incumbents reelected	129	10
Democratic incumbents defeated	16	2
Republican incumbents defeated	8	2
Democratic seats held [b]	258	57
Republican seats held	176	43
Democratic freshmen [c]	63	8
Republican freshmen	47	5
Party change from 102nd Congress	+10 Republicans	0

a. The Senate total does not include Senator Kent Conrad (D-N.D.), who retired from one North Dakota Senate seat, then ran for and was elected to the other one.

b. One House member is not included in either the Democratic or Republican total: Representative Bernard Sanders of Vermont, who runs as an Independent.

c. The Senate total includes the new member appointed to take the seat of Vice-President Al Gore. It does not include Senator Conrad (see note a).

most three-quarters had previously held elective office, slightly more than had the returning incumbents when they were first elected.[32] Nor did the concerns of the newcomers seem markedly different from those of their colleagues. The *Washington Post* summed up: "In a year when change has seemed the password to political office, Democrats elected to the House sound very much like the ones who are already there. The freshmen Democrats ... emphasized traditional Democratic concerns about creating jobs and expanding health services. And after a year in which the perks and privileges of Congress became campaign issues, these new members were more interested in committee assignments than rules."[33] As one writer put it, "the freshmen have canceled plans to torch Congress."[34]

Moreover, the party balance did not change greatly (see table 6.1). The net Democratic loss in the House was ten seats—a total well below the Republicans' early hopes and the Democrats' fears. In only one election since 1954 had there been less change in the party balance in the House. In the Senate, Democrats lost incumbents in Georgia and North Carolina, and Republicans lost one each in California and Wisconsin, leading to no net change. The Democrats now hold a 258–176 majority in the House (plus one Independent, Socialist Bernard Sanders of Vermont) and a 57–43 Senate majority: substantial, but not enough to silence a Republican filibuster in the upper house.

Percentage of those seeking reelection who won

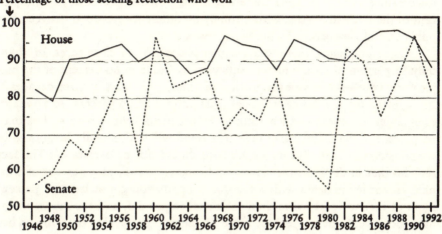

SOURCE: Norman J. Ornstein, Thomas E. Mann, and Michael J. Malbin, *Vital Statistics on Congress, 1991–1992*, 58–59. For 1992, *Congressional Quarterly Weekly Report*, 7 November 1992, 3579. The percentages include both primary and general elections.

FIGURE 6.3

REELECTION RATES OF HOUSE AND SENATE
INCUMBENTS, 1946–92

It was a disappointment for the Republican party. Republicans had long explained their deficit in the House by citing the big reelection advantages held by House incumbents, most of whom are Democrats. If there were more open seats, or if the playing field could be leveled by campaign finance reforms, they argued, Republicans would do better. There were unprecedented numbers of open seats in 1992, at least in comparison with the last forty-five years. But perhaps in part because of President Bush's drop in the polls, Democrats won 63 percent of the seats where no incumbent was running, or where one incumbent, because of redistricting, was facing another incumbent. Even worse for the Republicans, the impression that a number of marginal Democrats were helped by the Clinton-Gore ticket should give the Clinton administration greater leverage on these members' votes in Congress.

The most worrisome sign for incumbents was that their winning margins, though still healthy, had dropped a bit further from the lows recorded in 1990. The mean vote share of House incumbents with major-party opposition in 1988 was 68.4 percent. In 1990 it had dropped to 64.5 percent, the lowest since 1974.[35] In 1992 there was a slight further decrease, to 63.6 percent of the two-party vote, with virtually no difference recorded between Republican and Democratic incumbents' vote shares.

Correspondingly, there was a higher proportion of close races. In 1988, only 13 percent of House incumbents won by less than 60 percent of the major-party vote—the lowest proportion of "marginal" seats in three decades.[36] In 1990 the proportion of marginal seats jumped to 19 percent. In 1992, an even larger percentage—28 percent of House incumbents—won by less than 60 percent of the major-party vote. The trend will undoubtedly be noticed in congressional offices. But its significance should not be overstated. The fact remains that in the incumbent-bashing climate of 1992, 72.5 percent of winning House incumbents with major-party opposition got at least 20 percent more of the two-party vote than their challengers did, and the *average* winning incumbent got 27 percent more of the two-party vote than his or her challenger.

In recent years, researchers have found that freshmen running their first reelection races have done very well but that more senior members of the House, in the phase of their careers when they are spending more time on legislation and congressional leadership, can find themselves suddenly vulnerable. Gradual erosion of their base of support or larger swings in voter sentiment may have gone unnoticed by these incumbents; unexpected defeat may be the first (and, of course, the last!) sign of electoral weakness.[37] In 1992, the trend was continued; there were only three freshmen among the twenty-four House members defeated in the general election, and only one among the nineteen primary defeats. Those who lost the general election averaged 10.4 years of House service; those defeated in the primaries averaged 14 years.

Perhaps appropriately in a year when the institution was so heavily criticized, House leaders bore their share of the marginal victories. Speaker Thomas S. Foley, Majority Whip David E. Bonior, and the chair of the House Democratic Caucus, Steny H. Hoyer, all won with 55 percent of the vote. Republican Minority Leader Robert H. Michel and the Minority Whip, Newt Gingrich, both received less than 60 percent, as did Ways and Means Committee chair Dan Rostenkowski.

What, then, is the status of the incumbency advantage in the wake of the 1992 congressional races? That incumbency has two faces was clearly apparent. But the implications for congressional behavior lie in the explanations for the losses and the marginal races. If scandal and redistricting account for much of the congressional turnover and the lower victory margins, then it is tempting to conclude that there has been no sea change in House and Senate elections. Redistricting will not recur until after the year 2000, the risky use of perks can be curtailed, and thus incumbents would seem to retain a lot of control over their fates. If the defeats were more random, then it might be time for members of Congress to locate the lifeboats.

To What Extent Were Defeats Caused by Scandal or Redistricting?

The fate of the House Bank 325 suggests that scandal, writ large in 1992, was a major reason for the House turnover. Most of the biggest overdrafters were themselves bounced. But not in November. Most of their election losses came in the primaries, especially the early primaries, which were closer in time to the events of the scandal.

Of the seventeen members identified by the Ethics Committee in April as "abusers" of the House bank, the attrition rate was 65 percent: only eight had remained standing after the primaries, two of whom lost the general election. As table 6.2 shows, of the current members who were charged with a hundred or more overdrafts, twenty-five, or 54 percent, left the House at the end of 1992. Almost half of the twenty-five left voluntarily, and most of the others were defeated for renomination. Only seventeen percent of those who

TABLE 6.2
THE FATE OF THE HOUSE OVERDRAFTERS

Percentage who ...	*Number of overdrafts*									
	100+	(%)	*50–99*	(%)	*10–49*	(%)	*1–9*	(%)	*0*	(%)
Retired [a]	12	(26)	4	(12)	5	(9)	17	(13)	15	(9)
Lost House primary	8	(17)	0	(0)	0	(0)	6	(5)	5	(3)
Lost primary for another office	0	(0)	0	(0)	1	(2)	2	(2)	3	(2)
Lost general election	5	(11)	2	(6)	5	(9)	7	(5)	5	(3)
Lost general election for another office	0	(0)	2	(6)	0	(0)	1	(1)	0	(0)
Total	25	(54)	8	(25)	11	(20)	33	(26)	28	(17)
N	46		32		58		131		168	

SOURCE: *Congressional Quarterly Weekly Report*, 18 April 1992, 1006–7, modified by the state data on 1001–5 and 1008–12, compared with the election results provided by *Congressional Quarterly Weekly Report*, 7 November 1992, 3579.

NOTE: The totals exclude nonvoting and former House members. Two House members who died in office, Representatives Walter Jones and Ted Weiss, are included in the total Ns (and Jones in the category of those who retired, because he had previously announced his decision to do so).

a. Does not include those who left to run for other office.

had no overdrafts left the House, slightly more than half of whom decided to retire. Those with between one and ninety-nine overdrafts fell in between these two groups in their rates of retirement and defeat.

In short, the more overdrafts a member had, the more likely he or she was to leave Congress, voluntarily or otherwise. *Congressional Quarterly* called the bank scandal "a key, and perhaps decisive, issue in many of the incumbent losses."[38] It was the red flag by which challengers could call attention to incumbents' use of the other perks of office. Several of those defeated had what would have been termed safe seats until their names appeared high on the overdraft list. One was Representative Bob McEwen (R-Ohio); prior to 1992, and the 166 overdrafts with which he was charged, McEwen had won 70 percent of the vote in three straight elections.

Many of the big overdrafters sought to blunt the issue by stressing the benefits their seniority had brought to the district. Consider, for example, the race of Mary Rose Oakar. An eight-term Democrat from the Cleveland area, Oakar was one of the senior women in the House. She was also one of those named as the worst abusers of the House bank. There were further charges of ethics violations against her, including misuse of the House Post Office. Her conservative Republican challenger, Martin R. Hoke, called her "the most persuasive argument for term limitation." She, in response, stressed her intensive constituent service. It was not enough.

It is premature to conclude, however, that the voters would not tolerate ethical lapses. Of the forty-six House members with a hundred or more overdrafts, twenty-one were returned to office. (One of the twenty-one, Representative Barbara Boxer, won a Senate seat in California.) Representative Mavroules, of the seventeen criminal counts, was defeated, yet Representative Joseph M. McDade (R-Pa.) sailed unopposed into his sixteenth term despite his indictment in May 1992 on the charge of extorting $100,000 in bribes and favors.

As in the primaries, several of the losing incumbents marked by the House bank scandal were also the victims of redistricting. Five of the twenty-four defeats of House incumbents in the general election had been preordained by the redrawing of district lines that placed two incumbents in the same district. At least three other losing incumbents were running in districts redrawn to be less favorable to their party. Oakar, for example, ran in a substantially redrawn district that, although dominantly Democratic, now contained many new Republican voters. So scandal and redistricting were implicated (sometimes jointly) in almost half of the House general election losses.

Many incumbents, anticipating an unusually rough election, greatly stepped up their fund-raising efforts. By the end of September, Senate incumbents had a record advantage of 9–1 over their challengers in PAC contributions, according to Common Cause; incumbents had raised $32.6 million and challengers, $3.7 million. Overall, incumbents had raised three times the funds that their challengers had by the end of September.[39]

In the House, too, fund raising was Job One. In 1990, only six House members spent more than $1 million on their campaigns. By mid-October 1992, there were already fourteen million-dollar incumbent campaigns, with more on the way. All but one of those fourteen incumbents were reelected.[40] It is further evidence of the incumbency advantage—what Common Cause head Fred Wertheimer has called "the Washington equivalent of the fountain of youth"[41]—that House members and senators are able to step up their fund raising substantially in response to perceived electoral threat. In turn, those campaign funds, combined with the relative poverty of most challenges, probably kept the number of defeats low.

THE YEAR OF THE WOMAN?

Another important effect of the scandals was to open up opportunities for women candidates. Conventional wisdom suggests that there are so few women in Congress because incumbents, the great majority of whom are male, have so many advantages in winning reelection, not merely because voters discriminate against women candidates.[42] Redistricting and retirements in 1992 opened up unprecedented avenues into Congress for the growing number of women public officials at the state and local levels. Even the prevalence of gender stereotyping seemed to benefit women campaigners in 1992; given the high levels of public frustration with Congress, the stereotyping of women as more moral and less tainted by "politics as usual" put women, the ultimate congressional outsiders, in just the position that most male candidates were working to attain.

In addition to the opportunity, events of 1992 provided the motive for some women to run. The confirmation hearings on the nomination of Clarence Thomas, widely broadcast on radio and television, were a defining moment for many politically involved women. Some were propelled into candidacy by the sight of an all-male Senate Judiciary Committee grilling Professor Anita Hill on her charges of sexual harassment against Thomas. One was Lynn Yeakel, head of a fund-raising organization for women's issues. Yeakel's decision to run against Senator Arlen Specter (R-Pa.) was prompted by her disgust at the way in which Specter led the Judiciary Committee's charge against Hill. Another was Carol Moseley Braun, a Cook County, Illinois, official who astonished the political professionals by winning the Democratic Senate nomination from incumbent Senator Alan J. Dixon.

As the primary season advanced, the number of women running for

Congress increased. At the end of May there were 150 women candidates for the House—the largest number in history, by a considerable margin—106 of whom won their party's nomination in the primaries. A record eleven women won nomination to the Senate. Most were Democrats: seventy in the House races and all but one in the Senate. These candidates were greatly helped by the contributions of other women, which expanded substantially in 1992.[43]

But the two faces of incumbency were a potential hazard for these new women candidates. Although many women benefited from their image as outsiders, untainted by the scandals and the gridlock that dominate current perceptions of Congress, their outsider status could also, in the hands of a skilled opponent, be portrayed as a lack of experience and aggressiveness in bringing home benefits to the district. As Ellen Goodman wrote: "Gradually and predictably, The Year of the Woman became the year of individual women, each on her own turf, with her own strengths and weaknesses."[44]

In the end, the "year of the woman" turned out to be the year of *some* women. Four new Democratic women won Senate seats: Boxer and former San Francisco Mayor Dianne Feinstein in California, State Senator Patty Murray in Washington, and Braun in Illinois, the first black woman ever to serve in the Senate. They joined incumbents Barbara Mikulski (D-Md.), who won reelection easily, and Nancy Landon Kassebaum (R-Kan.) to push the number of women in the Senate to six—enough to convince the Senate to construct the first women members' restroom just off the Senate floor.

Lynn Yeakel, however, lost her initial lead during the summer and was unable to regain it during the fall, partly because of Specter's effective emphasis on his record of constituent service. One reporter wrote: "He struts his incumbency like a bodybuilder displaying his biceps ... and [he has] a way of squeezing blood out of the federal turnip that impresses even Democrats."[45] In addition to Yeakel, six other women Senate candidates lost their races.

The number of women voting members in the House jumped from twenty-eight in the 102nd Congress to forty-seven in the 103rd.[46] Other minorities greatly expanded their representation as well. The new House included a record number of African Americans (thirty-eight) and Hispanics (seventeen), many of whom ran in new districts drawn especially to help elect more minority representatives. Five southern states—Alabama, Florida, North and South Carolina, and Virginia—elected black House members for the first time since Reconstruction.

But the gains, particularly for women, must be kept in perspective. In order for women to hold about the same percentage of congressional seats as their proportion of the population as a whole, voters would have needed to elect 194 new women House members, not 19; and 49 new senators, not 4 (see table 6.3). Analysts may dispute whether parity in numbers between

TABLE 6.3

REPRESENTATION OF WOMEN, BLACKS, AND HISPANICS
IN CONGRESS, 1973–93

	Women		*Blacks*		*Hispanics*	
	%	N	%	N	%	N
1973						
% of population	51.3		11.1		4.6	
% of House membership	3.7	16 [b]	3.4	15	1.1	5
% of Senate membership	0.0	0	1.0	1	1.0	1
Representation ratio [a]	.06		.27		.24	
1983						
% of population	51.4		11.7		6.4	
% of House membership	5.1	22 [c]	4.8	21	2.3	10
% of Senate membership	2.0	2	0.0	0	0.0	0
Representation ratio	.09		.33		.30	
1993						
% of population	51.3		12.1		9.0	
% of House membership	10.8	47	8.7	38	3.9	17
% of Senate membership	6.0	6	1.0	1	0.0	0
Representation ratio	.19		.60		.35	

SOURCES: U.S. Bureau of the Census, *Congressional Quarterly Weekly Report*.

a. The ratio of the percentage of women (or blacks or Hispanics) in Congress (including both House and Senate) to the percentage of that group in the general population.

b. Includes two women members elected in special elections.

c. Includes one woman member elected in a special election.

women and men in Congress is a worthwhile goal; but the striking *lack* of parity certainly suggests that women remain seriously disadvantaged in the effort to win House and Senate seats, to a much greater extent than do blacks and Hispanics.

And the gap will close only slowly, if at all; a Voting Rights Act intended to benefit geographically concentrated minorities cannot be used to increase women's representation. Being a woman candidate clearly did not result in the free ride to victory that a trend-happy press had trumpeted. Mary Rose Oakar and two other female incumbents, Joan Kelly Horn (D-Mo.) and Liz Patterson (D-S.C.), were defeated for reelection (as was Beverly Byron, D-Md., in the primary) along with fifty-five of the seventy-nine nonincumbent women who ran in House races. Only two of the women House newcomers defeated male incumbents; all the other winners had contested open seats. Similarly, only two of the four new women senators had run against incumbents, one of whom had been appointed to the Senate only two years before; the others won open seats. All the other women Senate candidates who ran against incumbents lost. Many women candidates, in short, owed their seats to the great wave of incumbent retirements and primary defeats in 1992—an occurrence unlikely to recur with any regularity.

The new congressional women were not a group of political neophytes. A full three-quarters of those elected to the House had previously served in elective office. So had an even higher proportion of the new black and Hispanic House members; the least politically experienced group, in fact, was the new white male representatives. In the Senate, all four of the newly elected women members had previous experience in elective office, compared with five of the seven newly elected men. Political experience, it would seem, is even more central to the success of minority challengers than it is for white male challengers.

Will these demographic changes make any difference in congressional action? Some policy impact is likely: For example, every one of the newly elected women supports abortion rights. There may be some impact on the congressional agenda as well. A survey of half of all state legislators in 1991 found that "even when men and women shared the same party and ideology, women were much more likely to expend their energies on health care, children's and family questions and women's rights issues."[47] The survey also found that women public officials tended to bring government business out from behind closed doors and to involve private citizens in governmental processes, more than their male counterparts did. To the extent that women's life experiences differ from men's, the eyes through which Congress sees the nation could indeed have a different focus.

WILL THERE BE CHANGE IN CONGRESSIONAL BEHAVIOR?

The election brought other changes in the faces of Congress as well. Major committees gained a lot of new members, even though few committee chairs changed hands. Competition for committee seats was affected by members' anticipation of the Clinton agenda. Committees dealing with jobs, infrastructure, health, and environmental issues were expected to see more action in 1993, while those dealing with defense spending anticipated the agony of allocating spending cuts among the committees' constituencies.

There was little change in the congressional leadership. At organizational meetings in November, almost all of the party leaders of the 102nd Congress were reelected to their posts. They then turned their attention to the new freshman class, carrots and sticks at the ready. There had been no partisan swing comparable to those that had made possible the passage of Lyndon Johnson's Great Society legislation in 1965–66, or the Reagan agenda of tax cuts for upper-income people and corporations and the substantial defense buildup of the early 1980s. But there was the promise of something just as powerful: one-party control of both the executive and legislative branches.

Since World War II, the nation has had frequent experience with divided government, in which at least one house of Congress is controlled by a different party from that of the president. Divided-party control has occurred about two-thirds of the time since 1945, compared to only 12 percent of the time between 1897 and 1945.[48] That has prompted consternation by observers as disparate as David Broder and Dan Quayle. The charge is that a divided government is prone to gridlock and thus cannot be held accountable. We have elected Republican presidents on the basis of their pledge not to raise taxes, Jacobson argues, and Democratic members of Congress who have promised to protect and even expand domestic programs. The "fiscal fruit" is the constancy of budget deficits in recent years. "Neither side," he writes, "has been candid about the price."[49]

Divided government seemed to be at the root of problems in the 102nd Congress, which was described by the *Washington Post* as having "one of the thinnest records of legislative achievement within memory."[50] Action on the budget deficit, health care, and other major problems was notably absent. On issue after issue—gun control, reform of campaign finance laws, public school improvement, leave from work for family emergencies, abortion rights, simplified voter registration—"lawmakers brought a heavy load of legislation on a wide variety of issues to the verge of enactment, only to be thwarted by Republican filibusters in the Senate or by presidential vetoes that could not be overridden."[51]

The bill of charges against divided government is controversial, however. As logical as it sounds, research often contradicts it. Failure to pass a budget on time, increases in the national debt and in discretionary spending, and a decline in legislative productivity have been as common under unified governments as under divided governments.[52] Would the combination of a Democratic president and two Democratic houses of Congress resolve the stalemate? Clearly, there were no guarantees, as Jimmy Carter, the last president to serve with a Congress dominated by his party would readily attest.

Democratic congressional leaders worked to organize all House committees by Inauguration Day, about a month earlier than usual, in order to pass a raft of legislative proposals during the first hundred days of the Clinton administration. In early meetings with the president-elect, they spoke confidently of an end to gridlock. The prospects were complicated, however, by differences in their agendas.

Clinton, as he had during the campaign, stressed that his first step would be to "jump-start" the economy with an investment tax credit for businesses and more federal spending on job-creating infrastructure projects such as roads and sewers. But this effort at economic revival and job creation would inevitably delay moves to shrink the federal deficit, which many of the newly elected members had put high on their campaign agendas. These conflicting priorities were underscored by the need, in the first months of the Clinton administration, for Congress to increase the national debt ceiling (set at $4.1 trillion in 1990) to keep the Treasury from running out of authority to borrow money to pay the government's bills. Casting such a vote is politically painful, unless it is combined with a long-term deficit-reduction plan.

The freshmen will probably learn to live with the stimulus package. The budget deficit, worrisome as it is, remains less tangible to most constituents than are the pink slips of the unemployed. Despite the promises of many freshmen to seek a balanced-budget amendment and a line-item veto to restrain deficit spending, even more common were pledges to look after the interests of the folks back home. And the new members would not be pressured to act on the deficit by media interpretations of the congressional election results. In the first three weeks after election day, the explanations constructed by the national media emphasized the voters' desire for change, and their disgust at the scandals collectively represented by the House bank, much more than the impact of the economy or the deficit.[53]

Shadowing all these hopes for an end to gridlock, like the proverbial skunk at the garden party, was the lack of new money. The 1990 budget agreement required that new spending be funded either by budget cuts (with the further stipulation that money could not be shifted between domestic programs and defense) or new taxes. Much, then, rides on the shape of the 1993 budget agreement. If all new programs must be revenue neutral, then the wave of new members comes crashing into a most unpleasant choice: Their ideas for change must either cost nothing or be balanced by cuts in a program that some constituency values or lead to a tax increase. In that trio of unhappy options, the first—developing new programs that do not cost anything—is clearly the least painful. Yet the ideas that cost the federal government no revenues are often the very issues of social policy—abortion rights, family leave, campaign finance, regulations on gun sales—that are the most contentious, ideologically charged, and difficult to compromise.

President Clinton came into office, however, with twelve years of experience in working with legislators as governor of Arkansas and with substantial interpersonal skills; and congressional Democratic leaders were eager to work with him. Visions of the extraordinary productivity of Franklin D. Roosevelt's first hundred days, though wildly unrealistic in view of the nation's straitened economic circumstances, were widely mentioned. At the same time, Senate Republican Leader Robert Dole, while stepping around the word "obstruct," warned, "We're not going to be stampeded either.... It's not all going to be milk and honey for the Democrats."[54] A lobbyist close to the Senate Republican leadership stated more bluntly that the only Republican option was to "Throw sand in the gas tank."[55]

REFORM, TERM LIMITS, AND THE RESPONSIVENESS OF CONGRESS

Even as early as the previous spring, commentators were predicting that the expected turnover in the House would produce the fuel for internal reform. As political scientist Norman Ornstein put it, "We'll have 100 Wyatt Earps coming in to clean up the saloon."[56] One Earp hopeful, a Republican openseat candidate from California, took time during the campaign to plan a postelection meeting of newly elected House challengers in order to attack the seniority system and assure the new members of important committee positions. (He would not have been able to attend, however; he lost his race in November.)

As the election approached, continuing members debated changes that might head off the possibility of more drastic reforms. Representative Leon E. Panetta (D-Calif.): "The big fear is a class like that develops a dynamic of its own. That's the unknown quotient that's scaring the hell out of everyone."[57] Change was discussed in the areas of congressional perquisites and measures to reverse the decentralization that so often stymied congressional action. Liberal Democrats urged that the agenda-setting power of the party leadership and the rank and file be expanded at the expense of the "Old Bulls"—the powerful, long-time committee chairs. There were proposals to put term limits on committee chairs and ranking committee members and to streamline the number of subcommittees.

Continuing momentum for these changes would not necessarily come from the new members. In their early contact with the institution so many of them had portrayed in their campaigns as corrupt, the experienced politicians of the Class of 1992 managed to restrain their fervor for reform. The dynamic, however, was coming from outside Congress, in the movement to limit congressional terms. The theory was that if people could serve only a limited time in Congress, then competition would be restored and the status of members as a privileged class would be ended.

The term-limit movement began in earnest in 1990 when Colorado became the first state to vote to limit the terms of its congressional delegation. In the 1992 elections, fourteen states handily passed term-limit initiatives. Term-limit measures had an easy ride in most states, in part because few public figures had the incentive to make a case against them. Polls have consistently indicated that sizable majorities of the public favor a twelve-year limit for members of Congress.[58]

None of the measures was retroactive, so the only lawmakers likely to be affected would be the House members and senators elected for the first time in 1992. In all, and counting Colorado, fifty-eight new members began serving in the knowledge that their terms could be limited to between six and twelve years if the initiatives are upheld in the courts. Yet, ironically, in these same states, more than seventy incumbents were reelected who have already served longer than their state's term-limit measure would allow.

It is ironic as well that even without the initiatives, the average member of the House now serves no longer than he or she would be allowed to serve by many term-limitation measures: six two-year terms. And largely because of retirements, between 10 and 20 percent of House members in any given Congress are serving their first term—a larger proportion than one might expect after listening to arguments for limits (see figures 6.4 and 6.5). It seems

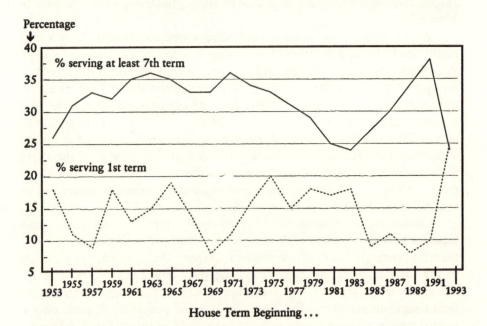

SOURCE: *Vital Statistics on Congress, 1991–1992,* 19–20. Figures for 1993 were calculated from *Congressional Quarterly Weekly Report,* 12 January 1991, 128–30, and 7 November 1992, 3577–78.

FIGURE 6.4

LENGTH OF SERVICE IN THE U.S. HOUSE, 1953–93

clear, then, that term limits are no more—and no less—than a symbolic expression of public frustration.

There are powerful arguments against limiting congressional terms.[59] None is more powerful, however, than that term limitation addresses the wrong problem. Term-limit measures rest on the assumption that members of Congress are unresponsive to public needs. In fact it is more realistic to argue that members are *hyper-responsive* to the demands of constituents. In spite of the continued incumbency advantage in elections, members continue to feel vulnerable.[60] The safest route to reelection, many feel, is through assiduous attention to servicing the requests of vocal groups and individuals. This route becomes even more attractive when, as is so often the case on major public problems, there is no broad consensus as to which policy is best.

But the collective result of all this individual responsiveness is not only an increasing debt but also a bankruptcy of direction.[61] If the reelection incentives all point in the direction of careful constituency service (and the

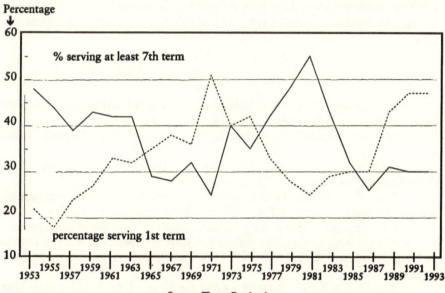

SOURCE: *Vital Statistics on Congress, 1991–1992,* 21. Figures for 1993 were calculated from *Congressional Quarterly Weekly Report,* 12 January 1991, 127, and 7 November 1992, 3558. The 1993 total includes the results of the Georgia and North Dakota races, and the successor to Senator Al Gore (Tenn.).

FIGURE 6.5

LENGTH OF SERVICE IN THE U.S. SENATE, 1953–93

group and individual contributions that it brings), combined with posturing on behalf of change, then the major policy issues facing the nation will remain unaddressed. Moreover, these incentives seriously hinder the development of stronger political parties, which could identify the policy choices and lead legislators to address them.

Term limits would certainly open up more congressional seats. But they would do nothing to change the incentive structure that now exists in congressional elections. Congressional reform could make it easier for the House and Senate to avoid gridlock. Unified government could permit those policies that do pass Congress to be tried. Media coverage could take Congress seriously as a policy-making institution, rather than primarily as a source of cheap shots (for which members, unfortunately, too often provide the material). Political parties could work to engage more voters, so as to stimulate more party voting in congressional races. Campaign finance reform could allow more challengers to give dissatisfied voters a real alternative. But until these events occur, with or without term limits, the increasing vulnerability felt by incumbents in 1992 will do no more than convince them that individual responsiveness, not collective problem solving, is the key to political success.

Notes

1. R.W. Apple, Jr., "Crystal Unclear: Will Tuesday's Disaffection Become Rejection at the 1992 Polls?" *New York Times*, 11 November 1990, sec. 4, p. 1.

2. W. Lance Bennett, *The Governing Crisis* (New York: St. Martin's, 1992), 9.

3. See Gary C. Jacobson, *The Politics of Congressional Elections*, 3d ed. (New York: HarperCollins, 1992), chap. 4.

4. Donald Gross and David Breaux, "Historical Trends in U.S. Senate Elections, 1912–1988," *American Politics Quarterly* 19 (July 1991): 284–309.

5. On campaign spending, see Jacobson, *Politics of Congressional Elections*.

6. Alan I. Abramowitz, "Incumbency, Campaign Spending, and the Decline of Competition in U.S. House Elections," *Journal of Politics* 53 (February 1991): 43, 47–49.

7. Kim Fridkin Kahn, "Incumbency and the News Media in U.S. Senate Elections: An Experimental Investigation," paper presented to the 1990 American Political Science Association annual meeting, August/September.

8. Richard Born, "Assessing the Impact of Institutional and Election Forces on Evaluations of Congressional Incumbents," *Journal of Politics* 53 (August 1991): 764–99.

9. Jacobson, *Politics of Congressional Elections*, 47–48.

10. David R. Mayhew, *Congress: The Electoral Connection* (New Haven: Yale University Press, 1974).

11. Abramowitz, "Incumbency, Campaign Spending," 35. But one study finds that the reverse is true: Narrow victories lead incumbents to work to secure more grants for their district. See Kenneth N. Bickers and Robert M. Stein, "Congressional Elections and the Pork Barrel," paper presented to the 1992 American Political Science Association annual meeting, September.

12. See Abramowitz, "Incumbency, Campaign Spending," 35.

13. Jacobson, *Politics of Congressional Elections*, 35.

14. Monica Bauer and John R. Hibbing, "Which Incumbents Lose in House Elections," *American Journal of Political Science* 33 (February 1989): 262–71.

15. Stephen Ansolabehere, David Brady, and Morris Fiorina, "The Vanishing Marginals and Electoral Responsiveness," *British Journal of Political Science* 22 (January 1992): 24.

16. Rhodes Cook, "Incumbents' National Status Breeds Local Distrust," *Congressional Quarterly Weekly Report*, 23 February 1991, 483.

17. Rhodes Cook, "Most House Members Survive, But Many Margins Narrow," *Congressional Quarterly Weekly Report*, 10 November 1990, 3798.

18. Cook, "Incumbents' National Status," 484.

19. Gary C. Jacobson, "Divided Government, Strategic Politicians, and the 1990 Congressional Elections," paper presented at the 1990 Midwest Political Science Association Annual Meeting, Chicago, 3–4.

20. For a valuable account of the events, see Phil Kuntz, "Check-Kiting at the House Bank: How It Worked, How It Didn't," *Congressional Quarterly Weekly Report*, 29 February 1992, 446–51.

21. Phil Kuntz, "Full Disclosure, Spin Control Await Beleaguered House," *Congressional Quarterly Weekly Report*, 14 March 1992, 599.

22. As reported in Craig Winneker, "Heard on the Hill," *Roll Call*, 8 October 1992, 14.

23. Jeffrey L. Katz, "Record Rate of Retirements Suggests Major Shakeup," *Congressional Quarterly Weekly Report*, 4 April 1992, 852.

24. Phil Kuntz, "McHugh Explains His Choice," *Congressional Quarterly Weekly Report*, 9 May 1992, 1227.

25. Rhodes Cook, "Incumbency Proves Liability in '92," *Congressional Quarterly Weekly Report*, 12 September 1992, 2774.

26. *Boston Globe*, 30 August 1992, 34.

27. Dave Kaplan and Bob Benenson, "The Hot, Hotter and Hottest of the November Contests," *Congressional Quarterly Weekly Report*, 19 September 1992, 2836–41.

28. Adam Clymer, "Voter Anger Propels Term-Limit Push," *New York Times*, 24 August 1992, A12.

29. Rep. Richard J. Durbin (D-Ill.), quoted in David S. Broder, "Democratic Incumbents Say Bush's Attacks Help," *Washington Post*, 3 September 1992, A13.

30. Rhodes Cook, "GOP Looking to Regain Footing," *Congressional Quarterly Weekly Report*, 8 August 1992, 9.

31. For a discussion of the diffusion of innovations in campaigns, see Marjorie Randon Hershey, *Running for Office* (Chatham, N.J.: Chatham House, 1984), 41–48 and chaps. 7, 8.

32. John R. Cranford, "The New Class: More Diverse, Less Lawyerly, Younger," *Congressional Quarterly Weekly Report,* 7 November 1992, 7.

33. Kenneth J. Cooper, "Freshmen House Democrats Stress Traditional Concerns of Party," *Washington Post,* 11 November 1992, A4.

34. Beth Donovan, "Freshmen Focus on the Product, Not on Legislative Process," *Congressional Quarterly Weekly Report,* 14 November 1992, 3626.

35. Data for 1988 and 1990 are from Jacobson, *Politics of Congressional Elections,* 190. The figures for 1992 were calculated from election data provided in *Congressional Quarterly Weekly Report,* 7 November 1992, 3600–3607.

36. Percentages for 1988 and 1990 are from Jacobson, *The Politics of Congressional Elections,* 187; and *Congressional Quarterly Weekly Report,* 10 November 1990, 3847–54. Figures for 1992 were calculated as indicated in note 35.

37. Jacobson, *Politics of Congressional Elections,* 55–58.

38. Phil Kuntz, "Overdrafts Were a Potent Charge," *Congressional Quarterly Weekly Report,* 7 November 1992, 3575.

39. Lou Cannon et al., "Senate Incumbents' PAC Advantage," *Washington Post,* 25 October 1992, A23.

40. Glenn R. Simpson, "Why Did So Few Incumbents Lose Nov. 3?" *Roll Call,* 9 November 1992, 2.

41. John W. Mashek, "Campaign System Turns Fund-raising into D.C. Addiction," *Birmingham News,* 14 October 1990, 5C.

42. R. Darcy, Susan Welch, and Janet Clark, *Women, Elections, and Representation* (New York: Longman, 1987).

43. Beth Donovan, "Women's Campaigns Fueled Mostly by Women's Checks," *Congressional Quarterly Weekly Report,* 17 October 1992, 3269–73.

44. "A Mood of Political Activism May Reveal Itself this Election," *Herald-Times* (Bloomington, Ind.), 9 October 1992, A8.

45. Dale Russakoff, "Arlen Specter on the Case," *Washington Post National Weekly Edition,* 14–20 September 1992, 9.

46. Eleanor Holmes Norton, the nonvoting delegate from Washington, D.C., is the forty-eighth.

47. R.W. Apple, Jr., "Steady Local Gains by Women Fuel More Runs for High Office," *New York Times,* 24 May 1992, sec. 4, p. 5.

48. James A. Thurber, "Representation, Accountability, and Efficiency in Divided Party Control of Government," *PS,* December 1991, 653.

49. Jacobson, "Divided Government," 8.

50. Helen Dewar, "102nd Congress Often Was Thwarted by Senate Filibusters and Bush Vetoes," *Washington Post,* 11 October 1992, A33.

51. Ibid.

52. See Thurber, "Representation"; and David R. Mayhew, *Divided We Govern: Party Control, Lawmaking, and Investigations, 1946–1990* (New Haven: Yale University Press, 1991).

53. On the process by which explanations are constructed for election results, see Marjorie Randon Hershey, "The Constructed Explanation: Interpreting Election Results in the 1984 Presidential Race," *Journal of Politics* 54 (November 1992): 943–76.

54. Pamela Fessler, "Clinton Plans for Smooth Start With Focus on the Economy," *Congressional Quarterly Weekly Report,* 7 November 1992, 3554.

55. Phil Kuntz, "Soon to Lose White House Clout, Republicans Rethink Strategy," *Congressional Quarterly Weekly Report,* 14 November 1992, 3625.

56. R.A. Zaldivar, "New Faces in House May Give Voters Hope for Internal Reform," *Miami Herald,* 22 March 1992, 5A.

57. Beth Donovan, "Visions of the Next Congress Inspire Reform Proposals," *Congressional Quarterly Weekly Report,* 3 October 1992, 3017.

58. Ronald E. Elving, "Foley Helps Put the Brakes on Drive for Term Limits," *Congressional Quarterly Weekly Report,* 9 November 1991, 3262.

59. Jacobson, *Politics of Congressional Elections,* 247.

60. See Richard F. Fenno, Jr., *Home Style* (Boston: Little, Brown, 1978).

61. See Ansolabehere et al., "Vanishing Marginals," 36.

7

The Meaning of the Election

WILSON CAREY MCWILLIAMS

And all the unsettled humours of the land . . .
Have sold their fortunes at their native homes,
Bearing their birthrights proudly on their backs,
To make a hazard of new fortunes here.

— *The Life and Death of King John* (II, i)

Half a millennium ago, Columbus, unwitting, landed in a new world, and Americans in 1992 suspected that, like him, they had arrived at some unexpected place, full of unfamiliar shadows.[1] In the election, most Americans allowed themselves to be drawn by hope, but they went wistfully, driven by worries and without much confidence, convinced that they had more to fear than fear itself.

Change was in the air: For the first time in more than half a century, a presidential election was not framed by war, present or rumored; voters were restless; new concerns and constituencies made themselves felt; and the victorious Democrats proclaimed themselves a "new" party. Yet no election has so often or so pervasively been compared to the American past; Americans wanted assurance of comparability if not continuity, looking for old landmarks and fixed stars in the strange new world they confronted.

The election was likened to the contest in 1932 and to earlier third-party elections, especially the races in 1912, 1968, and 1980.[2] Observers drew parallels between Bush and other defeated incumbents—Taft, Carter, and most insistently, Herbert Hoover.[3] On the other side, analysts sought Clinton's prototype in Carter, in Kennedy, even in Franklin Roosevelt.[4] For obvious reasons, Clinton was not often compared to Truman, that tower of straight talk

190

and private rectitude, but he did claim Truman's legacy. It was a heritage much in demand: Perot had designs on it and so, even more implausibly, did George Bush. Both comparisons were bizarre, and not only because Bush, a dutiful son of a Republican family, had voted for Dewey in 1948. Unlike Perot, Truman was a partisan and an insider, whose life was spent in the environs of politics and who never shook—or really sought to shake—his association with the Pendergast machine. And Truman, the come-from-behind campaigner Bush hoped to emulate, himself ran an almost completely partisan campaign, with few references to his opponent and no attacks on his character.[5] Lyndon Johnson, however, was not used as a model for the three candidates, although through Vietnam and racial politics he was a presence in the campaign; in 1992, Americans showed signs of making their peace with Johnson's lacerating failure and his equally troubling success.

In any event, a great many Americans, viewing the present, found themselves attracted to earlier times, especially to their moments of strength and exuberance. After the "numbness" of the presidential debates, Russell Baker wrote, "the mind finds itself shamefully yearning for a benighted time when vigor, sassiness, confidence, even arrogance, expressed itself in the national spirit."[6] In 1992, confidence did not point Americans to the future, it drew them to the past; and the election, a vote for change, was also a hope for renewal.

Economic Disorder and the American Civil Order

In one sense, the election is easily explained: Bush, R.W. Apple, Jr., noted, was "the economy's casualty."[7] The bad portents began to be apparent early on; by August 1991, Warren Brookes was arguing that the economy's woes might make Bush a "sitting duck" for the Democrats, and so it proved.[8] Democrats refused to be distracted and, in the end, achieved something close to their old fantasy, an election fought out simply on economic terms.[9]

The numbers were depressing. Unemployment was relatively high, job creation had virtually stopped, and the Gross National Product (GNP) was going nowhere.[10] Yet as Bush complained rather plaintively, the data were not *that* bad, especially when compared to other countries, and there were bright spots, such as low inflation and low interest rates.[11]

The greatest problem for the president lay behind the figures. Short-term calculations and immediate economic experiences, and even self-interest, narrowly defined, are less potent politically than judgments about the future and about the country as a whole.[12] In 1988, Bush parroted Ronald Reagan's 1980 question, "Are you better off than you were four years ago?" and the promise of improvement haunted him in 1992. But Reagan himself withstood worse economic conditions in the congressional elections of 1982, when the Republicans suffered relatively light losses because voters were convinced he had a star to steer by. In 1992, by contrast, the country felt no such assurance about times to come. Even during the Great Depression, Americans could take comfort in being the world's largest creditor, an industrial powerhouse with a favorable balance of trade and little public debt. All those consolations are now turned upside down, and the recession in 1992 differed from any since World War II "in the near certainty that it is not a prelude to any substantial recovery."[13]

Voters had been inclined to say that the country was on the "wrong track" even when Bush's ratings were high, and time only added to their pessimism.[14] Material well-being was only a part of the story: For many of the electorate in 1992, the economic issue was dignity for themselves and their country.

In the beginning of the republic, Jefferson observed that virtually all free men could enjoy the degree of economic independence necessary to self-governing citizenship. He relied, in his familiar thesis, on the existence of abundant land, available to yeoman proprietors, but it was also important, he wrote later on, that even those who worked for wages could expect to find "comfortable subsistence" and the ability to provide for old age.[15] In the latter argument, the critical factor is not income, although Jefferson presumes a socially adequate wage; his case relies on the worker's confidence that he will be able to find work at "satisfactory" pay so that no worker feels unduly dependent on a particular employer. And through much of our history, with only a little distortion, Americans have been able to take that condition as the ordinary rule.

Contemporary Americans are less likely to enjoy that good fortune. Blue-collar labor, once a kind of aristocracy, has been watching its position deteriorate for years: The 1991 *Economic Report to the President* indicated that the average weekly wage of blue-collar workers had fallen 20 percent since 1972.[16] Middle-class families generally have been able to keep incomes stable or rising, but only by relying on second wage earners, working longer hours, and borrowing, caught in the cycle of "work and spend."[17] More and more households, too, have found their health insurance threatened as employers seek to control costs.[18]

By a good many reckonings, the income of Americans in the middle sectors of society has been stagnant for a decade, and the U.S. Census Bureau recently noted a long-term decline in the percentage of Americans ranked in the middle class.[19] Inequality is growing, reaching "Great Gatsby levels," Paul Krugman says; even on the right, Charles Murray is troubled by the disparity between a considerable elite (10 to 20 percent) that can "bypass institutions it doesn't like" and the rest of the public, foreshadowing a society divided into the exempt and the trapped.[20]

During the Reagan years, this increase in inequality could be treated, in middle-class America, as only the other side of opportunity.[21] The recession of 1992, however, struck at the jobs of white-collar labor, its threat magnified by the fact that the middle class carries a burden of debt and expectations that makes its way of life exceptionally vulnerable.[22] Whole layers of management are disappearing, apparently for good, as companies strive to become "lean." Moreover, such jobs as are being created—blue and white collar—include a growing number of temporary positions, evidently less secure, with lower wages and benefits.[23]

Economic troubles, bad enough by themselves, were interwoven with concern for civil order and the decencies of private life. Despite devotion to "family values," the deterioration of families escalated during the Reagan-Bush years: the number of single-parent households increased by almost 50 percent, and too many of those families are desperately poor, while even in economically better-off homes with two parents, the demands of work drain time and quality from family life.[24] At best, families are losing autonomy; the media begin to inculcate their "hidden curriculum" in infancy, before literacy and to some extent even before speech.[25] Visible in the media, if not in day-to-day life, divorce, feminism, and the demand for gay rights, to say nothing of new ethnic diversities, are undermining old certainties. Change and mobility continue to make us hesitant about commitments to persons and places, and in a more overtly sinister way, crime keeps citizens away from public spaces, barring doors when it does not prompt a retreat to some place of relative safety.[26] The affluent are inclined to seek private solutions and immunities, while the less fortunate have their own forms of privatization, most destructively in the autoanesthesia of drugs.[27] Too many Americans are alone, frightened or uncivil, and all of us are at least a bit bewildered. Living in a state of anxious vulnerability, if not privation, multitudes of Americans in 1992 were disgusted with an administration that they saw as out of touch, indifferent, and ineffective.

Foreign policy, George Bush's strong suit, gave him little help. With some pride, the president argued that because of Republican successes, Americans could sleep without fear of nuclear war, but that claim moved few voters.[28] The collapse of Soviet communism softened the glue that had held the conservative coalition together, and for most Americans, foreign threats seemed distant, hypothetical or unpersuasive.[29] In August, Bush tried a little showy "toughness" with Iraq, but no other "October surprise" materialized, apart from the self-wounding search through the Clintons' passport files. Possibly the administration realized that, as Leslie Gelb observed, presidents "have so often abused the national interest for their own political ends" that Americans have come to take partisan purposes for granted.[30] Disillusionment hovered even around Bush's triumph in the Gulf war, which appeared more and more suspect and inconclusive, a mood typified by the bumper stickers that read *Saddam Has a Job. Do You?*[31]

In fact, foreign policy added to the American sense of economic and civic vulnerability. American borders are now permeated by foreign products, capital, and labor.[32] Foreign governments, too, play increasingly evident roles in American politics, as Ross Perot, with some exaggeration, so often observed. In 1988, Kevin Phillips claims, the Bank of Japan helped Bush so much "it should have registered as a Republican political action committee," and this year, the Miyazawa government, similarly inclined, ordered Japanese companies to ship fewer cars to the United States than they were allowed under Japan's self-imposed quota.[33] Americans became accustomed to hearing that their economy is no longer "world class," and already wounded by slighting comments from Japanese leaders, they were not reassured by Bush's feckless assertiveness in Tokyo, which came across as "bashing on bended knee."[34]

Clinton, an internationalist and, these days, a moderate hawk, demonstrated a respectable aptitude for foreign policy, and many observers ended by sharing Gelb's verdict that Bush, an able leader in dealing with the "old security and power issues," was not up to the economic concerns that now occupy center stage in international politics.[35]

The Skeptical Search for an Active Government

The clearest message of 1992 was the majority's demand for active government, engaged to relieve America's discontents and reclaim the future. Even in 1988, opinion had tended to side with the candidate who, on any given issue, supported the use of public power.[36] This time, the tide was unmistakable: 62 percent voted for the differing, but undeniably activist persuasions of Clinton and Perot.

It was a hard year for laissez-faire. Rhetorically, the high point of the Democratic campaign was Mario Cuomo's attack on Bush for relying on "the invisible hand of some cyclical economic god" to save the ship of state, and less elegantly, the Democratic campaign featured denunciations of "trickle-down economics."[37] Even conservatives, of course, now accept a considerable degree of economic intervention: Ronald Reagan promised a "safety net," the Reagan and Bush administrations committed billions to protect depositors in failing banks and savings and loans, and the administration took it for granted that the Federal Reserve should manage interest rates to promote growth.[38] In 1992, the current of activism ran even stronger. Among economists, there was something of a generational shift, reminiscent of the advent of Keynes, with practice brought to the critique of economic theory.[39] Clinton found no shortage of economists willing to agree, for example, that government is needed to promote saving and investment, especially since Reagan's reliance on the classical "equivalence theorem"—that government spending will lead to private saving—had proved misplaced.[40] By itself, moreover, investment may not be enough: Counter to much conventional wisdom, there is good evidence that American productivity is not low. The problem may be that relative efficiency is being purchased at the price of employment, and so that government is needed to link investment, productivity, and work.[41]

Americans were only a little less likely to look to government to shore up the social and moral foundations of society or to build new ones. Most were inclined to think that government should support the family in some way or other.[42] Conservative noise about family should not obscure the fact that liberals, though they differ in their definitions of the family and the policies they recommend, are eager to extend help.[43] The willingness to involve government in civil life extends beyond the family: The communitarian movement has attracted support from a broad spectrum of intellectuals, while in practice, 1992 saw several states attempt to link welfare rights with obligations.[44] Even the vogue of environmental protection, limits to growth, and historic preservation, while often tied to fairly narrow self-interest, also reflects an effort to enlist policy on the side of community.[45]

This is part of an old story, for conservatism's concern for "values," often bigoted and bumbling, touches a truth. Government by itself cannot make us good, but it can encourage decency by reducing its costs and by raising the price of indecent behavior.[46] In America, that role of government has been vital: Our customs and culture are not immemorial, but the result of a more or less conscious design, a people engaged in making itself.[47] American culture has been a perennially political issue, so it is no surprise that the contemporary "culture war" finds its way into democratic politics.[48] In fact, we ought to hope that the conflict can be expressed in, and confined to, democratic forms.

Unfortunately, our confidence on the point cannot be very great. Although Americans turned to government in 1992, they distrusted it and were apt to despise politics; a year earlier, Peter Hart and Douglas Bailey found that although voters "desperately want to believe in government," they were deeply disillusioned, so there was a "dangerously broad gulf between the governors and the governed."[49]

All our public pillars were more or less damaged.[50] Congress, which never stood too well with the public, was injured by legislative delay, the "scandal" at the House bank, and most of all, by the hearings on Justice Clarence Thomas's confirmation. Watching Thomas and Anita Hill before the Judiciary Committee, voters divided on the basis of gender and class, but virtually all felt contempt for politicians, and David Rohde saw the hearings as one event in the long-term "undermining of respect for institutions."[51]

Historically, the presidency has been less exposed to scorn than Congress, but a long series of abuses—Watergate, Iran-contra, and what the media began to call "Iraqgate"—has worked its hurt. Carter's perceived failure left its weight of doubt, as did Reagan's increasingly evident ineptitude, and George Bush never had Reagan's teflon charm.[52]

The decline of political parties, of course, has long been apparent, and this year the low level of partisan allegiance was reflected in the oscillation of the polls.[53] Voters, seeing money as dominant in elections and increasingly convinced that corruption is the political rule, feel a lack of voice and representation; in a 1990 Times-Mirror poll, 57 percent of respondents agreed that "people like me don't have any say about what government does."[54] This mood of disaffiliation and deauthorization in turn encourages citizens to look outside the institutions or to the negations of protest politics, a disposition especially clear among those attracted to Ross Perot—a candidate by "immaculate conception," Garry Wills said, untainted by politics.[55] Perot voters, Richard Marin and E.J. Dionne, Jr., found, had no good words for political parties, and while a large number expressed a desire for a third party, they did so not because of any positive convictions or any confidence in democratic politics, but simply because they were applying a free-market model to politics, relying on the logic of competition.[56]

It was to be expected, then, that along with some hope, the electorate harbored an abiding doubt that government can succeed.[57] And although it has been almost twenty-five years since an active president dealt with a legislature of the same party—in many ways, Carter was suspect on both counts —the voters' lack of confidence is not simply instrumental. It reflects an accentuated mistrust of government's moral title and the suspicion that politicians have no goal except self-perpetuation.[58] Divided government, after all, has been the creation of distrust, the mirror of deauthorization.[59] It also set in motion its own vicious cycle: The voters' disaffiliation has made leaders shy away from any policies with immediate costs, resulting in a "no pain" politics, full of posturings, such as the Balanced Budget Amendment, frustrating for leaders and citizens alike.[60] Political leaders have become more contemptuous of the electorate, not always so secretly, while the voters—on a generous reading—were left with a "grumpy cynicism."[61]

The prevailing discontents made it all the more striking that voter turnout in 1992 reversed the long decline in participation.[62] That the race was apparently closing undoubtedly helped, as did the fact that so many voters felt themselves immediately threatened by the recession. These factors, more or less specific to 1992, suggest that voters may easily lapse into their old indifference; over the long haul, individuals calculating self-interested utilities will find only inadequate reasons for going to the polls. Consistent participation presumes a fuller involvement in community life.[63] The signal in 1992 was faint, but Americans did hint that they are willing to be drawn back into the political system by any relatively entertaining show.[64]

Public Life and Private Politics

Clinton's great challenge, and the republic's, lies in the need to strengthen the dignity of citizenship and the quality of democratic consent. Knowing this, Clinton plans something approximating a permanent campaign, but the media, a part of his intended solution, are an even bigger part of the political problem.

Earlier in our history, Alexis de Tocqueville had no doubt that the press was an essentially representative institution, deriving much of its authority from the power of communities to hold it accountable. Like the media we know, the press of Tocqueville's day was inclined to slight principles in favor of personalities and to pursue public figures into their private lives. Tocqueville saw a press, however, that was local and intimate with its readers, enjoying less power than a mass press, but more authority, so that it was less likely to "give way to the current of the multitude."[65] Bound up with its communities, Tocqueville thought, the press was better able to instruct them and might even suggest from time to time that private and local interests should yield to the public good.[66] The "old news," Bill Moyers writes in the same spirit, "drew people to the public square" and helped teach the "vital habits of democracy."[67]

In contemporary America, in contrast, the dominant forms of the press are media by which information is communicated *to* us, but without any serious element of reciprocity or accountability.[68] We depend on the media and recognize their power, but our dependence is a mark of voicelessness and indignity.[69]

Recognizing our resentment and their lack of authority, the media are desperately anxious to please us, as Tocqueville would have expected, especially since few things are easier than changing channels. But in the first place, that disposition makes the media contemptible and incapable of self-regulation without limiting their power. In 1992, for example, the media's early resolution to forego sensational inquiries into the private lives of candidates crumbled under the impact of the supermarket tabloids, and the whole of the press was soon engaged in what one British paper called "sexual McCarthyism."[70] Similarly, concerned with criticism of the ever-shortening "sound bite"—down to 7.3 seconds, by one calculation, in 1988—CBS decided that all sound bites would, henceforth, be 30 seconds or more. But news editors, reaching the conclusion that such "bites" were unavailable or "unwieldy," eliminated them almost altogether, showing reporters more and candidates less.[71] And second, even the determination of *how* to please us is made by the media, on the basis of criteria and evidence they choose. This unauthorized decision making fuels the fear of some secret political design. In 1992, conservatives were particularly apt to detect a hostile conspiracy, or at least a tilt to the left, but plenty of liberals heard a tune called by Republican elites.[72] In fact, the media are probably shaped less by political intent than by "mass circulation images, themselves squeezed by commercial pressures," a principle just as troubling.[73]

The opinions that guide the media are not genuinely public, though they come from the people. The media reach us in private settings and address largely private concerns and feelings, relying on images more than words.[74] Where radio, as Russell Baker remembers, "intoxicated us with voices," the contemporary media discount speech, continuing the grand modern impulse, initiated by Machiavelli, to exalt the visible and nonverbal, the deed as opposed to the word.[75] To the extent that they are treated by the media at all, political speech and deliberation are presented as a kind of theater of deception, in which content matters only as clue to covert forces and schemes. In response to the president's State of the Union message, John Tierney noted that "the chief question raised by analysts on television was not whether his proposals made any sense, but how the Democrats would respond to his staff's strategy."[76]

This year, American resentment of the media turned so explosive that suddenly the campaign was dominated by "new" news—"weird media," Bush said—the talk shows and tabloids, Don Imus and Arsenio Hall, Larry King and the "infomercial."[77] Ross Perot was the first to see the advantages of the new vehicles; Clinton, damaged by the more orthodox media, soon followed. The new media have undeniable benefits: They are apt to be free, and they allow candidates to develop positions in depth, or at length, at any rate. Clinton turned to them in some relief. After a frustrating, much-trivialized primary in New York, Clinton sought to use his victory speech to direct public attention to the substance of his campaign, but after four minutes, all the networks except for CNN and C-Span stopped their coverage, and CNN dropped out after nine minutes. Network news reduced the speech to sound bites, and the next morning, on the "Today Show," Clinton's remarks had been shrunk to "I love

Wisconsin, Minnesota and Kansas, and I really love New York."[78] The talk shows, by contrast, allowed Clinton to display his virtuosity and command of the issues.[79] The new media, moreover, worked to diminish the advantage the party in power draws from its ability to dominate television news, and Republicans can be expected to cultivate them in force in 1996.[80]

For viewers, what mattered in the "new news" was face-to-face interaction with hosts and with audiences, or hearing candidates field called-in questions, an approximation, even if weak, of town-meeting democracy. But the "community," produced for the media, is only another image that can be managed. It comes into being around and because of leaders—the hosts or their guests—so that the talk shows only emphasize, as Ellen Hume put it, "that the media are our new political bosses—the direct filter that parties used to be."[81] The media audience cannot hold its studio "representatives" accountable, nor can the individuals who make up the "community" of questioners speak to one another without the assistance of the media themselves. The "electronic town hall," Gerald Marzorati wrote, is what passes for civic community when people live among strangers and the "friendliest colleagues are the computer, database and fax."[82] The new media, in sum, did not renew American citizenship, although they may have made citizenship seem interesting; as David Broder noted early on, they offered only the "catharsis" of "highly contrived dramas."[83]

Nothing in 1992 changed the fact that masses of Americans, inundated with information, know they lack the means of separating the false from the true.[84] As Michael Rogin argues, all too many citizens find themselves facing a baffling, overwhelming, and often arcane government in the "paranoid position" of "disordering powerlessness" and are tempted to equally paranoid analysis.[85] They are nudged further in that direction by the media's blurring of the line between politics and fiction, exemplified by the rise of the docudrama and movies like Oliver Stone's *JFK*.[86] This aspect of the media weakens the check of reality and encourages "splitting," the psychological process by which heroes or times past are idealized—as with John Kennedy or the "inheritance" denied to young Americans—while their negative qualities are disowned and identified with demonized and conspiratorial enemies.[87]

There were plenty of examples in 1992. Ross Perot, pushing aside evidence of his own use of investigators and personal threats, as well as his dealings with foreign governments, talked a good deal about the plots of Republican dirty tricksters and foreign agents in major-party campaigns.[88] Most pervasively, however, homosexuals—as Rogin pointed out—were identified with erotic and social disorder; this was true of the leftist fantasy of Oliver Stone, of the falangist rhetoric of Patrick Buchanan on the right, and of Perot's fear that appointing a gay cabinet member would cause "controversy" or that his daughter might be portrayed as a lesbian.

There was no shortage of Americans who, sharing such persuasions, were eager for a leader able to cut through the thicket of democratic politics. And others, less troubled, shared the same impatience.

The candidacy of Ross Perot epitomized many of the themes of 1992, but it would have been impossible without the media. On their battlefield, Perot proved a master strategist. He opened and promoted his candidacy through talk shows, trailing a stream of one-liners; he demonstrated the viability of the "infomercial"; and week by week, he spent more money purchasing time for his interrupted campaign than any previous candidate.[89] Perot showed that with grand salesmanship and enough money it is possible to become a major force without passing through the primaries or the parties, and dodging the press where he could not dominate it, he avoided almost all the scrutiny that goes with a traditional campaign.[90]

Of course, even Perot could not entirely sidestep the old modes, and Perot the candidate repeatedly undermined Perot the strategist, revealing too much of his testy, autocratic, and paranoid streak.[91] Yet at the beginning of the campaign, Perot was able to present himself as a candidate of force who could solve all problems magically, virtually without cost—"without breaking a sweat," as he liked to say—and otherwise, as a tabula rasa on which voters could write their own scripts and fantasies.[92]

Recognition that ending the deficit would call for taxes and for sacrifice of a high order helped persuade Perot to quit the race.[93] When he returned, he retained the image of "can do" forcefulness, now combined with a "message" that—vague in so many details—was presented as complete and tied to Perot's persona.[94]

The common thread of Perot's two campaigns was his demand for quick solutions and his unwillingness to do the prolonged work of persuasion and compromise within institutions. Hostility to institutions, in fact, was a major part of his appeal. In May, the great majority of Bush and Clinton supporters, while critical of Congress generally, approved the job being done by their own House members, but 55 percent of those supporting Perot disapproved.[95] That unhappiness fit neatly with Perot's discounting of representative government and his disdain for conflicts of interest and party, the messy charms of democratic politics.[96] The instinct of the entrepreneur, Michael Schrage observed, is the desire to create new forms, and hence to reject established institutions; Perot had the special attraction of an "outsider" who was knowledgeable about the system, one who did not offer to dismantle government but promised to make it stronger and more effective.[97] In addition, the nationalism of his antiforeign themes amounted to a pledge to restore the American imperium as a part of America's inheritance.

Repeatedly, Perot's campaign was linked to the "tradition of prairie populism," but the stark differences between his movement and the old Populism illustrate the difficulties of contemporary democratic life.[98] The Populists of 1892 grew out of and were composed of a dense forest of membership groups and face-to-face communities, so the People's party was a federation of localities and associations, held close to the grass roots.[99] The party abounded in policies, many spelled out in detailed plans: The Sub-Treasury system; free silver; the graduated income tax; the government ownership of railroads, telegraph, and telephone were only the most prominent.[100] But the Populists of 1892 had trouble finding a candidate. Their best bet, Polk of North Carolina, died before the convention, and Judge Walter Gresham turned them down. In the end, they nominated a veteran but rather uninspiring radical, General James B. Weaver, more or less because "there was little else left to do."[101]

By contrast, Perot's movement was constructed from the top down, its organization at least inspired and certainly sustained by Perot's money. It offered few policies; only the deficit-reduction program, the centerpiece of the second campaign, had much solidity. Above all, Perot's movement was centered on and defined by its candidate. Even Perot's version of the "electronic town hall," George Will pointed out, involved citizens giving information to the leader, not discussing or making decisions among themselves—an image, Will thought, shaped by the mystique of leadership with which Woodrow Wilson had invested the presidency.[102]

"I'm doing this for the American people," Perot often declared, "because they can't do it for themselves." Just so. Whatever the legacy of Perot's candidacy, it pointed to our distance from Populism's promise and to the endangered status of democratic citizenship.

The State of the Political Parties

Perot's candidacy, of course, also testified to discontent with the nominating process. In droves, voters rejected the primary system, grumbling about the choices offered and staying away from the polls. Many, a plurality at one point, found themselves supporting Perot despite the fact that he had avoided primaries altogether. The system, Russell Baker wrote, "is dead, dead, dead and ought to be buried before it kills the two major parties."[103]

Baker's obituary was premature. The primary system was wounded, but it will survive, especially because the Democrats won the election. Bush's nomination made many voters unhappy, but they saw that it was more or less inevitable; Clinton's candidacy was the source of more murmuring, and his success will quiet many critics.

Yet Clinton did emerge from the primary season as a flawed candidate, so damaged by doubts about his character that crowds of Democrats would have preferred someone else, just as they would have done when campaigning began.[104] The primary system, however, forced candidates to choose early, when Bush looked like a sure winner. The leading Democrats opted to wait for more likely times, leaving the field to long-shot players. Mario Cuomo might have entered relatively late in the game, but he took himself out, and the Democrats were left with the candidates in the field. The primary system has enough residual democratic legitimacy to prevent the party conventions from setting aside the verdict of its long string of elections.[105]

The primaries gave the Democrats two consolations in 1992. In the first place, President Bush was also scarred by Pat Buchanan's challenge. Moved to confess that he had made a "mistake" in agreeing to higher taxes, Bush added evident weakness to the sin of broken promises. And the president and his advisers responded curiously to the returns. In New Hampshire and after, Buchanan's supporters were mostly independents intent on "sending a message," voters who crossed the ideological spectrum. Bush, however, seemed to hear only the clamor on the right, setting a pattern for the campaign.[106]

Second, although the primaries ended with Perot ascendant and the Democrats near desperation, Clinton proved a supremely resilient candidate who played his hand well. Happy with the result, Democrats need to remember that Clinton's nomination was itself a chancy business, since it turned on Jesse Jackson's decision to stay out of the race and on the fact that Governor Douglas Wilder did not prove to be a viable candidate. Everywhere, Clinton had a decisive advantage among black voters, and that edge was critical to his victories. Had he lost those votes to Jackson or another African American candidate, he might have done no better on Super Tuesday than Senator Al Gore did in 1988, when Jackson won some southern primaries and Michael Dukakis squeaked by in Texas and Florida.[107] In this sense, Jackson, absent, was still a master spirit. His decision to forego the primaries allowed Clinton to build a class coalition across racial lines, the foundation for his success in November.

The Democrats have always been the more fractious party, a coalition of localities, ethnicities, and interests full of inner conflict and including ancient enemies united only by a sense of exclusion and opposition to the status quo. The GOP ordinarily has more positive bonds, with the defense of the established order—especially the private economy—as the party's bottom line.[108]

Social Issues: The Democrats and Race

For contemporary Democrats, race has been the bittersweet apple of discord.

This is not an entirely new story, since Democrats began to lose support in the South in the 1940s; but since 1964, Democratic championship of blacks and other minorities has led to defections that have been nationwide, chronic, and ordinarily decisive in presidential elections. Liberal Democrats did not acknowledge quickly enough that middle- and working-class whites were bearing a disproportionate part of the social and economic burden of the quest for equality, and their failure to redistribute those costs made it seem, to many traditional Democrats, that the party had deserted them in favor of minorities on one hand and liberal elites on the other.[109] And Republicans have been forward and effective in cultivating that view.

In 1992, however, race was a dog that did not bark, noteworthy for its relative absence as an issue in the campaign. In the second presidential debate, Carole Simpson had to prod her audience to ask about the politics of race, and even her insistence brought only a vapid inquiry about how soon minorities or women might be elected president or vice-president. The silence was more evident because the occasions of racial conflict were so thunderous: The rioting in Los Angeles that followed the verdict in the trial of the police officers who had arrested and beaten Rodney King, only an extreme case of urban ethnic conflict, forced more insulated Americans to look, briefly, at the ravaged ground and human desperation of the inner city. The sight was so dreadful that most Americans were happy to turn to something else, while for Americans of all races, economic conditions helped to discount other concerns.[110]

More specifically political factors were also at work. Ron Brown's visibility as national chairman symbolized the fact, recognized by an increasing number of African Americans, that blacks are no longer outsiders pressuring Democrats, but the new regulars, the heart of the party.[111] That perception strengthened the impulse, at least among leaders and activists, to find common ground, and with it, a willingness to speak the language of class rather than race.[112] Some of the most compelling African American voices showed themselves uneasy with the old shibboleths.[113] For Democrats of all races, moreover, the Los Angeles riots emphasized the need to win, making ideology less compelling than the need to end the decade of neglect, to do something to ease the agony of the inner city and the sense of superfluity that is the most terrible affliction of the underclass. It was part of the temper of 1992 that a surprisingly wide spectrum of African American leaders supported the principle that, just as all citizens have contributions to make, public assistance is rightly tied to responsibilities.[114] Clinton, William Julius Wilson wrote, spoke to "those who have grown weary of destructive racial rhetoric," and this year, that disposition counted.[115]

It allowed Clinton to distance himself from Sister Souljah and from Jesse

Jackson, a decisive gesture to "Reagan Democrats," without any significant loss of support from African Americans.[116] Although not enough blacks went to the polls, Clinton gathered the percentage of support among African Americans that Democrats have come to expect, in part because, whatever his other maneuvers, he addressed and appealed to their dignity as citizens.[117] Intermittently, in Clinton's rhetoric, there were intimations of a republic of equals.

Social Issues: The Republicans and Religion

Where the Democrats achieved a reasonable degree of unity, the Republicans called attention to their most troublesome divisions. The Reagan years made the GOP more discordant; its new accessions of strength, especially among social conservatives and the religious right, are also occasions for quarrel. The old rift between Main Street and Wall Street was, in large measure, a difference of interest; the new dissensions are matters of faith and culture.[118]

This year's Republican convention, the party's opening to the nation at large, was more or less given over to the cultural right. Its stridency, mirrored in the early part of the Bush campaign, presented Republicans in a role that, since 1964, had been claimed most often by Democrats, a party captured by ideologues and zealots.[119] The prominence of the right helped fracture the Republican coalition: In 1988, 90 percent of Republican voters supported Bush, but in 1992, his share fell to 73 percent, most of the defectors going to Perot.[120]

Still, while the Republicans ran a maladroit campaign, marked by arrogance and misjudgment, their strategists had reason to think that a turn to the right and an emphasis on "family values" was their best alternative.[121] Bush, always a poor candidate, was saddled with the stumbling economy, and it made matters worse that, by pledging to make voters "better off," he had invited them to desert him in hard times.[122] Unlike Reagan, Bush has no gift for political poetry. He is guided by certain working rules—good manners, confidence in the market economy, and devotion to the national interest—but, notoriously, he regards the "vision thing" as a word-spinning disturbance to the logic of practice, propriety, and power.[123] In 1988, Dukakis's emphasis on "competence" allowed Bush to present himself as the candidate of principles, but that opportunity was not offered in 1992, and in fact, Bush frequently seemed to be a weather vane, pointing in whatever direction he was blown by opinion or perceived political advantage.[124]

Needing an appeal that would be proof against economic distress, at a time when foreign policy no longer galvanized voters, Bush and his advisers fell back on the social issues. Bush's dependence on the right was greater, and the risks of that dependence smaller, in a three-way race, since Perot had already shaken Republican loyalties.[125] Despite all of Bush's liabilities, it was the right that kept him in the race: In 1992, the core support of the Republicans came from social conservatives, and the party will need their loyalty in the years to come.[126]

To assemble a winning coalition, the Republicans will need to moderate their stance on social issues, but doing so will call for art and delicacy. Social conservatives cannot be taken for granted: evangelical Protestants—and even more, socially conservative Catholics—can lean to the left on economic questions, and many might change sides if they feel abandoned, especially since Clinton keeps an open door.[127] Even in 1992, while white, born-again Christians heavily supported Bush, Clinton did better than Dukakis, winning about one vote in four, where Dukakis received only one in five.[128]

Paradoxically, the need for moderation points the Republicans right and not left. Bush had to curry favor with the right, stepping up his rhetoric where Reagan could be temperate because, unlike Reagan, the right did not see Bush as one of its own.[129] After all, in 1984, Bush had confessed his discomfort with the "elevation of the religion thing," and in practice, his support for the right-wing agenda had been modest at best.[130] Feeling its oats in 1992, the right made Bush pay the price. If Republicans want to lower that cost in 1996, they will need a candidate who is pragmatic but is perceived by the right as one of its champions, and that may be a tall order to fill.

On the other side, Democrats have reason to pause amid their ecstasies. Clinton's skillful race still fell far short of a national majority, and his victory can be explained by third-candidate defections more than any increase in Democratic strength.

Republican hopes of realignment were blunted. A higher percentage of college students began calling themselves liberal, and there was much comment about Clinton's appeal to the young.[131] But in the end, about the same percentage of younger voters went for Clinton as had gone Democratic four years earlier, while among younger married voters with children, Clinton did very badly indeed.[132] On the other hand, he apparently won an overwhelming majority among homosexuals.[133] Still, comparing Democratic support in 1988 and 1992, change was the exception and continuity the rule.

The Emerging American Politics

Clinton's victory, however, hinted at broader possibilities for redefining the Democratic coalition. On election night, Al Gore asserted that the election demonstrated the "end of sectionalism," and in a sense, it did confirm sectionalism's long decline.[134] But Clinton's southernness still made him seem alien to many northern audiences, and even Gore's argument pointed to the special sectional character of the Democratic ticket.[135] As the nomination of two border staters, it was not unprecedented; rather, it turned away from Dukakis's effort to re-create the Boston-Austin axis to that earlier success, the Truman-Barkley ticket of 1948. But unlike those predecessors, Clinton and Gore came from states that were members of the Confederacy: The 1992 nominations were a strong symbolic gesture to the South, part of a successful effort to dent that now-Republican bastion.[136]

The geography of the election was suggestive in another way. Sweeping the Northeast and the West Coast, Clinton and Gore also were almost universally successful in the broad, middle American region that Meredith Nicholson once called the "Valley of Democracy."[137] Except for Mississippi, Clinton carried every state bordering on the Mississippi River and every state on the Ohio except Indiana, equaling Lyndon Johnson (who took Indiana but lost Louisiana).[138] Only on the upper Missouri did Clinton's pluralities disappear.

Our stereotypes associate the two areas with the Democratic party's fundamental agon. We think of the coasts—somewhat unjustly, of course—as the homeland of liberals and neoliberals, a diverse grouping uniting partisans of high-tech industry and the cultural elite, mostly internationalists disposed toward free trade, almost all secular and inclined to relativism, people who defend policies in the idiom of rights.[139] Middle America, by contrast, symbolizes those in the middle sectors who "do the work, raise the kids, and pay the bills," the people to whom Clinton offered himself as champion and who probably gave him his margin of victory. For all their variety, these middle Americans are often tied to place and apt to be religious, not often moralists (at least, not those who voted for Clinton), but concerned with decency and justice—with families and safe communities and fair taxes—at least as much as they care about rights. And less confident about international politics, they include many unashamed patriots who sympathize with protection.[140]

The "character issue" chafed the line of friction between the two persuasions. The most bothersome side of Clinton's account of his doings during the Vietnam era was not that he tried to avoid military service—as the warm reception to his American Legion speech showed, that could have been dealt with rather easily—but that his stories varied, suggesting, as Dan Quayle argued during the vice-presidential debate, that "Bill Clinton has a problem telling the truth." It stirred fears among middle Americans that Clinton was too close to what they see as liberalism's moral flabbiness, too unwilling to offend, too prone to seek compromise, lacking any standard of justice except civil peace.[141]

The problem of guiding principles was exemplified in the debate over "family values." When they responded to Quayle, Russell Baker observed, liberals too often sounded "as though they're against love, marriage and family."[142] Unnecessarily so; recognizing that single-parent families face special difficulties does not entail rejection or ostracism but calls for appropriate assistance. Paradoxically, the liberal inclination to denounce as repressive any idea that the two-parent family is a standard leaves liberals only a limited, economic justification for aiding single-parent households, while conservatives, who accept the standard, are too niggardly to offer help.

Clinton avoided that ideological trap. He defused a good deal of the Republican appeal to "family values" by observing that, apart from restrictions on abortion and on gays, it was largely talk. And in his soft way, he was just as clear about the defects of liberalism: "Family values alone won't feed a hungry child, and material security can't provide a moral compass. We must have both."[143] Yet Clinton's shrewd claiming of the sensible middle ground left his family policy vague, like much of the agenda of the Clinton administration, still waiting to be defined.[144]

At the beginning of the campaign, the need for a moral compass led E.J. Dionne, Jr., to recommend the earlier, tougher liberalism symbolized by Humphrey Bogart in *Casablanca*.[145] To his detriment, a great many voters could not shake the fear that Clinton might be something closer to Claude Rains's portrayal of a smooth, unprincipled opportunist. But in the end, Rains's policeman went off with Bogart's Rick to join the Free French, and there is reason to hope that Clinton will do at least as well.

As a campaigner, Clinton kept his coalition pretty much together, but the presidency will be a harder test. More or less united against Bush and the Reagan legacy, Democrats will be more apt to squabble when the question is what they are for.[146] Even during the campaign, many of Clinton's middle American supporters were bothered by the exclusion of Robert Casey, Pennsylvania's antiabortion governor, from a convention platform that had been opened to pro-choice Republican women.[147] It was an example of the abiding fear of middle American Democrats that liberals will be more at ease in the corridors of power and that, in a Clinton administration, the "new" Democratic party will be swallowed by the "old." It will not help that some items high on the liberal agenda, including many aspects of abortion and gay rights, can be achieved fairly easily by executive order, while the hopes of middle Americans call for structural solutions, a long process of legislation and considerable pain.[148]

Judged by the campaign, Clinton can be expected to attend to such feelings and to the demand that burdens be shared fairly. But sacrifice, likely to be asked of all of us, will call for more than a gift for conciliation and the brokering of interests. It will demand a scale of justice and the conviction that our dignities and destinies are bound up with the common good.

Clinton shows every sign of concern to strengthen the government's title to rule and its claims on our allegiance. If he is wise, he will promote the use of public policy to rebuild the links between citizens and their government, not simply media gimmicks, but local governments, parties, and associations with the "power of meeting," where citizens can learn the habits of democracy and the arts of politics.[149]

Yet ultimately, both in relation to his party and the country as a whole, Clinton's success will depend on his ability to articulate measures of public purpose and policy. For a Democrat, equality is the enduring grail, and in his best moments, Clinton's rhetoric of citizenship pointed to equality's vital contemporary meanings. Civic equality is no prescription for uniformity, not even in the form of enforced diversity. As Barbara Jordan told the Democratic convention, equality and equal rights are the conditions of civil variety. For Americans, their differing faiths and cultures are sources of strength, but no one needs to be told, these days, that cultures are not always easily compatible with each other or with democratic politics, that cultures often include racism and sexism, or that some nurture a hunger for dominion or are otherwise at odds with democratic life. America's version of multiculturalism accepts diversity, but only on the understanding that all cultures yield any claim to rule that runs counter to equality and equal rights. From an egalitarian point of view, cultures are not "separate realities" but more or less adequate answers to the human problem, to which equality and the rights that go with it are qualitatively superior because, unlike stories and legends, they rest on the stark truth of human nature.[150]

An excellent campaign slogan, "Putting People First," also hints at broader meanings, just as the reconciliation with nature to which Al Gore calls America implies more than our relation to the nonhuman environment. From its Columbian beginnings, America has been caught up in the modern quest for the mastery of nature, the rejection of whatever humans have not chosen or made. It becomes ever clearer, however, that technological mastery subordinates us to the things we have made and, left to itself, tends to dispense with human craft and devotion.[151] Yet the United States also began by asserting the proposition that both our equality and our rights are things that we did not make and about which we have no choice, an unalienable heritage from nature. If people are to come first in public policy, human nature must be given its due. Human beings are more than consumers, and their dignity—their need to be needed—deserves to be afforded at least equal status with the pursuit of abundance and mastery. Equality implies more than rights; it suggests that, within the limits of our circumstances, we can and should be held accountable to equal standards, offered and expected to live up to the opportunity to contribute to the common life. Even in speech, Bill

Clinton's promise of a "new covenant" sounded chords of memory; it remains to be seen how far he can take Americans toward a rediscovery of the republic.

Notes

1. A century earlier, prophetically, Henry Adams saw the American people "wandering in a wilderness more sandy than ... Sinai," and in 1893, the Columbian Exposition seemingly "asked ... for the first time ... whether the American people knew where they were driving." Henry Adams, *The Education of Henry Adams,* edited by Ernest Samuels (Boston: Houghton Mifflin, 1974), 329, 343. But few Americans, back then, shared the vision.

2. Leslie Gelb, "1932 and 1992," *New York Times,* 7 February 1992, A29; R.W. Apple, Jr., "Close Three-Way Race Holds Opportunities for Clinton," *New York Times,* 23 June 1992, A18. Some voters compared their excitement with that of the first Roosevelt election, as they told Michael Winerip, "Fever Pitch: Democracy at Work," *New York Times,* 1 November 1992, L49.

3. "George Herbert Hoover Bush," *Economist,* 31 October 1992, 30.

4. David Broder, "Clinton's No Kennedy Either," *Washington Post National Weekly,* 12–18 October 1992, 4; Steven Greenhouse, "Clinton's Economic Plan Has a Roosevelt Tone," *New York Times,* 9 July 1992, 30.

5. David McCullough, *Truman* (New York: Simon and Schuster, 1992), 660–61, 668.

6. Russell Baker, "All Joy Departed," *New York Times,* 13 October 1992, A23.

7. R.W. Apple, Jr., "The Economy's Casualty," *New York Times,* 4 November 1992, A1.

8. *San Francisco Chronicle,* 20 August 1992, B3.

9. For the hope, see Robert Kuttner, *The Life of the Party: Democratic Prospects in 1988 and Beyond* (New York: Viking, 1987); by contrast, cultural cleavages were dominant in 1988. Joel Lieske, "Cultural Issues and Images in the 1988 Presidential Campaign," *PS* 24 (1991): 180–87.

10. Robert D. Hershey, Jr., "The Politics of Declining Incomes," *New York Times,* 9 March 1992, D6.

11. Jim Hoagland, "Bush: First of Many to Fall," *Washington Post National Weekly,* 12–18 October 1992, 29.

12. Michael S. Lewis-Beck, *Economics and Elections* (Ann Arbor: University of Michigan Press, 1988); Michael MacKuen, Robert S. Erickson, and James A. Stimson, "Peasants or Bankers: the American Electorate and the U.S. Economy," *American Political Science Review* 86 (1992): 597–611; Donald Kinder and D. Roderick Kiewiet, "Economic Grievances and Political Behavior: The Role of Personal Discontents and Collective Judgments in Congressional Voting," *American Journal of Political Science* 23 (1979): 495–527.

13. Hobart Rowen, "Misdiagnosing the Recession," *Washington Post National Weekly,* 27 January–12 February 1992, 5.

14. David Broder, "The Uneasy Electorate," *Washington Post National Weekly*, 22–28 July 1991, 4; Leonard Silk, "The Many Faces of the Electorate," *New York Times*, 10 April 1992, D2.

15. *Notes on Virginia*, Letter to John Jay, 31 August 1785, and Letter to John Adams, 28 October 1813, all in Adrienne Koch and William Peden, eds., *The Life and Selected Writings of Jefferson* (New York: Modern Library, 1944), 280, 377, 633.

16. William Schmidt, "Hard Work Can't Stop Hard Times," *New York Times*, 25 November 1990, 1ff. For the best days of industrial labor, see E.E. LeMasters, *Blue Collar Aristocrats* (Madison: University of Wisconsin Press, 1975).

17. Frank Levy, *Dollars and Dreams* (New York: Russell Sage Foundation, 1987); Juliet Shor, *The Overworked American* (New York: Basic Books, 1991); Jodie T. Allen, "It's Morning in America, All Right," *Washington Post National Weekly*, 4–10 November 1991, 23.

18. Paul Starr, "The New Politics of Health Care," *Harper's*, October 1991, 22–30.

19. *New York Times*, 22 February 1992, L9. See also Sylvia Nasar, "The 1980s: A Very Good Time for the Very Rich," *New York Times*, 5 March 1992, 1ff.

20. Sylvia Nasar, "Fed Gives New Evidence of '80's Gains by Richest," *New York Times*, 21 April 1992, 1ff; Charles Murray, "The Shape of Things to Come," *National Review*, 8 July 1991, 29–30.

21. As, to some extent, Mickey Kaus does in *The End of Equality* (New York: Basic Books, 1992).

22. Robert Samuelson, "White Collar Blues," *Washington Post National Weekly*, 6–12 January 1992, 29.

23. Rowen, "Misdiagnosing the Recession"; Anne Swardson, "The Swelling Ranks of the Underemployed," *Washington Post National Weekly*, 17–23 February 1992, 20; Peter Passell, "Clinton's Luck ... Or Albatross?" *New York Times*, 13 August 1992, D2. It is a sign of the times that, by October 1991, more Americans, by a margin of over half a million, worked for government than in manufacturing. When Reagan took office, manufacturing led by 25 percent. Floyd Norris, "The Jobs Are in Government, Not Industry," *New York Times*, 6 September 1992, F1.

24. Carl Rowan, "GOP Hasn't Been Kind to 'Family Values'," *Star Ledger*, 7 August 1992, 20; Steven Nock and P.W. Kingston, "Time with Children: The Impact of Couples' Work-Time Commitments," *Social Forces* 67 (1988): 59–85.

25. Uri Bronfenbrenner, "Contexts of Child Rearing," *American Psychologist* 34 (1979): 844–850; 74 percent of Americans, in one finding, consider that parents should have the greatest impact on their children's values, but a substantial plurality think that the media exert that influence. American Enterprise Public Opinion and Demographic Report, in *Public Perspective* 3 (Sept./Oct. 1992): 86.

26. Gerald M. Pomper, ed., *The Election of 1988* (Chatham, N.J.: Chatham House, 1989), 194–95; Kaus, 55–57; James Q. Wilson, "Crime, Race and Values," *Society*, December 1992, 90–93.

27. Robert Reich, "The Secession of the Successful," *New York Times Maga-

zine, 20 January 1991, 17ff; the term autoanesthesia is from Joseph Lyford's *The Airtight Cage* (New York: Harper, 1966).

28. Bush used the image of untroubled sleep so often that reporters began referring to the theme as "bedtime in America," parodying Reagan's "morning in America" slogan.

29. Norman J. Ornstein, "Foreign Policy in the 1992 Elections," *Foreign Affairs* 71 (Summer 1992): 3, 7; Sidney Blumenthal saw that 1988 was the "last campaign of the Cold War"; *Pledging Allegiance* (New York: Harper Collins, 1990).

30. Leslie Gelb, "No National Interest," *New York Times,* 18 October 1992, E15, and "Bush Gets Tough on Iraq," *New York Times,* 23 August 1992, E15.

31. Richard Marin, "How Quickly They Regret," *Washington Post National Weekly,* 20–26 January 1992, 37.

32. Jeffrey Frank, "Buy American or Bye, American," *Washington Post National Weekly,* 21–27 September 1992, 25; Lawrence Harrison, "Huddled Masses, Unskilled Labor," *Washington Post National Weekly,* 20–26 January 1992, 25.

33. Kevin Phillips, "The Old Boys' Club of the West is Getting Left in the Dust," *Washington Post National Weekly,* 13–19 July 1992, 23; Hobart Rowen, "A Little Help from His Friends," *Washington Post National Weekly,* 20–26 April 1992, 5; Benjamin Ginsberg and Martin Shefter describe "alliances with foreign governments" as one of the new modes of politics. *Politics by Other Means: The Declining Importance of Elections in America* (New York: Basic Books, 1990), 11.

34. Leslie Gelb, "Three Whine Mice," *New York Times,* 13 January 1992, A15.

35. Ibid. ; on Clinton, see William Safire, "Bush-Clinton Debate," *New York Times,* 2 April 1992, A23.

36. Pomper, ed., *The Election of 1988,* 189–90.

37. That the phrase hurt is indicated by Bush's effort to counter it by referring to "trickle-down" government.

38. Similarly, while Michael Novak rejects "socialist" versions of health insurance, he argued for a national plan based on tax credits. "Dead but Fair," *Forbes,* 16 March 1992, 112–13.

39. Steven Pearlstein, "First, Let's Kill All the Economists," *Washington Post National Weekly,* 30 November–5 December 1992, 31, cites Paul Krugman, "for people in their fifties, the cutting edge of economics was to show how markets were perfect. For people in their thirties, the cutting edge ... is now showing how markets are imperfect." See also Leonard Silk, "Is Liberalism Back in the Saddle?" *New York Times,* 17 April 1992, D2.

40. Frank Levy and Richard Michel, *The Economic Future of American Families* (Washington, D.C.: Urban Institute, 1991); on the failure of the equivalence theorem, see Leonard Silk, "The Crucial Issue Politicians Ignore," *New York Times,* 24 April 1992, D2.

41. Hobart Rowen, "Productivity Not the Problem," *Washington Post National Weekly,* 30 November–5 December 1992, 5.

42. According to the American Enterprise Public Opinion and Demographic

Report, 68 percent said candidates should talk about family values; 53 percent said government should concern itself. *Public Perspective* 3 (September/October 1992): 85.

43. For example, see Daniel P. Moynihan, "A Landmark for Families," *New York Times*, 16 November 1992, A13.

44. Peter Steinfels, "A Political Movement Blends Its Ideas from Left and Right," *New York Times*, 24 May 1991, E6; "in providing for the poor," *Commonweal* editorialized, "we must make reasonable demands on them—for work, schooling and, yes, sexual responsibility" (24 February 1992), 5. See also Christopher Jencks, *Rethinking Social Policy: Race, Poverty, and the Underclass* (Cambridge, Mass.: Harvard University Press, 1992).

45. Joel Garreau, "It's a Mall World After All," *Washington Post National Weekly*, 10–16 August 1992, 25.

46. Aristotle, *Ethics*, trans. J.A.K. Thompson (Harmondsworth, England: Penguin, 1956), book 2, chap. 1, pp. 55–56.

47. G.K. Chesterton noted that "what is unique is not America, but what is called Americanisation." *What I Saw in America* (New York: Dodd Mead, 1922), 14.

48. James Davison Hunter, *Culture Wars: The Struggle to Define America* (New York: Basic Books, 1991).

49. Tom Wicker, "An Alienated Public," *New York Times*, 13 October 1991, E15.

50. Humphrey Taylor, "The American Angst of 1992," *Public Perspective* 3 (July/August 1992): 3, table 1.

51. Rohde is cited by Dan Balz, "America the Morning After," *Washington Post National Weekly*, 21–27 October 1991, 13–14.

52. Jeffrey Schmalz, "Words on Bush's Lips in '88 Now Stick in Voters' Craw," *New York Times*, 14 June 1992, 1.

53. Martin P. Wattenberg, *The Decline of American Political Parties, 1952–1988* (Cambridge, Mass. : Harvard University Press, 1990).

54. Richard Zeiger, "Few Citizens Make Decisions for Everyone," *California Journal* 21 (November 1990): 517, 519; the belief in universal corruption is cited by Leslie Gelb, "Throw the Bums Out," *New York Times*, 23 October 1991, A23.

55. Garry Wills, "Ross Perot and the Immaculate Election," *Washington Post National Weekly*, 1–7 June 1992, 23; see also William Safire, "Protesting Too Much," *New York Times*, 6 April 1992, A19.

56. Richard Marin and E.J. Dionne, Jr., "Turning Down the Party Invitation," *Washington Post National Weekly*, 13–19 July 1992, 9; much the same position is espoused by Theodore Lowi, "The Party Crasher," *New York Times Magazine*, 23 August 1992, 28ff.

57. Anthony Lewis, "Time for a Change," *New York Times*, 9 April 1992, A25.

58. Russell Baker, "Potomac Breakdown," *New York Times*, 12 October 1991, 29; Lewis, "Time for a Change."

59. I am not persuaded by the notion that divided government is "accidental." See James Sundquist, "Needed: A Political Theory for the New Era of Coalition Government in the U.S.," *Political Science Quarterly* 103 (1988): 633–34. The more purposive model implied by Morris Fiorina in *Divided Government*

(New York: Macmillan, 1992), 128–29, is more compelling, especially since divided government need not result in "gridlock" and did not do so under Nixon. See also David Mayhew, *Divided We Govern* (New Haven: Yale University Press, 1991).

60. David Rosenbaum, "The Paralysis of No-Pain Politics," *New York Times,* 19 April 1992, E1; Roberto Suro, "Viewing Chaos in the Capital, Americans Express Outrage," *New York Times,* 19 November 1990, 1ff; Adam Clymer, "Citing Rise in Frustration, Dozens of Lawmakers Quit," *New York Times,* 5 April 1992, 1ff. On the Balanced Budget Amendment, see David Broder, "A Congressional Balancing Act," *Washington Post National Weekly,* 25–31 May 1992, 4.

61. James Q. Wilson, "The Newer Deal," *New Republic,* 2 July 1990, 34; Daniel Yankelovich, *Coming to Public Judgment* (Syracuse: Syracuse University Press, 1991), 4.

62. Jeffrey Schmalz, "Americans Sign Up in Record Numbers to Cast a Ballot," *New York Times,* 19 October 1992, 1ff; compare Paul R. Abramson and John H. Aldrich, "The Decline of Electoral Participation in America," *American Political Science Review* 76 (1982): 502–21.

63. Gerald Pomper and Loretta Sernekos, "Bake Sales and Voting," *Society,* July/August 1991, 10–16. Tocqueville argued that Americans were driven into politics by necessity but held there by the habits and pleasures of community life. See *Democracy in America* (New York: Schocken, 1961), 2:127.

64. Dan Balz, "They're Angry but Not Apathetic," *Washington Post National Weekly,* 26 October–1 November 1992, 13.

65. Tocqueville, *Democracy in America,* 1:210–11; 2:137.

66. Tocqueville *Democracy in America,* 2:134–37.

67. Bill Moyers, "The Old News and the New Civil War," *New York Times,* 22 March 1992, E15.

68. Russell Baker, "Hear America Listening," *New York Times,* 2 November 1991, 23.

69. Tom Wicker, "An Alienated Public."

70. Thomas Rosenstiel, "Networks Rethink Political Coverage," *Berkshire Eagle,* 17 July 1991, C6; Anthony Lewis, "Hair on their Chests," *New York Times,* 19 April 1992, E11; "Old News Deconstructed," *Economist,* 31 October 1992, 23.

71. *New York Times,* 11 July 1992, L7.

72. Harvey Mansfield refers to a "tendency toward the left." See *America's Constitutional Soul* (Baltimore: Johns Hopkins University Press, 1991), 167. By contrast, Deborah Tannen refers to the news media as manipulated by "mostly Republican" admakers in a review of Kathleen Hall Jamieson, *Dirty Politics* (New York: Oxford University Press, 1992). "Lies, Damned Lies and Political Ads," *Washington Post National Weekly,* 21–27 September 1992, 35.

73. Todd Gitlin, "On Being Sound-Bitten," *Boston Review,* December 1991, 17.

74. Mansfield, *America's Constitutional Soul,* 166–68. In an admittedly extreme example in 1990, Madonna, wrapped in an American flag, urged young Americans to vote on the principle that "freedom of speech is as good as sex," thus identifying public words with private passions and justifying the former in

terms of the latter. *New York Times*, 20 October 1990, 7.

75. Russell Baker, "You'd Hate It There," *New York Times*, 7 December 1991, 23; Roger Masters, Sigfried Frey, and Gary Bente, "Dominance and Attention: Images of Leaders in German, French and American TV News," *Polity* 23 (1991): 393.

76. John Tierney, "Now, Journalists Renege on Election Promises," *New York Times*, 31 January 1992, A12; newspaper coverage of TV ads similarly focused on strategy. Randall Rothenberg, "Newspapers Watch What People Watch in the TV Campaign," *New York Times*, 4 November 1990, E5.

77. Maureen Dowd, "Populist Media Forums and the Campaign of '92," *New York Times*, 3 November 1992, 14; Howard Kurtz, "The Year the Candidates Took to the Airwaves," *Washington Post National Weekly*, 2–8 November 1992, 14.

78. Elizabeth Kolbert, "Heard By Few, Clinton Speech Shows Candidates' Quandary," *New York Times*, 9 April 1992, A21.

79. Elizabeth Kolbert, "Perot Takes Issue while Clinton Takes on Issues," *New York Times*, 12 June 1992, A14.

80. Joe S. Foote, *Television Access and Political Power* (New York: Praeger, 1990).

81. Hume is cited by Richard Berke, "Campaign '92," *New York Times*, 26 June 1992, A13; Masters, et al. "Dominance and Attention"; Jan Hoffman, "Larry King: Kingmaker to the Pols," *New York Times*, 28 June 1992, H27.

82. Gerald Marzorati, "From Tocqueville to Perotville," *New York Times*, 28 June 1992, E17.

83. David Broder, "Tabloid Election," *Washington Post National Weekly*, 3–9 February 1992, 4. The importance of local media in 1992 is a somewhat more hopeful sign. See Phyllis Kaniss, "A Victory for Local News," *New York Times*, 5 December 1992, 19.

84. And politically, the truth matters. Intellectual champions of the view that reality is "constructed" and "plural" did not apply their teaching to the verdict constructed by the jury that tried the officers who arrested and beat Rodney King. "Postmodernists," Todd Gitlin writes, "enjoy skating on the surface, but they, we, are still probing for bedrock truth." Gitlin, "On Being Sound-Bitten," 17. On the King verdict, see Jeffrey Frank, "When Truth Becomes Image, History Becomes Myth," *Washington Post National Weekly*, 11–17 May 1992, 24.

85. Michael Paul Rogin, "JFK: The Movie," *American Historical Review* 97 (1992): 502, 505; Sidney Blumenthal saw many of the same themes in Jerry Brown's campaign. "He's a New Age Demagogue," *New York Times*, 5 April 1992, E17.

86. Caryl Rivers, "It's Tough to Tell a Hawk from a Lonesome Dove," *New York Times*, 10 February 1991, H29ff. We need to remember the spectacle of the vice-president of the United States in national dialogue with fictional TV characters. See Russell Baker, "To Cloud Men's Minds," *New York Times*, 23 May 1992, Y15.

87. Rogin, "JFK," 503; Lloyd Grove, "Looking for President Perfect," *Washington Post National Weekly*, 6–12 April 1992, 6–7.

88. Steven Holmes, "Perot-Bush 'Dirty Tricks' Feud Persists," *New York Times,* 27 October 1992, A1ff; on Perot's dealings with Hanoi, see *New York Times,* 4 June 1992, 1.

89. Gwen Ifill, "Perot's Popularity Sends Clinton into Frustration," *New York Times,* 25 May 1992, 8; see also Elizabeth Kolbert's report on Perot's spending, *New York Times,* 28 October 1992, A1.

90. Walter Goodman, "Perot Leaves a Field of Broken Rules," *New York Times,* 10 October 1992, 46.

91. Maureen Dowd, "Once Again, Questions of Character," *New York Times,* 28 June 1992, E1.

92. David Broder, "A Knight in Shining Armor," *Washington Post National Weekly,* 4–10 May 1992, 4; Peter Milius, "Ross Perot's Fuzz," *Washington Post National Weekly,* 11–17 May 1992, 29.

93. John Mintz and David Von Drehle, "The Day Perot Pulled the Plug," *Washington Post National Weekly,* 27 July–2 August 1992, 9.

94. Perot's style should be compared to Richard Rosenstone's observations in "Historical Fact/Historical Film," *American Historical Review* 97 (1992): 507.

95. Dan Balz and E.J. Dionne, Jr., "In a Quirky Year, Perot Could Be a Loose Cannon," *Washington Post National Weekly,* 4–10 May 1992, 8.

96. Wills, "Ross Perot and the Immaculate Election"; Michael Kelly, "Perot's Vision: Consensus by Computer," *New York Times,* 6 June 1922, 1ff; Richard Cohen, "Deconstructing Perot," *Washington Post National Weekly,* 18–24 May 1992, 28.

97. Michael Schrage, "Perot: A Man of Revolution, Not Evolution," *Washington Post,* 1 May 1992, B3; Steven Greenhouse, "Hardly Laissez-Faire," *New York Times,* 27 June 1992, L9.

98. Kevin Sack, "Why Perot Thrived in Fertile Kansas," *New York Times,* 6 November 1992, A20.

99. Lawrence Goodwyn, *Democratic Promise* (New York: Oxford University Press, 1976); the St. Louis Conference, early in 1892, seated delegates of twenty-two separate organizations. John Hicks, *The Populist Revolt* (Minneapolis: University of Minnesota Press, 1931), 225.

100. Matthew Josephson, a bit disdainful of the Populists as a party of "peasant proprietors," noted that "principles and platform" were central to them. *The Politicos* (New York: Harcourt Brace, 1938), 502–3.

101. Hicks, *Populist Revolt,* 234.

102. George Will, "Ross Perot: America's Rohrschach Test," *Washington Post National Weekly,* 8–14 June 1992, 29; Perot's third-party candidacy thus violated Lowi's crucial "proviso" that such a party be built "from bottom up." Lowi, "The Party Crasher," 33.

103. Russell Baker, "Stressed All Over," *New York Times,* 6 June 1992, A23; R.W. Apple, Jr., "The Voters' Message," *New York Times,* 8 April 1992. Even Edward Kearny and Robert Heineman, who predicted a centrist third party, overestimated the attachment of voters to the primaries. "Scenario for a Centrist Revolt: Third Party Prospects in a Time of Ideological Polarization," *Presidential Studies Quarterly* 22 (1992): 114.

104. It sometimes seemed that Democrats would be better off with a generic "Brand X" candidate. Robin Toner, "Bad News for Bush as Poll Shows National Gloom," *New York Times*, 28 January 1992, A1ff.

105. Cuomo certainly received plenty of advice akin to Leslie Gelb's counsel to wait for 1996, using the time to cope with his "inner demons." "To Cuomo or Not to Cuomo," *New York Times*, 27 November 1991, A21. Since the Democratic nomination is not likely to be doubtful in 1996, it might be a noncontroversial time to institutionalize Terry Sanford's proposal for a preprimary convention of superdelegates to screen candidates. See Walter Mondale's fine critique of primaries, "Primaries Are No Test of Character," *New York Times*, 26 February 1992, A23.

106. Thomas Byrne Edsall, "Those Crucial Voters Not Yet Heard From," *Washington Post National Weekly*, 30 March–5 April 1992, 12; my comments on the Buchanan vote derive from *New York Times* exit polls (e.g., 5 March 1992, A22).

107. *New York Times*, 5 March 1992, A22, for Clinton's vote on Super Tuesday. In New York, Tsongas—no longer an active candidate—had an edge among white Christians. Clinton depended on his margin among blacks and Jews. *New York Times*, 9 April 1992, A20.

108. With both parties, this is an old tradition. See Herbert Croly, "Democratic Factions and Insurgent Republicans," *North American Review* 191 (May 1910): 626–35.

109. Thomas Byrne Edsall with Mary D. Edsall, *Chain Reaction: The Impact of Race, Rights and Taxes on American Politics* (New York: Norton, 1992); Ronald P. Formisano, *Boston Against Busing* (Chapel Hill: University of North Carolina Press, 1991), 232–33.

110. The comments of Robert Huckfeldt and Carol Weitzel Kohfeld are apposite. See *Race and the Decline of Class in American Politics* (Champagne: University of Illinois Press, 1989), ix, 188.

111. David Broder, "Jackson's Decline, Brown's Ascent," *Washington Post National Weekly*, 20–26 July 1992, 4.

112. Ronald Brownstein, "New Studies of U.S. Tensions Put Focus on Class, Not Race," *Berkshire Eagle*, 28 July 1991, A3; William Julius Wilson, *The Truly Disadvantaged* (Chicago: University of Chicago Press, 1987).

113. Lena Williams, "In a 90s' Quest for Black Identity, Intense Doubts and Disagreement," *New York Times*, 30 November 1991, 1ff.

114. Lena Williams, "Growing Black Debate on Racism: When Is It Real, When an Excuse," *New York Times*, 5 April 1992, 1ff. "To join the public household of this great nation," Orlando Patterson wrote after the election, "is to share responsibility for its fortunes and for one's failings." "Our History vs. Clinton's Covenant," *New York Times*, 13 November 1992, A29.

115. William Julius Wilson, "The Right Message," *New York Times*, 17 March 1992, A25.

116. It helped, of course, that Bush's record on the politics of race showed a combination of indifference and backsliding, while Perot was clearly impossible after his early gaffes. Ruth Marcus, "The Shifting Sands of George Bush's Civil Rights Positions," *Washington Post National Weekly*, 24–30 August 1992, 8–9.

117. Patterson, "Our History and Clinton's Covenant."

118. William Schneider, "The Political Legacy of the Reagan Years," in *The Reagan Legacy*, edited by Sidney Blumenthal and Thomas Byrne Edsall (New York: Pantheon, 1988), 12. At that, Republican divisions are probably less severe than those among Democrats. Corwin Smidt and James Penning, "A Party Divided?" *Polity* 23 (1990): 138.

119. John J. Farmer, "Republicans Sound Like the Ideologues Now," *Star-Ledger*, 13 August 1992, 24; Garry Wills, "George Bush: Prisoner of the Crazies," *New York Times*, 16 August 1992, E17.

120. *New York Times*, 5 November 1992, B9.

121. Andrew Rosenthal, "The Politics of Morality," *New York Times*, 22 May 1992, A19; on the Republican campaign, see Robin Toner, "How Bush Lost Five Chances to Save the Day," *New York Times*, 11 October 1992, E1ff.

122. Mansfield, *America's Constitutional Soul*, 69.

123. David Rosenbaum, "Missing from Politics: The Blueprints for the Future," *New York Times*, 2 February 1992, E1; Blumenthal, *Pledging Allegiance*, 49–76.

124. "President Noodle," *New York Times*, 5 March 1992, A26; George Will, "Serious People Flinch," *Washington Post National Weekly*, 31 August–6 September 1992, 29.

125. Mary McGrory, "You Say Potato and I Say It Takes Only 35 Percent to Win," *Washington Post National Weekly*, 29 June–5 July 1992, 25; Kevin Phillips, "GOP Crackup," *New York Times*, 4 June 1992, A23.

126. John Green and James Guth, "The Christian Right in the Republican Party," *Journal of Politics* 50 (1988): 150–65.

127. David Moraniss, "Clinton's Journey of the Spirit," *Washington Post National Weekly*, 13–19 July 1992, 10–11.

128. The figures are 23 percent and 18 percent respectively. *New York Times*, 5 November 1992, B9.

129. Garry Wills, "The Hostage," *New York Review of Books*, 13 August 1992, 21–27.

130. Alan Geyer identifies Bush with "political docetism," a creed of vague, disembodied values. See *Christianity and Crisis*, 21 September 1992, 291; David Broder, "Value Added Politics," *Washington Post National Weekly*, 1–7 June 1992, 4.

131. Thomas Byrne Edsall, "The GOP May Be Losing Its Realignment Linchpin," *Washington Post National Weekly*, 21–27 September 1992, 15; Mary Jordan, "More Freshmen Lean to Left," *Washington Post National Weekly*, 20–26 January 1992, 37.

132. Clinton drew 44 percent of voters aged 18–29. Dukakis had attracted 47 percent. *New York Times*, 5 November 1992, B9; Barbara Vobejda, "Family Value Voting," *Washington Post National Weekly*, 30 November–5 December 1992, 36.

133. Peter Cellupica, "The Political Dawn Arrives for Gays," *New York Times*, 7 November 1992, 21; David Broder argues that homophobia among Republicans and from Perot, by guaranteeing that Jackson's gay financial backers

had no alternative, helped encourage Clinton to criticize Sister Souljah. Broder, "Jackson's Decline, Brown's Ascent."

134. Harvey Schantz, "The Erosion of Sectionalism in American Elections" *Polity* 24 (1992): 355–77.

135. Robin Toner, "Clinton's Southern Roots Trip Him in New York," *New York Times*, 1 April 1992, A20.

136. Bush helped by calling Arkansas "the lowest of the low" in the third debate, which to sensitive ears, sounded like regional and class contempt. *New York Times*, 1 November 1992, A1.

137. Meredith Nicholson, *The Valley of Democracy* (New York: Scribners, 1918).

138. Even in Mississippi, Clinton carried all the counties that touch the river except Warren and De Soto, if county-by-county maps are accurate.

139. Mary Ann Glendon, *Rights Talk: The Impoverishment of Political Discourse* (New York: Basic Books, 1991).

140. The Democrats' internal conflict is well presented by David Carlin, "Blame the Message," *Commonweal*, 8 May 1992, 9–10; and Margaret O'Brien Steinfels, "Safe, Legal and Rare," *Commonweal*, 20 November 1992, 4–5.

141. This critique of liberalism was the message of Ben Wattenberg's PBS special on the Democrats. (See Walter Goodman's review, *New York Times*, 16 October 1992, B16.) Clinton's record provides some support for his critics: David Moraniss, "Clinton's Arkansas Legacy," *Washington Post National Weekly*, 26 October–1 November 1992, 7.

142. Baker, "To Cloud Men's Minds."

143. Gwen Ifill, "Clinton Sees Bush Engaging in Empty Talk on Families," *New York Times*, 22 May 1992, A18.

144. For a realistic "family agenda," see Timothy Bates, "Paying for Values: The Real Needs of Real Families," *Commonweal*, 9 October 1992, 6–7.

145. E.J. Dionne, Jr., "Bogart in '92: The Fundamental Things Apply," *Washington Post National Weekly*, 16–22 December 1991, 25. Ironically, Dionne's own defense of the moral center in *Why Americans Hate Politics* (Simon and Schuster, 1991) has been criticized by David O'Brien as "too easy and too conciliatory." *American Political Science Review* 86 (1992): 800.

146. Thomas Byrne Edsall, "Nibbling Rivalry: Democrats Are One Big, Scrappy Family," *Washington Post National Weekly*, 16–22 November 1992, 23.

147. Walter Goodman, "The Convention Images: Plenty for Both Sides," *New York Times*, 18 July 1992, 49.

148. David Rosenbaum, "No Painless Way Out for the Next President," *New York Times*, 4 October 1992, E1.

149. *Democracy in America*, 1:217–18; 2:124.

150. Bill Moyers, "Old News and the New Civil War."

151. Raising the too-present danger, Albert Borgmann observes that the public will be reduced to sullen consumers on one hand and hyperactive careerists on the other. *Crossing the Postmodern Divide* (Chicago: University of Chicago Press, 1992).

Appendix

My fellow citizens, today we celebrate the mystery of American renewal.

This ceremony is held in the depth of winter, but by the words we speak and the faces we show the world, we force the spring. A spring reborn in the world's oldest democracy that brings forth the vision and courage to reinvent America.

When our Founders boldly declared America's independence to the world and our purposes to the Almighty, they knew that America to endure would have to change. Not change for change's sake but change to preserve America's ideals—life, liberty, the pursuit of happiness. Though we march to the music of our time, our mission is timeless. Each generation of Americans must define what it means to be an American.

On behalf of our nation, I salute my predecessor, President Bush, for his half-century of service to America. And I thank the millions of men and women whose steadfastness and sacrifice triumphed over depression, fascism, and communism.

Today, a generation raised in the shadows of the cold war assumes new responsibilities in a world warmed by the sunshine of freedom but threatened still by ancient hatreds and new plagues.

Raised in unrivaled prosperity, we inherit an economy that is still the world's strongest but is weakened by business failures, stagnant wages, increasing inequality, and deep divisions among our own people.

When George Washington first took the oath I have just sworn to uphold, news traveled slowly across the land by horseback and across the ocean by boat. Now the sights and sounds of this ceremony are broadcast instantaneously to billions around the world. Communications and commerce are global; investment is mobile; technology is almost magical; and ambition for a better life is now universal. We earn our livelihood in America today in peaceful competition with people all across the earth.

Profound and powerful forces are shaking and remaking our world. And the urgent question of our time is whether we can make change our friend and not our enemy.

This new world has already enriched the lives of millions of Americans who are able to compete and win in it. But when most people are working harder for less, when others cannot work at all, when the cost of health care devastates families and threatens to bankrupt our enterprises great and small, when the fear of crime robs law-abiding citizens of their freedom, and when millions of poor children cannot even imagine the lives we are calling them to lead—we have not made change our friend.

We know we have to face hard truths and take strong steps, but we have not done so. Instead, we have drifted, and that drifting has eroded our re-sources, fractured our economy, and shaken our confidence. Though our challenges are fearsome, so are our strengths. Americans have ever been a restless, questing, hopeful people, and we must bring to our task today the vi-sion and will of those who came before us.

From our Revolution to the Civil War, to the Great Depression, to the civil rights movement, our people have always mustered the determination to construct from these crises the pillars of our history.

Thomas Jefferson believed that to preserve the very foundations of our nation we would need dramatic change from time to time. Well, my fellow Americans, this is our time. Let us embrace it.

Our democracy must be not only the envy of the world but the engine of our own renewal. There is nothing wrong with America that cannot be cured by what is right with America.

And so today we pledge an end to the era of deadlock and drift, and a new season of American renewal has begun.

To renew America we must be bold. We must do what no generation has had to do before. We must invest more in our own people—in their jobs and in their future—and at the same time cut our massive debt. And we must do so in a world in which we must compete for every opportunity.

It will not be easy; it will require sacrifice. But it can be done and done fairly. Not choosing sacrifice for its own sake, but for our own sake. We must provide for our nation the way a family provides for its children.

Our Founders saw themselves in the light of posterity. We can do no less. Anyone who has ever watched a child's eyes wander into sleep knows what posterity is. Posterity is the world to come—the world for whom we hold our ideals, from whom we have borrowed our planet, and to whom we bear sacred responsibility. We must do what America does best: Offer more opportunity to all and demand more responsibility from all. It is time to break the bad habit of expecting something for nothing from our government or from each other. Let us all take more responsibility not only for ourselves and our families but for our communities and our country.

To renew America we must revitalize our democracy.

This beautiful capital, like every capital since the dawn of civilization, is often a place of intrigue and calculation. Powerful people maneuver for position and worry endlessly about who is in and who is out, who is up and who is down, forgetting those people whose toil and sweat sends us here and pays our way.

Americans deserve better, and in this city today there are people who want to do better. And so I say to all of you here, let us resolve to reform our politics so that power and privilege no longer shout down the voice of the people. Let us put aside personal advantage so that we can feel the pain and see the promise of America. Let us resolve to make our government a place for what Franklin Roosevelt called bold, persistent experimentation, a government for our tomorrows, not our yesterdays.

Let us give this capital back to the people to whom it belongs. To renew America, we must meet challenges abroad as well as at home. There is no longer a clear division between what is foreign and what is domestic. The world economy, the world environment, the world AIDS crisis, the world arms race—they affect us all.

Today, as an old order passes, the new world is more free but less stable. Communism's collapse has called forth old animosities and new dangers. Clearly, America must continue to lead the world we did so much to make. While America rebuilds at home, we will not shrink from the challenges nor fail to seize the opportunities of this new world. Together with our friends and allies we will work to shape change lest it engulf us. When our vital interests are challenged or the will and conscience of the international community is defied, we will act, with peaceful diplomacy whenever possible, with force when necessary. The brave Americans serving our nation today in the Persian Gulf and Somalia, and wherever else they stand, are testament to our resolve.

But our greatest strength is the power of our ideas, which are still new in many lands. Across the world we see them embraced and we rejoice. Our hopes, our hearts, our hands are with those on every continent who are building democracy and freedom. Their cause is America's cause.

The American people have summoned the change we celebrate today. You have raised your voices in an unmistakable chorus. You have cast your votes in historic numbers and you have changed the face of Congress, the presidency, and the political process itself.

Yes, you, my fellow Americans, have forced the spring. Now we must do the work the season demands.

To that work I now turn with all the authority of my office. I ask the Congress to join with me. But no president, no Congress, no government can undertake this mission alone. My fellow Americans, you, too, must play your part in our renewal.

I challenge a new generation of young Americans to a season of service—to act on your idealism by helping troubled children, keeping company with those in need, reconnecting our torn communities. There is so much to be done—enough, indeed, for millions of others who are still young in spirit to give of themselves in service, too. In serving, we recognize a simple but powerful truth: We need each other. And we must care for one another.

Today we do more than celebrate America, we rededicate ourselves to the very idea of America: an idea born in revolution and renewed through two centuries of challenge; an idea tempered by the knowledge that, but for fate, we—the fortunate and the unfortunate—might have been each other; an idea ennobled by the faith that our nation can summon from its myriad diversity the deepest measure of unity; an idea infused with the conviction that America's long, heroic journey must go forever upward.

And so, my fellow Americans, as we stand at the edge of the twenty-first century, let us begin anew with energy and hope, with faith and discipline, and let us work until our work is done. The Scripture says, "And let us not be weary in well-doing, for in due season we shall reap, if we faint not."

From this joyful mountaintop of celebration we hear a call to service in the valley.

We have heard the trumpets, we have changed the guard. And now —each in our own way, and with God's help—we must answer the call.

Thank you, and God bless you all.

TABLE A.1. THE CLINTON ADMINISTRATION

Position	Name	Age	Residence	Occupation	Previous experience	Education
President	William J. Clinton	46	Arkansas	Lawyer	Governor of Arkansas	B.A., Georgetown; Rhodes Scholar, Oxford; J.D., Yale
Vice-President	Albert A. Gore, Jr.	44	Tennessee	Journalist	U.S. Senator	B.A., Harvard
Secretary of State	Warren M. Christopher	67	California	Lawyer	Deputy Secretary of State	B.A., USC; LL.B., Stanford
Secretary of Treasury	Lloyd M. Bentsen	71	Texas	Lawyer	Chair, Senate Finance Committee	J.D., University of Texas
Secretary of Defense	Leslie Aspin	54	Wisconsin	Economist	Chair, House Armed Services Committee	B.A., Yale; M. Phil., Oxford; Ph.D., MIT
Attorney-General	Janet Reno	54	Florida	Lawyer	State Attorney, Miami, Florida	A.B, Cornell; LL.B., Harvard
Secretary of the Interior	Bruce Babbitt	54	Arizona	Lawyer	Governor of Arizona	B.S., Notre Dame; M. Phil. Geophysics, Newcastle (Marshall Scholar); J.D., Harvard
Secretary of Agriculture	Mike Espy	39	Mississippi	Lawyer	U.S. Representative	B.A., Howard; J.D., Santa Clara
Secretary of Commerce	Ronald H. Brown	51	District of Columbia	Lawyer	Chair, Democratic National Committee	B.A., Middlebury; J.D., St. John's
Secretary of Labor	Robert B. Reich	46	Massachusetts	Lawyer	Lecturer, Harvard University	B.S., Dartmouth; M. Phil. Economics, Oxford (Rhodes Scholar); J.D., Yale
Secretary of Health	Donna E. Shalala	51	Wisconsin	Political scientist	Chancellor, University of Wisconsin	B.A., Western College for Women; Ph.D., Syracuse
Secretary of Housing	Henry G. Cisneros	45	Texas	Administrator	Mayor, San Antonio, Texas	B.A., M.A., Texas A&M; M.A., Harvard; Ph.D., G. Washington
Secretary of Transportation	Federico F. Peña	45	Colorado	Lawyer	Mayor, Denver, Colorado	B.A., J.D., University of Texas, Austin

TABLE A.I. — CONTINUED

Position	Name	Age	Residence	Occupation	Previous experience	Education
Secretary of Education	Richard W. Riley	59	South Carolina	Lawyer	Governor of South Carolina	B.A., Furman; J.D., University of South Carolina
Secretary of Energy	Hazel R. O'Leary	55	Minnesota	Business executive	Corporate executive vice-president	B.A., Fisk; J.D., Rutgers
Secretary of Veterans Affairs	Jesse Brown	48	District of Columbia	Administrator	Director, Disabled American Veterans	Chicago City College
Administrator, E.P.A.	Carol M. Browner	37	Florida	Lawyer	Florida Secretary of Environment	B.A., J.D., University of Florida
National Security Adviser	W. Anthony Lake	53	Massachusetts	Political scientist	Director of Policy, State Department	B.A., Harvard; Ph.D., Princeton
Director of Central Intelligence	R. James Woolsey	51	District of Columbia	Military officer	Under-Secretary of Navy	B.A., Stanford; M.A., Oxford (Rhodes Scholar); LL.B., Yale
Ambassador to United Nations	Madeleine K. Albright	55	Maryland	Political scientist	President, Center for National Policy	B.A., Wellesley; M.A., Ph.D., Columbia
Director of the Budget	Leon E. Panetta	54	California	Lawyer	Chair, House Budget Committee	B.A., J.D., Santa Clara
Chair, National Economic Council	Robert E. Rubin	54	New York	Investment banker	Co-Chair, Goldman, Sachs	B.A., Harvard; LL.B, Yale
Chair, Council of Economic Advisers	Laura D. Tyson	45	California	Economist	Professor, University of California	B.A., Smith; Ph.D., MIT
U.S. Trade Representative	Michael Kantor	53	California	Lawyer	Director, Clinton for President	B.A., Vanderbilt; J.D., Georgetown
White House Chief of Staff	Thomas F. McLarry	46	Arkansas	Business executive	Chairman, Arkla Natural Gas Co.	B.A., University of Arkansas

Index